Advanced Turbo C®

Advanced Turbo C®

Herbert Schildt

BORLAND·OSBORNE/McGRAW·HILL
PROGRAMMING SERIES

Osborne **McGraw-Hill**
2600 Tenth Street
Berkeley, California 94710
U.S.A.

For information on translations and book distributors outside of the U.S.A., please write to Osborne **McGraw-Hill** at the above address.

A complete list of trademarks appears on page 387.

Advanced Turbo C®

1234567890 DODO 8987

ISBN 0-07-881280-1

C O N T E N T S

FOREWORD

The C language is firmly established as the favorite programming language of serious developers. The freedom, unmatched portability, and remarkable access of this language have made it the choice of computer professionals around the world.

It makes sense that Borland, a software company dedicated to serving programmers and known for its exceptional programming tools, should create Turbo C. Turbo C's power, versatility, and simplicity of design allow programmers to create better tools, utilities, and applications more quickly and more easily than they could in any other language development environment. Users will appreciate Turbo C's incredible compilation speed and the quality of the code it generates.

Now Herbert Schildt, veteran C programmer and author of five previous books on C, has written *Advanced Turbo C* for developers ready for power programming. In these pages he leads readers through a thorough discussion of C's components and their uses. In addition, he covers the conversion of Turbo Pascal to Turbo C.

This readable instruction guide and reference is the power programmer's key to that most powerful of programming language environments — Turbo C.

Philippe Kahn
President
Borland International, Inc.

PREFACE

I admit it: I'm hooked on C. There is a subtle elegance combined with raw power inherent in its design that I find irresistible. However, Borland's Turbo C adds another dimension: speed. In the past many C compilers were painfully slow, and compiling was an almost unbearably tedious process. Using Turbo C, it is now possible to compile, link, and execute programs in a matter of seconds. With Turbo C available, there is no longer an excuse to program in any other language.

This book helps you unlock the power of Turbo C through an applications-oriented approach. Each chapter examines a specific programming topic and develops programs that address that topic. Through this process, you will see many of the advanced features of Turbo C applied to some common programming problems, while, at the same time, you will sharpen your programming skills.

Chapter 1 covers sorting and searching. Chapter 2 deals with queues, stacks, linked lists, and binary trees. Chapter 3 discusses dynamic allocation and sparse arrays. Chapter 4 presents an overview of operating system interfacing and Chapter 5 covers the use of assembly language with Turbo C programs. Chapter 6 discusses graphics and develops several graphics functions, including line and circle functions. Chapter 7 discusses statistics and includes a complete statistics program.

Chapter 8 discusses codes, ciphers, and data compression. It includes a short history of cryptography, which is quite interesting. Chapter 9 details random number generators and then discusses how to use them in two simulations. The first is a check-out line in a store and the second is a random-walk portfolio management program.

Chapter 10 is my personal favorite because it contains the complete code to a recursive descent parser. Years ago, I would have given just about anything to have had that code.

Chapter 11 examines the conversion of Turbo Pascal code into Turbo C. Finally, Chapter 12 discusses efficiency, porting, and debugging.

There are two appendixes in this book: Appendix A explores Turbo C's memory model options and Appendix B contains a brief review of the Turbo C language.

There are many useful and interesting functions and programs in this book. If you're like me, you probably would like to use them, but would hate typing them into the computer. When I key in routines from a book, it seems that I always type something wrong and spend hours trying to get the program to work. For this reason, I am offering a diskette containing the source code to all the functions and programs contained in this book for $24.95. To obtain your copy, fill in the order blank on the next page and mail it, along with your payment, to the address shown. Or, if you're in a hurry, call my consulting office at (217) 586-4021 to place your order by telephone (Visa and MasterCard are accepted).

—H.S.

Please send me ____ copies, at $24.95 each, of the programs in *Advanced Turbo C*. Foreign orders, please add $5 shipping and handling.

_____

Name

_____

Address

_____

City   State   ZIP

_____

Telephone

Method of payment: check ____ Visa ____ MC ____

Credit card number: _____

Expiration date: _____

Signature: _____

Send to:

    Herbert Schildt
    RR 1, Box 130
    Mahomet, IL 61853
    or phone: (217) 586-4021

This is solely the offering of Herbert Schildt. Osborne/McGraw-Hill takes no responsibility for the fulfillment of this offer.

Sorting and Searching

CHAPTER 1

In the world of computer science perhaps no other tasks are more fundamental or as extensively analyzed as those of sorting and of searching. These routines are used in virtually all database programs, as well as in compilers, interpreters, and operating systems. This chapter introduces the basics of sorting and searching information. Because sorting data generally makes searching the data easier and faster, sorting is discussed first.

Sorting

Sorting is the process of arranging a set of similar information into an increasing or decreasing order. Specifically, given a sorted list i of n elements, then:

$$i_1 <= i_2 <= \ldots <= i_n$$

Though Turbo C supplies the standard **qsort( )** function as part of the standard library, the study and understanding of sorting is important for three main reasons. First, a generalized function like **qsort( )** cannot be applied to all situations. Second, because **qsort( )** is parameterized to operate on a wide variety of data, it will run slower than a similar sort that operates on only one type of data. (The generalization process inherently increases run time because of the extra processing time needed to handle various data types.) Finally, the Quicksort algorithm (used by **qsort( )**), although very good for the general case, may not be the best type of sort for specialized situations.

The two general categories of sorting algorithms are the sorting of arrays (both in memory and in random access disk files), and the sorting of sequential disk (or tape) files. This chapter focuses mostly on the first category because it is of the most interest to the average programmer. However, the general method of sorting sequential files is also discussed.

The main difference between sorting arrays and sorting sequential files is that each element of the array is available all the time. That is, any element may be compared or exchanged with any other element at any time. With a sequential file, only one element is available at any one time. Because of this difference, sorting techniques differ greatly between the two.

Generally, when information (such as a mailing list) is sorted, only a portion of that information is used as the *sort key*. This key is used in comparisons, but when an exchange is made the entire data structure is swapped. In a mailing list, for example, the ZIP code field might be used as the key, but the entire address is sorted. For the sake of simplicity while developing the various sorting methods, you will be sorting character arrays. Later, you will learn how to adapt any of these methods to any type of data structure.

Classes of Sorting Algorithms

The three general methods that can be used to sort arrays are

- By exchange
- By selection
- By insertion

To understand these three methods, imagine a deck of cards. To sort the cards using *exchange*, you would spread the cards, face up, on a table and then proceed to exchange out-of-order cards until the deck is ordered.

To sort by *selection*, you would spread the cards on the table, select the lowest-value card, take it out of the deck, and hold it in your hand. Then you would select from the remaining cards on the table the lowest card and place it behind the one already in your hand. This process would continue until all the cards were in your hand. Because you always select the lowest card from those remaining on the table, the cards in your hand would be sorted when the process was complete.

To sort the cards using *insertion*, you would hold the cards in your hand and would take one at a time. As you took cards from the deck, you would place them into a new deck on the table, always inserting them in the correct position. The deck would be sorted when you had no cards in your hand.

Judging Sorting Algorithms

Many different algorithms exist for each of the three sorting methods. Each algorithm has its merits, but the general criteria for judging a sorting algorithm are based on the following questions:

- How fast can it sort information in an average case?
- How fast is its best and worst case?
- Does it exhibit *natural* or *unnatural* behavior?
- Does it rearrange elements with equal keys?

How fast a particular algorithm sorts is of great concern. The speed with which an array can be sorted is directly related to the number of comparisons and the number of exchanges (exchanges take more time). A *comparison* occurs when one array element is compared to another. An *exchange* happens when two elements are swapped in the array. Later in this chapter you will see that some sorts require an exponential amount of time per element to sort and some require logarithmic time.

The best and worst-case run times are important if you expect to encounter one of these situations frequently. Often a sort will have a good average case, but a terrible worst case.

A sort is said to exhibit *natural behavior* if it works least when the list is already in order, harder as the list becomes less ordered, and hardest when a list is in inverse order. How hard a sort works is based on the number of comparisons and moves that must be executed.

To understand the importance of rearranging elements with equal keys, imagine a database that is sorted on a main key and a subkey —for example, a mailing list with the ZIP code as the main key and the last name within the same ZIP code as the subkey. When a new address is added to the list, and the list sorted again, you do not want the subkeys (that is, last names within ZIP codes) to be rearranged. To guarantee this, a sort must not exchange main keys of equal value.

In the following sections, representative sorts from each class of sorting algorithms are analyzed to judge their efficiency. Later, improved sorting methods are studied.

The Bubble Sort The best-known (and most infamous) sort is the *Bubble sort*. Its popularity is derived from its catchy name and its simplicity. For reasons that will become evident, this is one of the worst sorts ever conceived.

The Bubble sort uses the exchange method of sorting. The general concept behind the Bubble sort is the repeated comparisons and, if necessary, exchanges of adjacent elements. Its name comes from the method's similarity to bubbles in a tank of water, where each bubble seeks its own level. In this simplest form of the Bubble sort

```
void bubble(item,count)  /* bubble sort */
char *item;
int count;
{
  register int a,b;
  register char t;

  for(a=1;a<count;++a)
    for(b=count-1;b>=a;--b) {
      if(item[b-1] > item[b]) {
        /* exchange elements */
        t=item[b-1];
        item[b-1]=item[b];
        item[b]=t;
    }
  }
}
```

item is a pointer to the character array to be sorted and **count** is the number of elements in the array.

The Bubble sort is driven by two loops. Given that there are **count** elements in the array, the outer loop causes the array to be scanned **count−1** times. This ensures that, in the worst case, every element is in its proper position when the function terminates. The inner loop performs the actual comparisons and exchanges. (A slightly optimized version of the Bubble sort will terminate if no exchanges occur, but this also adds another comparison to each pass through the inner loop.)

This version of the Bubble sort can be used to sort a character array into ascending order. For example, this short program sorts a string typed in from the keyboard:

```
void bubble();

/* sort driver */
main()  /* sort a string from the keyboard */
{
  char s[80];

  printf("enter a string:");
  gets(s);
  bubble(s,strlen(s));
  printf("the sorted string is: %s\n",s);
}
```

To illustrate how the Bubble sort works, here are the passes used to sort **dcab**.

initial	d c a b
pass 1	a d c b
pass 2	a b d c
pass 3	a b c d

When analyzing any sort, you must determine how many comparisons and exchanges will be performed for the best, average, and worst case. With the Bubble sort, the number of comparisons is always the same because the two **for** loops will still repeat the specified number of times, whether or not the list is initially ordered. This means that the Bubble sort will always perform $1/2(n^2-n)$ comparisons, where n is the number of elements to be sorted. This formula is derived from the fact that the outer loop executes $n-1$ times and the inner loop $n/2$ times. Multiplying these together gives the formula.

The number of exchanges is 0 for the best case—an already sorted list. The numbers are $3/4(n^2-n)$ for the average case and $3/2(n^2-n)$ for the worst case. It is beyond the scope of this book to explain the derivation of these cases, but you can see that as the list becomes less ordered, the number of elements that are out of order approaches the number of comparisons. (Remember, there are three exchanges in a Bubble sort for every element out of order.) The Bubble sort is said to be an *n-squared algorithm* because its execution time is a multiple of the square of the number of elements. A Bubble sort is bad for a large number of elements because execution time is directly related to the number of comparisons and exchanges.

For example, if you ignore the time it takes to exchange any out-of-position element, and if each comparison takes 0.001 seconds, then sorting 10 elements will take about 0.05 seconds, sorting 100 elements will take about 5 seconds, and sorting 1000 elements will take about 500 seconds. A 100,000-element sort (the size of a small telephone book) would take about 5,000,000 seconds, or about 1400 hours—about two months of continuous sorting! Figure 1-1 shows how execution time increases in relation to the size of the array.

You can make some slight improvements to the Bubble sort to speed it up and to help its image. For example, the Bubble sort has one peculiarity: an out-of-order element at the large end (such as the **a** in the **decab** array example) will go to its proper position in one pass, but a misplaced element in the small end (such as the **d**) will rise very slowly to its proper place. This suggests an improvement to the Bubble sort.

Instead of always reading the array in the same direction, subsequent passes could reverse direction. Greatly out-of-place elements will travel more quickly to their correct positions. Shown here, this version of the Bubble sort is called the *Shaker sort* because of its shaking motion over the array:

```
void shaker(item,count) /* Shaker sort, an improved bubble sort */
char *item;
int count;
{
   register int a,b,c,d;
   char t;

   c=1;
   b=count-1; d=count-1;

   do {
     for(a=d; a>=c; --a) {
       if(item[a-1]>item[a]) {
         t=item[a-1];
         item[a-1]=item[a];
         item[a]=t;
```

```
      b=a;
    }
  }
  c=b+1;
  for(a=c;a<d+1;++a) {
    if(item[a-1]>item[a]) {
      t=item[a-1];
      item[a-1]=item[a];
      item[a]=t;
      b=a;
    }
  }
  d=b-1;
} while (c<=d);
}
```

Although the Shaker sort does improve the Bubble sort, it still executes on the order of n^2 because the number of comparisons is unchanged and because the number of exchanges has only been reduced by a relatively small constant. Although the Shaker sort is better than the Bubble sort, better sorts do exist.

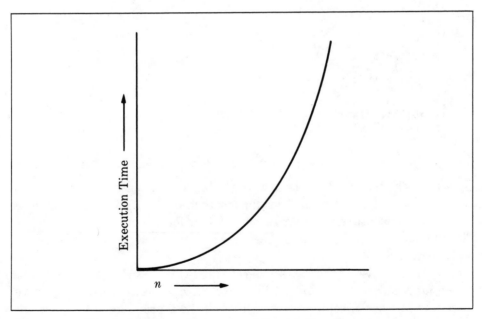

Figure 1-1. Execution time of an n^2 sort in relation to array size

Sorting by Selection   A *Selection sort* selects the element with the lowest value and exchanges that with the first element. Then from the remaining $n-1$ elements, the element with the least key is found and exchanged with the second element, and so forth, up to the last two elements. For example, if the selection method were to be used on the array **bdac**, each pass would look like this:

initial	b d a c
pass 1	a d b c
pass 2	a b d c
pass 3	a b c d

The basic Selection sort is shown here:

```
void select(item,count)   /* selection sort */
char *item;
int count;
{
  register int a,b,c;
  char t;

  for(a=0; a<count-1;++a) {
    c=a;
    t=item[a];
    for(b=a+1; b<count;++b) {
      if(item[b]<t) {
        c=b;
        t=item[b];
      }
    }
    item[c]=item[a];
    item[a]=t;
  }
}
```

Unfortunately, like the Bubble sort, the outer loop executes $n-1$ times and the inner loop $1/2(n)$ times. This means that the Selection sort requires $1/2(n^2-n)$ comparisons, which makes it too slow for a large number of items. The number of exchanges for the best case is $3(n-1)$ and for the worst case is $n^2/4+3(n-1)$.

For the best case, if the list is ordered, then only $n-1$ elements need to be moved, and each move requires three exchanges. The worst case approximates the number of comparisons. Although the average case is beyond the scope of this book to develop, it is $n(\ln n+y)$ where y is Euler's constant (about

0.577216). This means that although the number of comparisons for both the Bubble sort and the Selection sort is the same, the number of exchanges in the average case is far less for the Selection sort.

Sorting by Insertion   The *Insertion sort* is the last of the simple sorting algorithms. The Insertion sort initially sorts the first two members of the array. Next, the algorithm inserts the third member into its sorted position in relation to the first two members. Then, the fourth element is inserted into the list of three elements. The process continues until all elements have been sorted. For example, given the array **dcab**, each pass of the Insertion sort would look like this:

initial	d c a b
pass 1	c d a b
pass 3	a c d b
pass 4	a b c d

A version of the Insertion sort is shown here:

```
void insert(item,count) /* sorting by straight insertion */
char *item;
int count;
{

  register int a,b;
  char t;

  for(a=1; a<count; ++a) {
    t=item[a];
    b=a-1;
    while(b>=0 && t<item[b] ) {
      item[b+1]=item[b];
      b--;
    }
    item[b+1]=t;
  }
}
```

Unlike the Bubble sort and the Selection sort, the number of comparisons that occur while the Insertion sort is used will depend on how the list is initially ordered. If the list is in order, then the number of comparisons is $n-1$. If the list is in inverse order, then the number of comparisons is $1/2(n^2+n)-1$, while its average number of comparisons is $1/4(n^2+n-2)$.

The number of exchanges for each case is as follows:

best	$2(n-1)$
average	$1/4(n^2+9n-10)$
worst	$1/2(n^2+3n-4)$

Therefore, the number for the worst case is as bad as those for the Bubble and Selection sorts, and for the average case it is only slightly better.

The Insertion sort does have two advantages, however. First, it behaves *naturally*: it works the least when the array is already sorted and the hardest when the array is sorted in inverse order. This makes the Insertion sort useful for lists that are almost in order. Second, it leaves the order of equal keys unchanged: if a list is sorted using two keys, then it remains sorted for both keys after an Insertion sort.

Even though the comparisons may be fairly good for certain sets of data, the fact that the array must always be shifted over each time an element is placed in its proper location means that the number of moves can be very significant. However, the Insertion sort still behaves naturally, with the least exchanges occurring for an almost sorted list and the most exchanges for an inversely ordered array.

Improved Sorts

All of the algorithms thus far had the fatal flaw of executing in n^2 time. For large amounts of data, the sorts would be slow — in fact, at some point, too slow to use. Every computer programmer has heard, or told, the horror story of the "sort that took three days." Unfortunately, these stories are often true.

When a sort takes too long, it may be the fault of the underlying algorithm. However, a sad commentary is that the first response is often "write it in assembly code." Although assembler code will sometimes speed up a routine by a constant factor, if the underlying algorithm is bad, the sort will be slow no matter how optimal the coding. Remember, when the run time of a routine is relative to n^2, increasing the speed of the coding or of the computer will only cause a slight improvement because the rate at which the run time increases changes exponentially. (The graph in Figure 1-1 is shifted to the right slightly, but the curve is unchanged.) Keep in mind that if something is not fast enough in Turbo C, then it will generally not be fast enough in assembler. The solution is to use a better sorting algorithm.

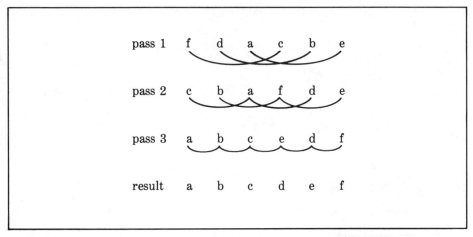

Figure 1-2. The Shell sort

In this section, two excellent sorts are developed. The first is the Shell sort, and the second is the Quicksort, which is generally considered the best sorting routine. These sorts run so fast that if you blink, you will miss them.

The Shell Sort   The *Shell sort* is named after its inventor, D.L. Shell. However, the name seems to have stuck because its method of operation resembles sea shells piled upon one another.

The general method, derived from the Insertion sort, is based on diminishing increments. Figure 1-2 gives a diagram of a Shell sort on the array **fdacbe**. First, all elements that are three positions apart are sorted. Then all elements that are two positions apart are sorted. Finally, all those adjacent to each other are sorted.

It may not be obvious that this method yields good results, or even that it will sort the array, but it does both. This algorithm is efficient because each sorting pass involves relatively few elements, or elements that are already in reasonable order; therefore each pass increases the order of the data.

The exact sequence for the increments can be changed. The only rule is that the last increment must be 1. For example, the sequence 9, 5, 3, 2, 1 works well and is used in the Shell sort shown here. Avoid sequences that are powers of 2 because, for mathematically complex reasons, they reduce the efficiency of the sorting algorithm. (However, even if you use them, the sort would still work.)

```
void shell(item,count)   /* a shell sort */
char *item;
int count;
{

   register int i,j,k,s,w;
   char x, a[5];

   a[0]=9; a[1]=5; a[2]=3; a[3]=2; a[4]=1;

   for(w=0; w<5; w++) {
     k=a[w]; s=-k;
     for(i=k; i<count;++i) {
       x=item[i];
       j=i-k;
       if(s==0){ s=-k;
         s++;
         item[s]=x;
       }
       while(x<item[j] && j>=0 && j<=count) {
         item[j+k]=item[j];
         j=j-k;
       }
       item[j+k]=x;
     }
   }
}
```

You may have noticed that the inner **while** loop has three test conditions. The **x<item[j]** is a comparison necessary for the sorting process. The tests **j>=0** and **j<=count** are used to keep the sort from overrunning the boundary of the array **item**. These extra checks degrade the performance of Shell sort to some extent. Slightly different versions of the Shell sort employ special array elements, called *sentinels*, which are not actually part of the array to be sorted. Sentinels hold special termination values that indicate the least and greatest possible elements. In this way the boundary checks are unnecessary. However, using sentinels requires a specific knowledge of the data, which limits the generality of the sort function.

The analysis of the Shell sort presents some very difficult mathematical problems that are far beyond the scope of this text. However, execution time is proportional to $n^{1.2}$ for sorting n elements. This is a very significant improvement over the n^2 sorts of the previous section. To understand how great an improvement, see Figure 1-3, which graphs both an n^2 and an $n^{1.2}$ curve together. However, before you decide to use the Shell sort, you should know that the Quicksort is even better.

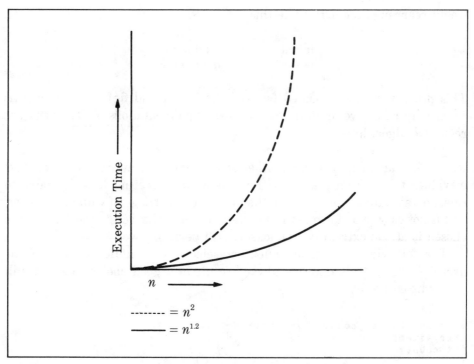

Figure 1-3. The n^2 and $n^{1.2}$ curves

The Quicksort   The *Quicksort*, invented and named by C.A.R. Hoare, is generally considered the best sorting algorithm currently available. It is based on the exchange method of sorting. This is surprising if you consider the terrible performance of the Bubble sort, which is also based on the exchange method.

The Quicksort is built on the idea of partitions. The general procedure is to select a value (called the *comparand*) and then to partition the array into two parts with all elements greater than or equal to the partition value on one side and those less than the partition value on the other. This process is then repeated for each remaining part until the array is sorted. For example, given the array **fedacb** and using the value **d**, the first pass of the Quicksort would rearrange the array like this:

```
initial       f e d a c b
pass 1        b c a d e f
```

This process is then repeated for each half (**bca** and **def**). The process is essentially recursive; indeed, the cleanest implementations of Quicksort are recursive algorithms.

The selection of the middle comparand value can be accomplished two ways. The value can be chosen either at random or by averaging a small set of values taken from the array. For the optimal sorting it is desirable to select a value that is precisely in the middle of the range of values. However, this is not easy to do for most sets of data. Even in the worst case—the value chosen is at one extremity—Quicksort still performs well.

The following version of Quicksort selects the middle element of the array. Although this may not always result in a good choice, the sort still performs correctly.

```c
void quick(item,count)   /* quicksort set up */
char *item;
int count;
{

  qs(item,0,count-1);

}
void qs(item,left,right)   /* quicksort */
char *item;
int left,right;
{

  register int i,j;
  char x,y;

  i=left; j=right;
  x=item[(left+right)/2];

  do {
    while(item[i]<x && i<right) i++;
    while(x<item[j] && j>left) j--;

    if(i<=j) {
      y=item[i];
      item[i]=item[j];
      item[j]=y;
      i++; j--;
```

```
   }
} while(i<=j);

if(left<j)  qs(item,left,j);
if(i<right) qs(item,i,right);
}
```

In this version, the function **quick()** sets up a call to the main sorting function, called **qs()**. While this maintains the same common interface of **item** and **count**, it is not essential because **qs()** could have been called directly using three arguments.

The derivation of the number of comparisons and number of exchanges that Quicksort performs requires mathematics beyond the scope of this book. However, you can assume that the number of comparisons is $n \log n$ and that the number of exchanges is approximately $n/6 \log n$. These are significantly better than any of the previous sorts discussed so far.

The equation

$$N = a^x$$

can be rewritten as

$$x = \log_a N$$

This means, for example, that if 100 elements were to be sorted, Quicksort would require 100 * 2, or 200, comparisons because log 100 is 2. Compared with the Bubble sort's 990 comparisons, this number is quite good.

You should be aware of one particularly nasty aspect to Quicksort. If the comparand value for each partition happens to be the largest value, then Quicksort degenerates into "slowsort" with an n^2 run time. Generally, however, this does not happen.

You must carefully choose a method of determining the value of the comparand. Often the value is determined by the actual data you are sorting. In large mailing lists where the sorting is often by ZIP code, the selection is simple, because the ZIP codes are fairly evenly distributed and a simple algebraic function can determine a suitable comparand. However, in certain databases, the sort keys may be so close in value (with many being the same value) that a random selection is often the best method available. A common and fairly effective method is to sample three elements from a partition and take the middle value.

Choosing a Sort

Generally, the Quicksort is the sort of choice because it is so fast. However, when only very small lists of data are to be sorted (less than 100), the overhead created by Quicksort's recursive calls may offset the benefits of a superior algorithm. In rare cases like this, one of the simpler sorts (perhaps even the Bubble sort) will be quicker.

Sorting Other Data Structures

Until now, you have only been sorting arrays of characters. This has made it easy to present each of the sorting routines. Obviously, arrays of any of the built-in data types can be sorted simply by changing the data types of the parameters and variables to the sort function. However, generally complex data types like strings, or groupings of information like structures, need to be sorted. Most sorting involves a key and information linked to that key. To adapt the algorithms to sort other structures, you need to alter either the comparison section or the exchange section, or both. The algorithm itself will remain unchanged.

Because Quicksort is one of the best general-purpose routines available at this time, it will be used in the following examples. The same techniques will apply to any of the sorts described earlier.

Sorting Strings   The easiest way to sort strings is to create an array of character pointers to those strings. This allows you to maintain easy indexing and keeps the basic Quicksort algorithm unchanged. The string version of Quicksort shown here will accept an array of **char** pointers that point to the strings to be sorted. The sort rearranges the pointers to the strings, not the actual strings in memory. This version sorts the strings in alphabetical order.

```
void quick_string(item,count)  /* quick sort for strings setup */
char *item[];
int count;
{
   qs_string(item,0,count-1);
}

void qs_string(item,left,right)  /* quick sort for strings */
char *item[];
int left,right;
{
   register int i,j;
```

```
char *x,*y;

i=left; j=right;
x=item[(left+right)/2];

do {
   while(strcmp(item[i],x)<0 && i<right) i++;
   while(strcmp(item[j],x)>0 && j>left) j--;
   if(i<=j) {
      y=item[i];
      item[i]=item[j];
      item[j]=y;
      i++; j--;
   }
} while(i<=j);

if(left<j)  qs_string(item,left,j);
if(i<right) qs_string(item,i,right);
}
```

The comparison step has been changed to use the function **strcmp()**, which returns a negative number if the first string is lexicographically less than the second, 0 if the strings are equal, and a positive number if the first string is lexicographically greater than the second. The exchange part of the routine has been left unchanged because only the pointers are being exchanged — not the actual strings. To exchange the actual strings, you would have to use the function **strcpy()**.

The use of **strcmp()** will slow down the sort for two reasons. First, it involves a function call, which always takes time; second, the **strcmp()** function itself performs several comparisons to determine the relationship of the two strings. If speed is absolutely critical, the code for **strcmp()** can be duplicated in line inside the routine. However, there is no way to avoid comparing the strings, since this is by definition what the task involves.

Sorting Structures   Most application programs that require a sort will need to have a grouping of data sorted. A mailing list is an excellent example because a name, street, city, state, and ZIP code are all linked together. When this conglomerate unit of data is sorted, a sort key is used, but the entire structure is exchanged. To see how this is done, you first need to create a structure. For the mailing-list example, a convenient structure is

```
struct address {
        char name[40];
        char street[40];
        char city[20];
        char state[3];
        char zip[10];
};
```

The **state** is three characters long and **zip** is ten characters long because a string array always needs to be one character longer than the maximum length of any string in order to store the null terminator.

Since it is reasonable to arrange a mailing list as an array of structures, assume for this example that the sort routine sorts an array of structures of type **address**, as shown here.

```
void quick_struct(item,count)  /* quick sort for structures */
             /* setup */
struct address item[];
int count;
{
   qs_struct(item,0,count-1);
}

void qs_struct(item,left,right)  /* quick sort for structures */
struct address item[];
int left,right;
{

   register int i,j;
   char *x,*y;

   i=left; j=right;
   x=item[(left+right)/2].zip;

   do {
     while(strcmp(item[i].zip,x)<0 && i<right) i++;
     while(strcmp(item[j].zip,x)>0 && j>left) j--;
     if(i<=j) {
       swap_all_fields(item,i,j);
       i++; j--;
     }
   } while(i<=j);

   if(left<j)  qs_struct(item,left,j);
   if(i<right) qs_struct(item,i,right);
}
```

Notice that both the comparison code and the exchange code needed to be altered. Because so many fields needed to be exchanged, a separate function, **swap_all_fields( )**, was created to do this. You will need to create **swap_all_fields( )** in accordance with the nature of the structure being sorted.

Sorting Disk Files

The two types of disk files are *sequential* and *random-access*. If a disk file is small enough, it may be read into memory and the array-sorting routines presented earlier sort it most efficiently. However, many disk files are too large to be sorted easily in memory and require special techniques. Most microcomputer database applications use random access files. For this reason they are examined first.

Sorting Random-Access Disk Files as Arrays Random-access disk files have two major advantages over sequential disk files. First, they are easy to maintain: you can update information without having to recopy the entire list. Second, random-access disk files can be treated as an array on disk, allowing (with small modification) any of the array sorting routines to be applied to them.

Applying this method means that you can use the basic Quicksort with modifications to seek different records on the disk, much like indexing an array. Unlike sorting a sequential disk file, sorting a random file in place means that a full disk does not need to have room for both the sorted and unsorted files.

Each sorting situation differs with the exact data structure that is sorted and the key that is used. However, the general idea of sorting random-access disk files can be understood by developing a sort program to sort the mailing-list structure called **address** that was defined earlier. This sample program assumes that the number of elements is fixed at 100, but in a real application, a record count would have to be dynamically maintained. The mailing-list sorting program is given here.

```
/* disk sort for structures of type address */
#include "stdio.h"
#define NUM_ELEMENTS 100  /* this is an arbitrary number
                             that should be determined
                             dynamically for each list */

struct address {
  char name[30];
  char street[40];
  char city[20];
  char state[3];
  char zip[10];
}ainfo;

void quick_disk(), qs_disk(), swap_all_fields();

main()
{
  FILE *fp;
  int t;

  if((fp=fopen("mlist","rb+"))==0) {
```

```
      printf("cannot open file for read/write\n");
      exit (0);
   }

   quick_disk(fp,NUM_ELEMENTS);
   fclose(fp);
   printf("List sorted.\n");
}

void quick_disk(fp,count)  /* quick sort for random files */
                     /* setup */
FILE *fp;
long int count;
{
   qs_disk(fp,0L,(long) count-1);
}

void qs_disk(fp,left,right)  /* quick sort for random files */
FILE *fp;
long int left,right;
{

   long int i,j;
   char x[100],*y,*get_zip();

   i=left; j=right;

   strcpy(x,get_zip(fp,(long)(i+j)/2)); /* get the middle zip */

   do {
     while(strcmp(get_zip(fp,i),x)<0 && i<right) i++;
     while(strcmp(get_zip(fp,j),x)>0 && j>left) j--;

     if(i<=j) {
       swap_all_fields(fp,i,j);
       i++; j--;
     }
   } while(i<=j);

   if(left<j)  qs_disk(fp,left,j);
   if(i<right) qs_disk(fp,i,right);
}

void swap_all_fields(fp,i,j)
FILE *fp;
long int i,j;
{

   char a[sizeof(ainfo)],b[sizeof(ainfo)];
   register int t;

   /* first read in record i and j */
   fseek(fp,sizeof(ainfo)*i,0);
   fread(a,sizeof(ainfo),1,fp);
```

```
    fseek(fp,sizeof(ainfo)*j,0);
    fread(b,sizeof(ainfo),1,fp);

    /* then write them back in opposite slots */
    fseek(fp,sizeof(ainfo)*j,0);
    fwrite(a,sizeof(ainfo),1,fp);

    fseek(fp,sizeof(ainfo)*i,0);
    fwrite(b,sizeof(ainfo),1,fp);
}

char *get_zip(fp,rec)
FILE *fp;
long int rec;
{
    struct address *p;
    register int t;

    p=&ainfo;

    fseek(fp,rec*sizeof(ainfo),0);
    fread(p,sizeof(ainfo),1,fp);

    return ainfo.zip;
}
```

Several support functions had to be written to sort the address records. For the comparison section of the sort, the **get_zip( )** function returns a pointer to the ZIP code of the comparand and the record being checked. The **swap_all_fields( )** function performs the actual exchange of the data. Under most operating systems, the order of reads and writes has a great impact on the speed of this sort. The code, as it is written, forces a **seek** to record **i**, then to **j**. While the head of the disk drive is still positioned at **j**, the data of **i** is written. This means that it is not necessary for the head to move a great distance. Had the code been written with the data of **i** to be written first, then an extra **seek** would have been necessary.

Sorting Random Access Files Using Index Files   Sometimes, depending upon the application, it is possible to not physically sort the information in a disk data file, but rather to sort another file that contains the keys and the data file record numbers of the information associated with each key. In this case, the much smaller *index file* is sorted in memory. Figure 1-4 shows this approach. This greatly reduces the time it takes to sort the data. Of course, to access the actual data you first read the index file to find the location of each entry. Because of the complexity involved, no example of this method is shown. However, the general procedure should be clear.

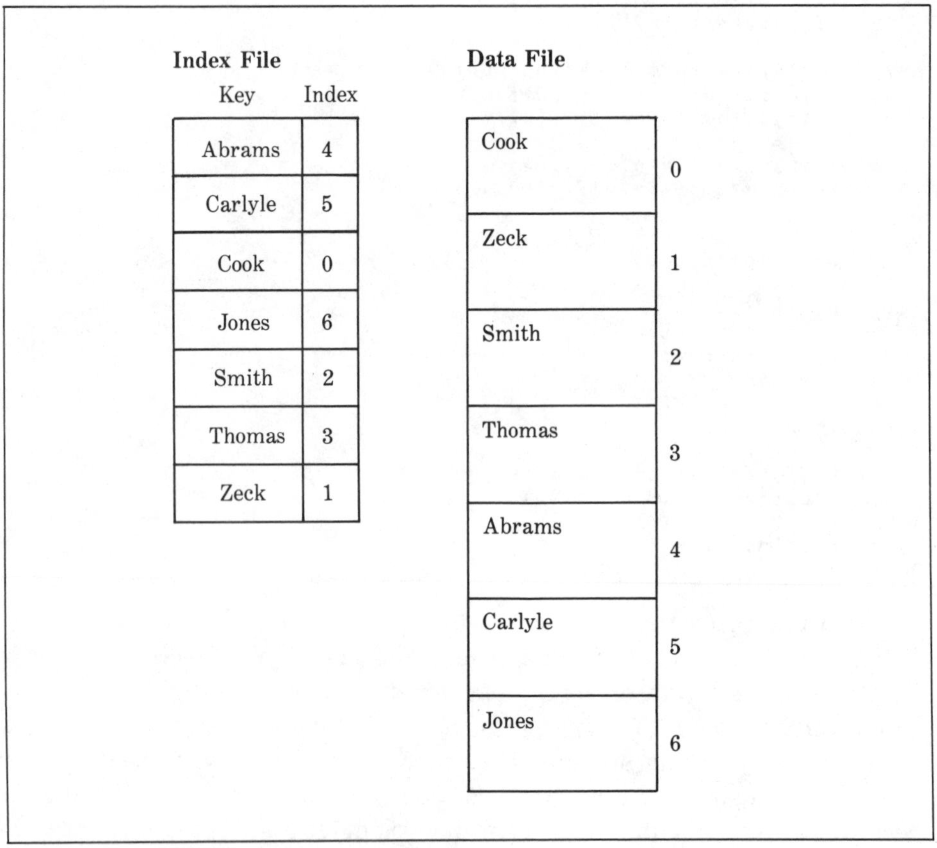

Index File	
Key	Index
Abrams	4
Carlyle	5
Cook	0
Jones	6
Smith	2
Thomas	3
Zeck	1

Data File	
Cook	0
Zeck	1
Smith	2
Thomas	3
Abrams	4
Carlyle	5
Jones	6

Figure 1-4.   Using an index file with a data file

Sorting Sequential Files   Unlike random-access files, sequential files generally have no fixed record lengths and they may be organized on storage devices that do not allow easy random access. Despite these limitations, sequential disk files are common because a specific application is best suited to variable record lengths or because the storage device is sequential in nature. For example, most text files are sequential.

Although sorting a disk file as if it were an array has several advantages, this method cannot be used with sequential files because there is no way to achieve quick enough access to any arbitrary element. For example, no quick way exists to reach arbitrary records of a sequential file that is located on tape. For this reason, it would be difficult to apply any of the previously presented array-sorting algorithms to sequential files.

There are two main approaches to sorting sequential files. The first approach reads the information into memory and sorts with one of the standard array-sorting algorithms. Although this approach is fast, memory constraints limit the size of the file that can be sorted.

The second approach is to divide the file into two pieces and perform a *Merge sort.* The Merge sort divides the file to be sorted into two files of equal length. Using these files, the sort reads an element from each file, orders that pair, and writes elements to a third disk file. This new file is then split in half, and the ordered doubles are merged into ordered quadruples. The new file is split again, and the same procedure followed until the list is sorted. For historical reasons, this Merge sort is called a *three-tape merge* because it requires three files (tape drives) to be active at one time.

To understand how this works, consider the following sequence:

$$1\ 4\ 3\ 8\ 6\ 7\ 2\ 5$$

The first split produces

$$1\ 4\ 3\ 8$$
$$6\ 7\ 2\ 5$$

The first merge yields

$$1\ 6\quad 4\ 7\quad 2\ 3\quad 5\ 8$$

This is split again to be

$$1\ 6\quad 4\ 7$$
$$2\ 3\quad 5\ 8$$

The final split is

$$1\ 2\ 3\ 6$$
$$4\ 5\ 7\ 8$$

with the outcome

$$1\ 2\ 3\ 4\ 5\ 6\ 7\ 8$$

As you may have guessed, the three-tape merge requires passes equal to $\log_2 n$ where n is the number of total elements to sort.

A simple version of the Merge sort is shown here. It assumes that the input file is a character stream (such as a text file) and that the file is an even power of 2 in length. You can easily alter this version to sort any type of data file.

```
#include "stdio.h"

#define LENGTH 16   /* arbitrary */
void merge();

main(argc,argv)  /* merge sort for disk files */
int argc;
char *argv[];
{
   FILE *fp1,*fp2,*fp3;

   if((fp1=fopen(argv[1],"rw"))==0) {
     printf("cannot open file 1%s\n",argv[1]);
     exit(0);
   }

   if((fp2=fopen("sort1","rw"))==0) {
     printf("cannot open file 2\n");
     exit(0);
   }

   if((fp3=fopen("sort2","rw"))==0) {
     printf("cannot open file 3\n");
     exit(0);
   }

   merge(fp1,fp2,fp3,LENGTH);

   fclose(fp1); fclose(fp2); fclose(fp3);

}
void merge(fp1,fp2,fp3,count)
FILE *fp1,*fp2,*fp3;
int count;
{
   register int t,n,j,k,q;
   char x,y;

   for(n=1;n<count;n=n*2) {

     /* split file */
     for(t=0;t<count/2;++t) putc(getc(fp1),fp2);
     for(;t<count;++t) putc(getc(fp1),fp3);

     reset(fp1,fp2,fp3);

     for(q=0;q<count/2;q+=n) {
         x=getc(fp2);
         y=getc(fp3);
         for(j=k=0;;) {
```

```
      if(x<y) {
        putc(x,fp1);
        j++;
        if(j<n) x=getc(fp2);
        else break;
      }
      else {
        putc(y,fp1);
        k++;
        if(k<n) y=getc(fp3);
        else break;
      }
      }
      if(j<n)  {
    putc(x,fp1);
    j++;
      }
      if(k<n)  {
    putc(y,fp1);
    k++;
      }
      for(;j<n;++j) putc(getc(fp2),fp1);
      for(;k<n;++k) putc(getc(fp3),fp1);
    }
    reset(fp1,fp2,fp3);
  }
}


reset(fp1,fp2,fp3)
FILE *fp1,*fp2,*fp3;
{
  rewind(fp1);
  rewind(fp2);
  rewind(fp3);
}
```

All three files have been opened for read/write mode and **reset()** was created to rewind the files each time.

Searching

Databases of information exist so that, from time to time, a user can locate a record by knowing its key. There is only one method of finding information in an unsorted file or array, and another for a sorted file or array. Many compilers supply search functions as part of the standard library. However, as with sorting, general-purpose routines sometimes are simply too inefficient for use in demanding situations because of the extra overhead created by the generalization.

Searching Methods

Finding information in an unsorted array requires a sequential search starting at the first element and stopping either when a match is found or when the end of the array is reached. This method must be used on unsorted data, but can also be applied to sorted data. If the data has been sorted, then a binary search can be used, which greatly speeds up any search.

The Sequential Search   The *sequential search* is easy to code. The following function searches a character array of known length until a match is found with the specified key.

```
sequential_search(item,count,key)
char *item;
int count;
char key;
{
  register int t;
  for(t=0;t<count;++t)
    if(key==item[t]) return t;
  return -1;  /* no match */
}
```

This function will return the index number of the matching entry if there is one, or −1 if there is not.

A straight sequential search will, on the average, test $n/2$ elements. In the best case, it will test only one element and in the worst case n elements. If the information is stored on disk, the search time can be very long. But if the data is unsorted, this is the only method available.

The Binary Search   If the data to be searched is in sorted order, then a superior method, called the *binary search*, can be used to find a match. The method uses the "divide-and-conquer" approach. It first tests the middle element; if the element is larger than the key, it then tests the middle element of the first half; otherwise, it tests the middle element of the second half. This process is repeated until either a match is found, or there are no more elements to test.

For example, to find the number 4 in the array **1 2 3 4 5 6 7 8 9**, the binary search would first test the middle, which is **5**. Since this is greater than 4, the search would continue with the first half, or

In this example, the middle element is **3**. This is less than 4, so the first half is discarded and the search continues with

4 5

This time the match is found.

In the binary search, the number of comparisons given the worst case is $\log_2 n$. With average cases, the number is somewhat better; in the best case, the number is 1.

A binary search function for character arrays is shown here. You can make this search any arbitrary data structure by changing the comparison portion of the routine.

```
binary(item,count,key)    /* Binary search */
char *item;
int count;
char key;
{
  int low,high, mid;

  low=0; high=count-1;
  while(low<=high) {
    mid=(low+high)/2;
    if(key<item[mid]) high=mid-1;
    else if(key>item[mid]) low=mid+1;
    else return mid;  /* found */
  }
  return -1;
}
```

Queues, Stacks, Linked Lists, and Binary Trees

CHAPTER 2

Programs consist of *algorithms* and *data structures*. The good program is a blend of both. Choosing and implementing a data structure are as important as the routines that manipulate the data. The way that information is organized and accessed is usually determined by the nature of the programming problem. Therefore, as a programmer, you must have in your "bag of tricks" the right storage and retrieval method for a variety of situations.

How closely the logical concept of an item of data is bound with its physical machine representation is in inverse correlation to its abstraction. That is, as data types become more complex, the way the programmer thinks of them bears an ever-decreasing resemblance to the way they are actually represented in memory. For example, simple types such as **char** and **int** are tightly bound to their machine representation. In this case, the value that an integer has in its machine representation closely approximates that which the programmer conceives of it having.

Simple arrays, which are organized collections of the simple data types, are not quite as tightly bound as the simple types themselves because an array may not appear in memory the way the programmer thinks of it. Less tightly bound yet are **floats** because the actual representation inside the machine is unlike the average programmer's conception of a floating-point number. The structure, which is a conglomerate data type accessed under one name, is even more abstracted from the machine representation.

The final level of abstraction transcends the mere physical aspects of the data and concentrates instead on the sequence in which the data will be accessed (that is, *stored* and *retrieved*). In essence, the physical data is linked with a "data engine" that controls the way information can be accessed by your program. The four types of these engines are

- A queue

- A stack

- A linked list

- A binary tree

Each method provides a solution to a class of problems; each is essentially a "device" that performs a specific storage and retrieval operation on the given information according to the requests it receives. The methods share two operations, *store an item* and *retrieve an item*, in which an item is one informational unit. This chapter shows you how to implement these methods in Turbo C for use in your own programs.

Queues

A queue is a linear list of information that is accessed in *first-in, first-out* order (sometimes called FIFO). The first item placed on the queue is the first item retrieved, the second item put in is the second item retrieved, and so on. This order is the only means of storage and retrieval; a queue does not allow random access of any specific item.

Queues are very common in everyday life. For example, lines at a bank or a fast-food restaurant are queues. To visualize how a queue works, consider two functions: **qstore( )** and **qretrieve( )**. **Qstore( )** places an item onto the end of the queue and **qretrieve( )** removes the first item from the queue and returns its value. Figure 2-1 shows the effect of a series of these operations.

Action	Contents of Queue
qstore(A)	A
qstore(B)	A B
qstore(C)	A B C
qretrieve( ) returns **A**	B C
qstore(D)	B C D
qretrieve( ) returns **B**	C D
qretrieve( ) returns **C**	D

Figure 2-1. A queue in action

Keep in mind that a retrieve operation removes an item from the queue, and if it is not stored elsewhere, destroys it. Therefore, even though the program is still active, a queue may be empty because all of its items have been removed.

Queues are used in many types of programming situations such as simulations (discussed later in their own chapter), event or appointment scheduling (such as in a PERT or Gant chart), and I/O buffering.

For example, consider a simple appointment-scheduler program that allows you to enter a number of events. As each appointment is performed it is taken off the list. You might use a program like this to organize a day's appointments. For the sake of simplicity, the program uses an array of pointers to the event strings. It limits each appointment description to 256 characters and the number of entries to 100. First, here are the functions **qstore( )** and **qretrieve( )** that will be used for the simple scheduling program:

```
/* store an appointment */
void qstore(q)
char *q;
{
  if(spos==MAX) {
    printf("List full\n");
    return;
  }
  p[spos]=q;
  spos++;
}
```

```
/* retrieve an appointment */
char *qretrieve()
{
  if(rpos==spos) {
    printf("No (more) appointments.\n");
    return NULL;
  }
  rpos++;
  return p[rpos-1];
}
```

These functions require two global variables: **spos**, which holds the index of the next free storage location, and **rpos**, which holds the index of the next item to retrieve. It is possible to use these functions to maintain a queue of other data types by simply changing the base type of the array on which they operate.

The function **qstore( )** places pointers to new events on the end of the list and checks whether the list is full. **Qretrieve( )** takes events off the queue as they occur. With each new appointment scheduled, **spos** is incremented, and with each appointment removed, **rpos** is incremented. In essence, **rpos** "chases" **spos** through the queue. Figure 2-2 shows the way this may appear in memory as the program executes. If **rpos** and **spos** are equal, no events are left in the schedule. Keep in mind that even though the information stored in the queue is not actually destroyed by the **qretrieve( )** function, it can never be accessed again and is in effect destroyed.

Here is the entire program for this simple appointment scheduler. You may want to enhance this program for your own use.

```
#include "stdlib.h"
#include "stdio.h"
#define MAX 100

char *p[MAX], *qretrieve();
int spos;
int rpos;
void enter(), qstore(), review(), delete();

main()  /* Mini Appointment-Scheduler */
{
  char s[80];
  register int t;

  for(t=0;t<MAX;++t) p[t]=NULL; /* init array to nulls */
  spos=0; rpos=0;

  for(;;) {
    printf("Enter, List, Remove, Quit: ");
    gets(s);
    *s=toupper(*s);
```

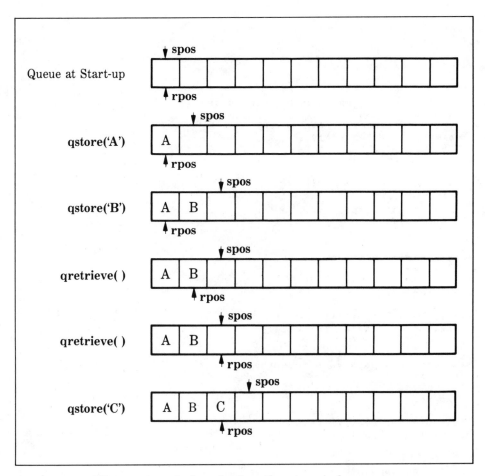

Figure 2-2. The retrieve index chasing the store index

```
switch(*s) {
  case 'E':
    enter();
    break;
  case 'L':
    review();
    break;
  case 'R':
    delete();
    break;
  case 'Q':
    exit(0);
  }
 }
}
```

```
/* enter appointments */
void enter()
{
  char s[256], *p;

  do {
    printf("enter appointment %d: ",spos+1);
    gets(s);
    if(*s==0) break;  /* no entry */
    p=malloc(strlen(s));
    if(!p) {
      printf("out of memory.\n");
      return;
    }
    strcpy(p,s);
    if(*s) qstore(p);
  }while(*s);
}

/* see what's in the queue */
void review()
{
  register int t;

  for(t=rpos;t<spos;++t)
    printf("%d. %s\n",t+1,p[t]);
}

/* delete an appointment from the queue */
void delete()
{
  char *p;

  if(!(p=qretrieve())) return;
  printf("%s\n",p);
}

/* store an appointment */
void qstore(q)
char *q;
{
  if(spos==MAX) {
    printf("list full\n");
    return;
  }
  p[spos]=q;
  spos++;
}

/* retrieve an appointment */
char *qretrieve()
{
  if(rpos==spos) {
    printf("No (more) appointments.\n");
    return NULL;
```

```
    }
    rpos++;
    return p[rpos-1];
}
```

A sample run of the appointment scheduler is shown here:

```
Enter, List, Remove, Quit: E
enter appointment 1: Jon at 9 about the phone system
enter appointment 2: Ted at 10:30 - wants that raise...humm.
enter appointment 3: lunch with Mary and Tom at Harry's
enter appointment 4: <cr>
Enter, List, Remove, Quit: L
1. Jon at 9 about the phone system
2. Ted at 10:30 - wants that raise...humm.
3. lunch with Mary and Tom at Harry's
Enter, List, Remove, Quit: R
Jon at 9 about the phone system
Enter, List, Remove, Quit: L
2. Ted at 10:30 - wants that raise...humm.
3. lunch with Mary and Tom at Harry's
Enter, List, Remove, Quit:
```

The Circular Queue

In studying the appointment-scheduler program in the previous section, an improvement may have occurred to you. Instead of having the program stop when the limit of the array used to store the queue was reached, you could have both the store index (**spos**) and the retrieve index (**rpos**) loop back to the start of the array. This would allow any number of items to be placed on the queue, as long as items were also being taken off. This method of implementing a queue is called a *circular queue* because it uses its storage array as if it were a circle instead of a linear list.

To create a circular queue for use in the appointment-scheduler program, the **qstore( )** and **qretrieve( )** functions need to be changed, as shown here:

```
void qstore(q)
char *q;
{
  /* The queue is full if either spos is one less than rpos
     or if spos is at the end of the queue array and rpos
     is at the beginning.
  */
  if(spos+1==rpos || (spos+1==MAX && !rpos)) {
    printf("list full\n");
    return;
```

```
    }
    p[spos]=q;
    spos++;
    if(spos==MAX) spos=0; /* loop back */
}

char *qretrieve()
{
    if(rpos==MAX) rpos=0; /* loop back */
    if(rpos==spos) {
      printf("No (more) appointments.\n");
      return NULL;
    }
    rpos++;
    return p[rpos-1];
}
```

In essence, the queue is only full when both the store index and the retrieve index are equal; otherwise, the queue has room for another event. However, this means that when the program starts, the retrieve index (**rpos**) must not be set to 0, but rather to **MAX** so that the first call to **qstore( )** does not produce the **queue full** message. It is important to note that the queue will hold only **MAX-1** elements because **rpos** and **spos** must always be at least one element apart; otherwise, it would be impossible to know whether the queue was full or empty. Figure 2-3 is a conceptual representation of the array used for the circular version of the appointment-scheduler program.

Perhaps the most common use of a circular queue is in operating systems that buffer the information read from and written to disk files or the console. Another common use of the circular queue is in real-time application programs that must continue to process information while buffering I/O requests. Many word processors do this when they reformat a paragraph or justify a line. A brief period elapses during which what is being typed is not displayed until after the other process the program is working on is completed. To accomplish this, the application program must continue to check for keyboard entry during the execution of the other process. If a key has been typed, it is quickly placed in the queue, and the process continues. Once the process is complete, the characters are retrieved from the queue.

To see how this can be done, consider the simple program presented next, which contains two processes. The first process in the program will print the numbers 1 through 32,000 on the screen. The second process places characters in a circular queue as they are typed, without echoing them on the screen until a semicolon is struck. The characters you type will not be displayed because the first process is given priority over the screen at this time. After the semicolon has been struck, the characters in the queue are retrieved

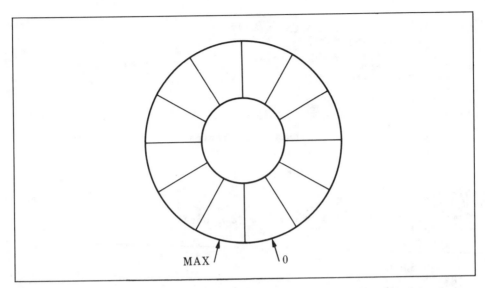

Figure 2-3. The circular array for the appointment-scheduler program

and printed. The proposed ANSI standard does not define library functions that check keyboard status or read keyboard characters without echoing them to the display because these functions are highly dependent on the operating system. However, Turbo C does supply routines to do these things.

The short program shown here works with the IBM PC and uses **kbhit( )** to determine the keyboard status and **getch( )** to read a character without echoing it to the screen.

```
#include "stdio.h"

#define MAX 80

char buf[MAX+1];
int spos=0;
int rpos=MAX;

void qstore();
char qretrieve();

main() /* circular queue example - keyboard buffer */
{
   register char ch;
   int t;

   buf[80]=NULL;
```

```
  for(ch=' ',t=0; t<32000 && ch!=';'; ++t) {
    printf("%d",kbhit());
    if(kbhit()) {
      ch=getch();
      qstore(ch);
    }
    printf("%d ",t);
  }

  while((ch=qretrieve())!=NULL) putchar(ch); /* display buf */
}

/* store characters in queue */
void qstore(q)
char q;
{
  if(spos+1==rpos || (spos+1==MAX && !rpos)) {
    printf("list full\n");
    return;
  }
  buf[spos]=q;
  spos++;
  if(spos==MAX) spos=0; /* loop back */
}

/* retrieve a character */
char qretrieve()
{
  if(rpos==MAX) rpos=0; /* loop back */
  if(rpos==spos) {
    return NULL;
  }
  rpos++;
  return buf[rpos-1];
}
```

Stacks

A *stack* is the opposite of a queue because it uses *last-in, first-out* accessing (sometimes called LIFO). Imagine a stack of plates. The bottom plate in the stack is the last to be used, and the top plate (the last plate placed on the stack) is the first to be used. Stacks are used a great deal in system software including compilers and interpreters. In fact, Turbo C uses the computer's stack when passing arguments to functions.

For historical reasons, the two basic operations — *store* and *retrieve* — are usually called *push* and *pop*, respectively. Therefore, to implement a stack you need two functions: **push()**, which places a value on the stack, and **pop()**, which retrieves a value from the stack. You also need a region of memory to use as the stack: you could either use an array, or you could allocate a region of memory using Turbo C's dynamic memory allocation functions. Like the queue, the retrieval function takes a value off the list and, if the value is not stored elsewhere, destroys it. The general forms of **push()** and **pop()** using an integer array are shown here. You may maintain stacks of other data types by changing the base type of the array on which the **push()** and **pop()** functions operate.

```
int stack[MAX];
int tos=0;   /* top of stack */

void push(i)  /* place element on the stack */
int i;
{

  if(tos>=MAX) {
    printf("stack full\n");
    return;
  }
  stack[tos]=i;
  tos++;
}


int pop()   /* retrieve top element from the stack */
{
  tos--;
  if(tos<0) {
    printf("stack underflow\n");
    return HUGH_VAL;
  }
  return stack[tos];
}
```

Action	Contents of Stack
push(A)	A
push(B)	B A
push(C)	C B A
pop( ) retrieves C	B A
push(F)	F B A
pop( ) retrieves F	B A
pop( ) retrieves B	A
pop( ) retrieves A	*empty*

Figure 2-4. A stack in action

The variable **tos** is the index of the next open stack location. When implementing these functions, always remember to prevent overflow and underflow. In these routines, if **tos** equals 0, the stack is empty; if **tos** is greater than the last storage function, the stack is full. Figure 2-4 shows how a stack works.

An excellent example of the use of a stack is a four-function calculator. Most calculators today accept a standard form of expression called *infix notation*, which takes the general form *operand-operator-operand*. For example, to add 100 to 200, you would enter **100**, then press + , enter **200**, and press press the equal-sign key. However, many early calculators, in an attempt to save memory, used a form of expression evaluation called *postfix notation* in which both operands are entered before the operator is entered. For example, using postfix notation to add 100 to 200, you would first enter **100**, then enter **200**, and then press the + key. As operands are entered, they are placed on a stack; when an operator is entered, two operands are removed from the stack, and the result is pushed back on the stack. The advantage of the postfix form is that expressions can be evaluated easily by the calculator without much code.

Before developing the full four-function calculator for postfix expressions, you need to modify the basic **push( )** and **pop( )** functions. Turbo C's dynamic allocation routines provide memory for the stack. These functions, as used in the calculator example later, are shown here:

```
int *p;    /* will point to a region of free memory */
int *tos; /* points to top of stack */
int *bos; /* points to bottom of stack */


void push(i)  /* place element on the stack */
int i;
{
  if(p>bos) {
    printf("stack full\n");
    return;
  }
  *p=i;
  p++;
}

pop()    /* retrieve top element from the stack */
{
  p--;
  if(p<tos) {
    printf("stack underflow\n");
    return 0;
  }
  return *p;
}
```

Before you can use these functions, you must allocate a region of free memory using **malloc( )**. You must also assign the address of the beginning of that region to **tos** and assign the address of the end to **bos**.

The entire calculator program is shown here. In addition to the operators plus, minus, times, and divide, you may also enter a period, which causes the current value on the top of the stack to be displayed.

```
/* a simple four-function calculator */

#include "stdlib.h"
#define MAX 100

int *p;    /* will point to a region of free memory */
int *tos; /* points to top of stack */
int *bos; /* points to bottom of stack */
void push();

main()
{
  int a,b;
  char s[80];

  p=(int *)malloc(MAX*sizeof(int));   /* get stack memory */
  if(!p) {
    printf("allocation failure\n");
    exit(1);
  }
  tos=p;
```

```
    bos=p+MAX-1;

  printf("Four Function Calculator\n");

  do {
    printf(": ");
    gets(s);
    switch(*s) {
      case '+':
        a=pop();
        b=pop();
        printf("%d\n",a+b);
        push(a+b);
        break;
      case '-':
        a=pop();
        b=pop();
        printf("%d\n",b-a);
        push(b-a);
        break;
      case '*':
        a=pop();
        b=pop();
        printf("%d\n",b*a);
        push(b*a);
        break;
      case '/':
        a=pop();
        b=pop();
        if(a==0) {
            printf("divide by 0\n");
            break;
        }
        printf("%d\n",b/a);
        push(b/a);
        break;
      case '.': /* show  contents of top of stack */
        a=pop();
        push(a);
        printf("Current value on top of stack: %d\n", a);
        break;
      default:
        push(atoi(s));
    }
  } while(*s!='q');
}

void push(i)  /* place element on the stack */
int i;
{
  if(p>bos) {
    printf("stack full\n");
    return;
  }
```

```
  *p=i;
  p++;
}

pop()    /* retrieve top element from the stack */
{
  p--;
  if(p<tos) {
    printf("stack underflow\n");
    return 0;
  }
  return *p;
}
```

A sample session at the calculator is shown here:

```
Four Function Calculator
: 10<cr>
: 10<cr>
: +<cr>
20
: 5<cr>
: /<cr>
4
: .<cr>
Current value on top of stack: 4
: q<cr>
```

Linked Lists

Queues and stacks share two common traits. First, both have strict rules for referencing the data stored in them. Second, the retrieval operations are, by nature, *consumptive;* that is, accessing an item in a stack or queue requires its removal, and, unless stored elsewhere, its destruction. Both stacks and queues also require, at least conceptually, a contiguous region of memory to operate.

Unlike a stack or a queue, a *linked list* may access its storage in a random fashion, because each piece of information carries with it a link to the next data item in the chain. A linked list requires a complex data structure, whereas a stack or queue can operate on both simple and complex data items. A linked-list retrieval operation does not remove and destroy an item from the list; a specific *deletion* operation must be added to do this.

Linked lists are used for two main purposes. The first purpose is to create arrays of unknown size in memory. If you know the amount of storage in advance, you can use an array; but if you do not know the actual size of a list, you must use a linked list. The second main usage is for disk-file storage of databases. The linked list allows you to insert and delete items quickly and easily without rearranging the entire disk file. For these reasons, linked lists are used extensively in database managers.

Linked lists can be either singly linked or doubly linked. A *singly linked list* contains a link to the next data item. A *doubly linked list* contains links to both the next and the previous element in the list. The type you use depends upon your application.

Singly Linked Lists

A singly linked list requires that each item of information contain a link to the next element in the list. Each data item generally consists of a structure that contains information fields and a link pointer. The concept of a singly linked list is shown in Figure 2-5.

There are two ways to build a singly linked list. The first simply puts each new item on the end of the list. The other adds items into specific places in the list (for example, by ascending sorted order). The manner in which you build the list determines the way the *store function* is coded, as shown in the simpler case of creating a linked list by adding items on the end.

Before beginning, you need to define a data structure to hold the information and the links. Because mailing lists are common, this example uses one.

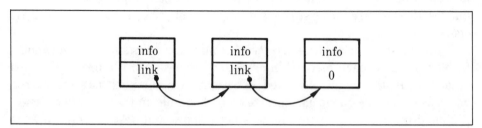

Figure 2-5.   Singly linked list in memory

The data structure for each element in the mailing list is defined here:

```
struct address {
  char name[40];
  char street[40];
  char city[20];
  char state[3];
  char zip[10];
  struct address *next;
} info;
```

The function **slstore( )** builds a singly linked list by placing each new element on the end. It must be passed a pointer to a structure of type **address**, as shown here:

```
void slstore(i)
struct address *i;
{
  static struct address *last=NULL; /* start with null link */

  if(!last) last=i; /* first item in list */
  else last->next=i;
  i->next=NULL;
  last=i;
}
```

Notice the use of the **static** variable **last**. Because initialization of a **static** occurs once at the start of the program, it can be used to start the list-building process.

Although you can sort the list created with the **slstore( )** function as a separate operation, it is easier to sort while building the list by inserting each new item in the proper sequence of the chain. Also, if the list is already sorted, then it is advantageous to keep it sorted by inserting new items in their proper locations. To do this, sequentially scan the list until the proper location is found, insert the new address at that point, and rearrange the links as necessary.

Three possible situations can occur when you insert an item in a singly linked list. First, the item can become the new first item; second, it can be inserted between two other items; third, it can become the last element. Figure 2-6 shows how the links are changed for each case.

If you change the first item in the list, you must update the entry point to the list elsewhere in your program. To avoid this overhead, you can use a sentinel as a first item. (Remember, a sentinel is a special value that will

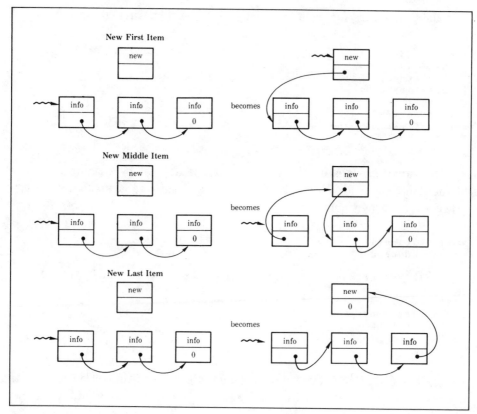

Figure 2-6.   Inserting an item into a singly linked list

always, under all circumstances, be first in the list.) Using this method, you can keep the entry point to the list unchanged. This method does have the disadvantage of using one extra storage location to hold the sentinel.

The function **sls_store( )**, shown here, inserts addresses into the mailing list in ascending order based on the **name** field. It returns a pointer to the first element in the list and also requires that the pointer to the start of the list be passed to it. When the first element is inserted, both **top** and **i** are the same.

```
struct address *sls_store(i,top)  /* store in sorted order */
struct address *i;     /* new element to store */
struct address *top;   /* start of list */
{
```

```
  static struct address *last=0; /* start with null link */
  struct address *old,*start;

  start=top;

  if(!last) {  /* first element in list */
    i->next=NULL;
    last=i;
    return i;
  }

  old=NULL;
  while(top) {
    if(strcmp(top->name,i->name)<0) {
      old=top;
      top=top->next;
    }
    else {
      if(old) {  /* goes in middle */
        old->next=i;
        i->next=top;
        return start;
      }
      i->next=top; /* new first element */
      return     i;
    }
  }
  last->next=i; /* put on end */
  i->next=NULL;
  last=i;
  return start;
}
```

In a linked list it is uncommon to find a specific function dedicated to the *retrieve process*, which returns item after item in list order. This code is usually so short that it is simply placed inside another routine, such as a search, delete, or display function. For example, the following routine displays all the names in a mailing list:

```
void display(top)
struct address *top;
{
  while(top) {
    printf(top->name);
    top=top->next;
  }
}
```

Here, **top** is a pointer to the first structure in the list. Retrieving items from the list is as simple as following a chain. A search routine based on the **name** field could be written like this:

```
struct address *search(top,n)
struct address *top;
char *n;
{
  while(top) {
    if(!strcmp(n,top->name)) return top;
    top=top->next;
  }
  return NULL;  /* no match */
}
```

Because **search()** is returning a pointer to the list item that matches the search name, **search()** must be declared as returning a structure pointer of type **address**. If there is no match, a null is returned.

The process of deleting an item from a singly linked list is straightforward. As with insertion, there are three cases: deleting the first item, deleting a middle item, and deleting the last item. Figure 2-7 shows each of these operations.

This function deletes a given item from a list of structures of type **address**.

```
struct address *sldelete(p,i,top)
struct address *p; /* previous item */
struct address *i; /* item to delete */
struct address *top; /* start of list */
{
  if(p) p->next=i->next;
  else  top=i->next;

  return top;
}
```

Pointers to the deleted item, the item before it in the chain, and to the start of the list must be sent to **sldelete()**. If the first item is to be removed, then the previous pointer must be null. The function must return a pointer to the start of the list because of the case in which the first item is deleted—the program must know where the new first element is located.

Singly linked lists have one major drawback that prevents their extensive use: the list cannot be followed in reverse order. For this reason, doubly linked lists are generally used.

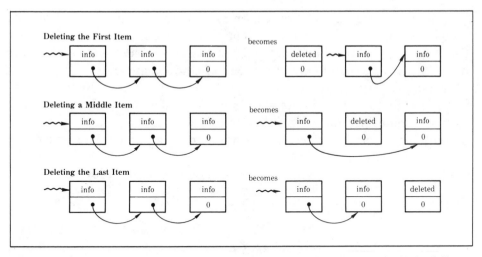

Figure 2-7.   The three cases of deleting an item from a singly linked list

Doubly Linked Lists

Doubly linked lists consist of data and links to both the next item and the preceding item. Figure 2-8 shows how these links are arranged. A list that has two links instead of just one has two major advantages. First, the list can be read in either direction. This not only simplifies sorting the list but also,

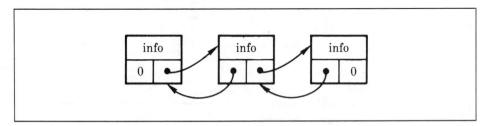

Figure 2-8.   A doubly linked list

the case of a database, allows a user to scan the list in either direction. Second, because either a forward link or a backward link can read the entire list, if one link becomes invalid, the list can be reconstructed using the other link. This is meaningful only in the case of equipment failure.

Three primary operations can be performed on a doubly linked list: insert a new first element, insert a new middle element, and insert a new last element. These operations are shown in Figure 2-9.

Building a doubly linked list is similar to building a singly linked list, except that the structure must have room to maintain two links. Using the mailing-list example again, you can modify the structure **address** as shown

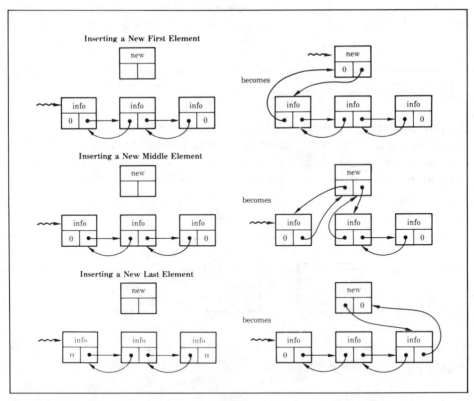

Figure 2-9. The three primary operations that can be performed on a doubly linked list

here to accommodate this:

```
struct address {
  char name[40];
  char street[40];
  char city[20];
  char state[3];
  char zip[10];
  struct address *next;
  struct address *prior;
} info;
```

Using structure **address** as the basic data item, the **dls—store( )** function builds a doubly linked list.

```
void dlstore(i)
struct address *i;
{
  static struct address *last=NULL; /* start with null link */

  if(last==NULL) last=i; /* first item in list */
  else last->next=i;
  i->next=NULL;
  i->prior=last;
  last=i;
}
```

This function places each new entry on the end of the list.

Like the singly linked list, a doubly linked list can have a function that stores each element in a specific location in the list as it is built, instead of always placing each new item on the end. The **dls—store( )** function creates a list that is sorted in ascending order.

```
/* Create a doubly linked list in sorted order.
   A pointer to the first element is returned because
   it is possible that a new element will be inserted
   at the start of the list.
*/
struct address *dls_store(i,top)  /* store in sorted order */
struct address *i;    /* new element */
struct address *top;  /* first element in list */
{
  struct address *old,*p;

  if(last==NULL) {  /* first element in list */
    i->next=NULL;
    i->prior=NULL;
```

```
    last=i;
    return i;
}

  p=top; /* start at top of list */

  old=NULL;
  while(p) {
    if(strcmp(p->name,i->name)<0){
      old=p;
      p=p->next;
    }
    else {
      if(p->prior) {
        p->prior->next=i;
        i->next=p;
        i->prior=p->prior;
        p->prior=i;
        return top;
      }
      i->next=p; /* new first element */
      i->prior=NULL;
      p->prior=i;
      return   i;
    }
  }
  old->next=i; /* put on end */
  i->next=NULL;
  i->prior=old;
  last=i;
  return start;
}
```

Because an item may be inserted at the top of the list, this function must return a pointer to the first item so that other parts of the program will know where the list begins. As with the singly linked list, to retrieve a specific data item, the program follows the links until the proper element is found.

There are three cases to consider when deleting an element from a doubly linked list: deleting the first item, deleting a middle item, and deleting the last item. Figure 2-10 shows how the links are rearranged.

The following function will delete an item of type **address** from a doubly linked list:

```
struct address *dldelete(i,top)
struct address *i; /* item to delete */
struct address *top;  /* first item in list */
{
  if(i->prior) i->prior->next = i->next;
  else { /* new first item */
    top=i->next;
```

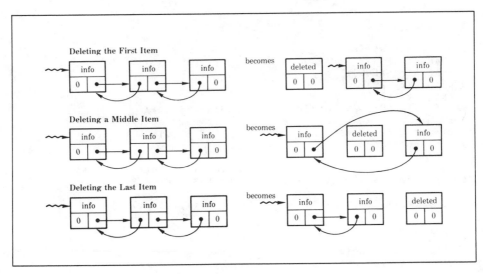

Figure 2-10. Deleting three items from a doubly linked list

```
     /* if deleting only element in list skip */
        if(top) top->prior=NULL;
  }

  if(i->next) i->next->prior = i->prior;
  return top;
}
```

This function requires one less pointer to be passed to it than the singly
linked list version, because the data item being deleted already carries with
it a link to the previous element and to the next element. Because the first
element in the list could change, the pointer to the top element is passed back
to the calling routine.

A Mailing List with a Doubly Linked List

Here is a simple mailing-list program that shows the use of a doubly linked
list. The entire list is kept in memory while in use. However, it can be stored
in a disk file and loaded for later use.

```
#include "stdio.h"

struct address {
  char name[30];
  char street[40];
  char city[20];
  char state[3];
  char zip[10]; /* hold US and Canadian zips */
  struct address *next;  /* pointer to next entry */
  struct address *prior;  /* pointer to previous record */
} list_entry;

struct address *start;  /* pointer to first entry in list */
struct address *last;  /* pointer to last entry */

void enter(), display(), search(), save(), load();

main()
{
  char s[80], choice;
  struct address *info;

  start=last=NULL;  /* zero length list */
  for(;;) {
    switch(menu_select()) {
      case 1: enter();
        break;
      case 2: delete();
        break;
      case 3: list();
        break;
      case 4: search(); /* find a street */
        break;
      case 5: save();  /* save list to disk */
        break;
      case 6: load();  /* read from disk */
        break;
      case 7: exit(0);
    }
  }
}

/* select an operation */
menu_select()
{
  char s[80];
  int c;

  printf("1. Enter a name\n");
  printf("2. Delete a name\n");
  printf("3. List the file\n");
  printf("4. Search\n");
  printf("5. Save the file\n");
  printf("6. Load the file\n");
```

```
  printf("7. Quit\n");
  do {
    printf("\nEnter your choice: ");
    gets(s);
    c=atoi(s);
  } while(c<0 || c>7);
  return c;
}

/* enter names and address */
void enter()
{
  struct address *info,*dls_store();

  for(;;) {
    info=(struct address *)malloc(sizeof(list_entry));
    if(!info) {
      printf("\nout of memory");
      return;
    }

    inputs("enter name: ",info->name,30);
    if(!info->name[0]) break;  /* stop entering */
    inputs("enter street: ",info->street,40);
    inputs("enter city: ",info->city,20);
    inputs("enter state: ",info->state,3);
    inputs("enter zip: ",info->zip,10);

    start=dls_store(info,start);
  } /* entry loop */
}

inputs(prompt,s,count) /* this function will input a string up to
      the length in count.  This will prevent
      the string from overrunning its space and
      display a prompt message. */
char *prompt;
char *s;
int count;
{
  char p[255];

  do {
    printf(prompt);
    gets(p);
    if(strlen(p)>count) printf("\ntoo long\n");
  } while(strlen(p)>count);
  strcpy(s,p);
}

/* Create a doubly linked list in sorted order.
   A pointer to the first element is returned because
   it is possible that a new element will be inserted
   at the start of the list.
```

```
*/
struct address *dls_store(i,top)   /* store in sorted order */
struct address *i;      /* new element */
struct address *top;  /* first element in list */
{
   struct address *old,*p;

   if(last==NULL) {   /* first element in list */
     i->next=NULL;
     i->prior=NULL;
     last=i;
     return i;
   }

   p=top; /* start at top of list */

   old=NULL;
   while(p) {
     if(strcmp(p->name,i->name)<0){
       old=p;
       p=p->next;
     }
     else {
       if(p->prior) {
         p->prior->next=i;
         i->next=p;
         i->prior=p->prior;
         p->prior=i;
         return top;
       }
       i->next=p; /* new first element */
       i->prior=NULL;
       p->prior=i;
       return   i;
     }
   }
   old->next=i; /* put on end */
   i->next=NULL;
   i->prior=old;
   last=i;
   return start;
}

/* remove an element from the list */
delete()
{
   struct address *info, *find();
   char s[80];

   printf("enter name: ");
   gets(s);
   info=find(s);
   if(info) {
     if(start==info) {
       start=info->next;
```

```
      if(start) start->prior=NULL;
      else last=NULL;
    }
    else {
      info->prior->next=info->next;
      if(info!=last)
          info->next->prior=info->prior;
      else
        last=info->prior;
    }
    free(info);  /* return memory to system */
  }
}

struct address *find(name)
char *name;
{
  struct address *info;

  info=start;
  while(info) {
    if(!strcmp(name,info->name)) return info;
    info=info->next;  /* get next address */
  }
  printf("name not found\n");
  return NULL;  /* not found */
}

list()
{
  register int t;
  struct address *info;

  info=start;
  while(info) {
    display(info);
    info=info->next;  /* get next address */
  }
  printf("\n\n");
}

void display(info)
struct address *info;
{
    printf("%s\n",info->name);
    printf("%s\n",info->street);
    printf("%s\n",info->city);
    printf("%s\n",info->state);
    printf("%s\n",info->zip);
    printf("\n\n");
}

void search()
{
  char name[40];
```

```
  struct address *info,*find();

  printf("enter name to find: ");
  gets(name);
  if(!(info=find(name))) printf("not found\n");
  else display(info);
}

void save()
{
  register int t;
  struct address *info;

  FILE *fp;
  if((fp=fopen("mlist","wb"))==NULL) {
    printf("cannot open file\n");
    exit(1);
  }
  printf("\nsaving file\n");

  info=start;
  while(info) {
    fwrite(info,sizeof(struct address),1,fp);
    info=info->next;  /* get next address */
  }
  fclose(fp);
}

void load()
{
  register int t;
  struct address *info, *temp=NULL;
  FILE *fp;

  if((fp=fopen("mlist","rb"))==NULL) {
    printf("cannot open file\n");
    exit(1);
  }

  while(start) {
    info=start->next;
    free(info);
    start=info;
  }

  printf("\nloading file\n");

  start=(struct address *) malloc(sizeof(struct address));
  if(!start) {
    printf("out of memory\n");
    return;
  }
  info=start;
  while(!feof(fp)) {
    if(1!=fread(info,sizeof(struct address),1,fp)) break;
```

```
  /* get memory for next */
  info->next=(struct address *) malloc(sizeof(struct address));
  if(!info->next) {
    printf("out of memory\n");
    return;
  }
  info->prior=temp;
  temp=info;
  info=info->next;
  }
  temp->next=NULL;   /* last entry */
  last=temp;

  start->prior=NULL;
  fclose(fp);
}
```

Binary Trees

The fourth data structure is the *binary tree*. Although there can be many different types of trees, binary trees are special because, when they are sorted, they lend themselves to rapid searches, insertions, and deletions. Each item in a binary tree consists of information with a link to the left member and a link to the right member. Figure 2-11 shows a small tree.

The special terminology needed to discuss trees is a classic case of mixed metaphors. The *root* is the first item in the tree. Each data item is called a *node* (sometimes called a *leaf*) of the tree, and any piece of the tree is called a *subtree*. A node that has no subtrees attached to it is called a *terminal node*. The *height* of the tree equals the number of layers deep that its roots grow. Throughout this discussion, think of binary trees as appearing in memory as they do on paper, but remember that a tree is only a way to structure data in memory, which is linear in form.

The binary tree is a special form of linked list. Items can be inserted, deleted, and accessed in any order. Also, the retrieval operation is non-destructive. Although trees are easy to visualize, they present some very difficult programming problems that this section will only introduce.

Most functions that use trees are recursive because the tree itself is a recursive data structure; that is, each subtree is a tree. Therefore, the routines that are developed are recursive as well. Nonrecursive versions of these functions do exist, but code for them is much more difficult to understand.

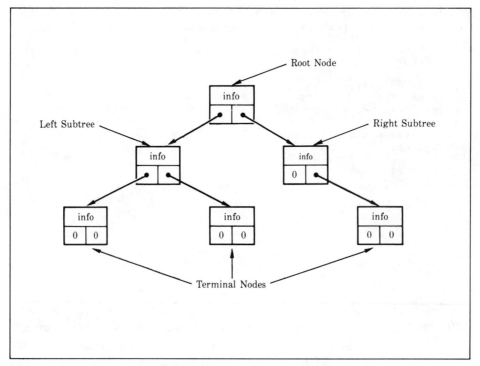

Figure 2-11.   A sample binary tree of height of 3

The order of a tree depends on how the tree is going to be referenced. The process of accessing each node in a tree is called a *tree traversal.* Consider the following tree:

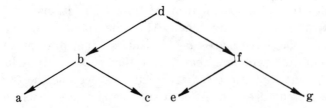

There are three ways to traverse a tree: *inorder, preorder,* and *postorder.* Using inorder, you visit the left subtree, visit the root, and then visit the right subtree. In preorder, you visit the root, then the left subtree, and then the right subtree. With postorder, you visit the left subtree, then the right subtree, and then the root. The order of access for the tree just shown, using each method, is as follows:

inorder	a	b	c	d	e	f	g
preorder	d	b	a	c	f	e	g
postorder	a	c	b	e	g	f	d

Although a tree need not be sorted, most uses require it. What constitutes a sorted tree depends on how you will be traversing the tree. The examples in the rest of this chapter access the tree inorder. In a sorted binary tree, the subtree on the left contains nodes that are less than or equal to the root, while those on the right are greater than the root. The following function, **stree()**, builds a sorted binary tree:

```
struct tree *stree(root,r,info)
struct tree *root;
struct tree *r;
char info;
{

  if(!r) {
    r=(struct tree *) malloc(sizeof(struct tree));
    if(!r) {
      printf("out of memory\n");
      exit(0);
    }
    r->left=NULL;
    r->right=NULL;
    r->info=info;
    if(!root) return r; /* first entry */
    if(info<root->info) root->left=r;
    else root->right=r;
    return r;
  }

  if(info<r->info) stree(r,r->left,info);
  else
  if(info>r->info) stree(r,r->right,info);
}
```

This algorithm simply follows the links through the tree, going left or right based on the **info** field. To use this function you need a global variable that holds the root of the tree. This global must be set initially to null, and a pointer to the root will be assigned on the first call to **stree()**. Subsequent calls will not need to reassign the root. If you assume the name of this global is **rt**, then to call the **stree( )** function, you would use

```
/* call stree()  */
if(!rt) rt=stree(rt,rt,info);
else stree(rt,rt,info);
```

In this way both the first and subsequent elements can be inserted correctly.

The **stree( )** function is a recursive algorithm, as are most tree routines. The same routine would be several times longer if straight iterative methods were employed. The function must be called with a pointer to the root, the left or right node, and information. For simplicity, only a single character is used here as the information, but you can substitute any simple or complex data type you like.

To traverse the tree built using **stree( )** inorder, and to print the **info** field of each node, you could use the **inorder( )** function shown here:

```
void inorder(root)
struct tree *root;
{
  if(!root) return;

  inorder(root->left);
  printf("%c ",root->info);
  inorder(root->right);
}
```

This recursive function returns when it encounters a terminal node (a null pointer). The functions to traverse the tree in preorder and in postorder are shown here:

```
void preorder(root)
struct tree *root;
{
  if(!root) return;

  printf("%c ",root->info);
  preorder(root->left);
  preorder(root->right);
}

void postorder(root)
struct tree *root;
{
  if(!root) return;

  postorder(root->left);
  postorder(root->right);
  printf("%c ",root->info);
}
```

You can write a short program that builds a sorted binary tree and prints the tree sideways on the screen of your computer. You need only a small modification to the **inorder()** function. The new **print_tree()** function prints a tree in inorder fashion.

```
void print_tree(r,l)
struct tree *r;
int l;
{
  int i;

  if(r==NULL) return;

  print_tree(r->left,l+1);
  for(i=0;i<l;++i) printf("    ");
  printf("%c\n",r->info);
  print_tree(r->right,l+1);
}
```

The entire tree-printing program is given here. You should try entering various trees to see how each one is built.

```
#include "stdlib.h"
#include "stdio.h"

struct tree {
  char info;
  struct tree *left;
  struct tree *right;
};

struct tree *root;  /* first node in tree */
void print_tree();
struct tree *stree();

main()  /* treeprint program */
{
  char s[80];
  struct tree *stree();

  root=NULL;  /* initialize the root */

  do {
    printf("enter a letter: ");
    gets(s);
    if(!root) root=stree(root,root,*s);
    else stree(root,root,*s);
  } while(*s);

  print_tree(root,NULL);

}
```

```
struct tree *stree(root,r,info)
struct tree *root;
struct tree *r;
char info;
{

  if(!r) {
    r=(struct tree *) malloc(sizeof(struct tree));
    if(!r) {
      printf("out of memory\n");
      exit(0);
    }
    r->left=NULL;
    r->right=NULL;
    r->info=info;
    if(!root) return r; /* first entry */
    if(info<root->info) root->left=r;
    else root->right=r;
    return r;
  }

  if(info<r->info) stree(r,r->left,info);
  else
  if(info>r->info) stree(r,r->right,info);
}

void print_tree(r,l)
struct tree *r;
int l;
{
  int i;

  if(!r) return;

  print_tree(r->left,l+1);
  for(i=0;i<l;++i) printf("    ");
  printf("%c\n",r->info);
  print_tree(r->right,l+1);
}
```

This program actually is sorting the information you give it. This is a variation on the Insertion sort that was given in Chapter 1. For the average case, its performance can be quite good, but the QuickSort is still a better general-purpose sorting method because it uses less memory and has lower processing overhead. However, if you have to build a tree from scratch, or maintain an already sorted tree, you should always insert new entries in sorted order using the **stree( )** function.

If you have run the Treeprint program, you have probably noticed that some trees are *balanced*—each subtree is the same or nearly the same height as any other—and that other trees are far out of balance. In fact, if you entered the tree **abcd**, it would be built looking like this:

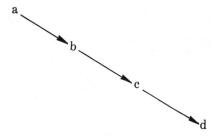

There would be no left subtrees. This is called a *degenerate tree* because it has degenerated into a linear list. In general, if the data you use to build a binary tree is fairly random, the tree produced will approximate a balanced tree. However, if the information is already sorted, a degenerate tree will result. (It is possible to readjust the tree with each insertion to keep the tree in balance. The algorithms to do this are fairly complex; if you are interested in them, refer to books on advanced programming algorithms.)

Search functions are easy to implement for binary trees. The following function returns a pointer to the node in the tree that matches the key; otherwise it returns null:

```
struct tree *search_tree(root,key)
struct tree *root;
char key;
{
  if(!root) return root;  /* empty tree */
  while(root->info!=key) {
    if(key<root->info) root=root->left;
    else root=root->right;
    if(root==NULL) break;
  }
  return root;
}
```

Unfortunately, deleting a node from a tree is not as simple as searching the tree. The deleted node may be either the root, a left node, or a right node. The node may also have from zero to two subtrees attached to it. The process of rearranging the pointers lends itself to a recursive algorithm, as the next program shows.

```
struct tree *dtree(root,key)
struct tree *root;
char key;
{
   struct tree *p,*p2;

   if(root->info==key) { /* delete root */
     /* this means an empty tree */
     if(root->left==root->right){
       free(root);
       return NULL;
     }
     /* or if one subtree is null */
     else if(root->left==NULL) {
       p=root->right;
       free(root);
       return p;
     }
     else if(root->right==NULL) {
       p=root->left;
       free(root);
       return p;
     }
     /* or both tree present */
     else {
       p2=rootr>right;
       p=root->right;
       while(pr>left) p=p->left;
       p->left=root->left;
       free(root);
       return p2;
     }
   }
   if(root->info<key) root->right=dtree(root->right,key);
   else root->left=dtree(root->left,key);
   return root;
}
```

Remember to update the pointer to the root in the rest of your program, because the node deleted could be the root of the tree.

Binary trees offer tremendous power, flexibility, and efficiency when used with database management programs because the information for these databases must reside on disk and because access times are important. Because a balanced binary tree has, as a worst case, $\log_2 N$ comparisons in searching, it performs far better than a linked list, which must rely on a sequential search.

Dynamic Allocation

CHAPTER 3

The dynamic allocation system of Turbo C has several uses. One is for creating variable-length lists of information (such as in a database application), as described in the previous chapter. The second is for supporting sparse arrays. A *sparse array* is one in which not all the elements of the array are actually present—or necessary. You create an array like this when the application's array dimensions are larger than will fit in the memory of the machine, but when not all array locations actually will be used.

Recall that arrays (especially multidimensional arrays) can consume vast quantities of memory because their storage needs are exponentially related to their size. For example, a character array of 10×10 needs only 100 bytes of memory, a 100×100 needs 10,000, but a 1000×1000 needs 1 million bytes of memory—clearly too much for many computers.

Before you explore the ways that dynamic allocation can be used in your Turbo C programs, a brief review of the dynamic allocation system might be helpful.

The Turbo C
Dynamic Allocation System

Before you can understand Turbo C's allocation system, you must visualize how a program compiled by Turbo C organizes memory, as shown in Figure 3-1. (Compiling with different memory models causes this organization to change somewhat, but the essence of it is correct.)

The stack grows downward as it is used, so your program design determines the amount of memory needed by the stack. For example, a program

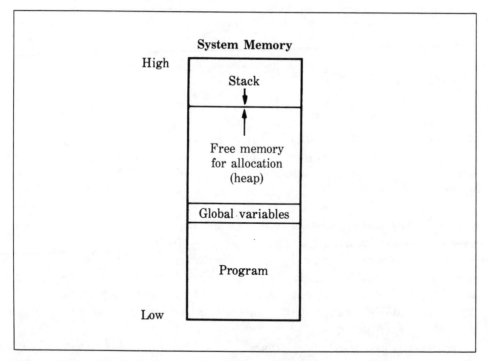

Figure 3-1. Conceptual view of a Turbo C program's memory usage

with many recursive functions demands greater stack memory than one that does not have recursive functions, because local variables and function return addresses are stored on the stack. The memory required for the program and global data is fixed during the execution of the program. Memory to satisfy an allocation request is taken from the free-memory area, starting just above the global variables and growing toward the stack. This region is called the heap. Under fairly extreme cases, it is possible for the stack to run into allocated memory. (Or, if the program has been compiled for a large data model, the entire 64K segment used for the heap may become exhausted.)

Of the several functions included in the dynamic allocation system the most important are **malloc()** and **free()**.

Malloc and Free

The **malloc()** and **free()** functions form the core of the dynamic allocation system in Turbo C and are part of its standard library. Using the heap, they work together to establish and maintain a list of available storage. Each time a memory request is made using **malloc()**, a portion of the remaining free memory is allocated. Each time **free()** is called, memory is returned to the system.

In Turbo C, **malloc()** is declared as

```
void *malloc(unsigned int size)
```

Here, *size* represents the number of bytes to allocate. If *size* bytes can be allocated, then a pointer is returned to the first byte. You must use an explicit type cast to make the **void** pointer returned by **malloc()** compatible with the type of pointer to which it is being assigned. If there is not enough available memory to satisfy the **malloc()** request, an allocation failure occurs and **malloc()** returns a null value. You must confirm that a valid pointer has been returned by **malloc()** prior to using it. Using a null pointer on the left side of an assignment statement generally will cause a system crash, because you will be overwriting some important memory locations. The code fragment at the top of the following page shows the proper way to allocate memory (in this case for a **float**).

```
float *f;

f = (float *) malloc(sizeof(float));

if(!f) {
  printf("memory allocation error");
  exit(1);  /* or call error handling routine */
}
```

As the preceding fragment shows, use **sizeof** to determine the exact number of bytes needed for the type of data you are storing (instead of manually adding up the bytes). Not only does this make your program portable to a variety of systems, but it also makes it easier to maintain when changes to the dynamically allocated object occur. This is especially important when you are using dynamic allocation to store structure variables. Because many computers require that data be aligned on even-word boundaries, the actual size of a structure may be one or more bytes larger that the sum of the sizes of the individual fields.

The **free( )** function is the opposite of **malloc( )** because it returns to the system previously allocated memory. Once the memory has been released, it may be reused by a subsequent call to **malloc( )**. The **free( )** function is declared as

$$free(void *p);$$

Remember that you must *never* call **free( )** with an invalid argument. Using an invalid argument could destroy the free list, thus causing the allocation system to cease working.

Good programming practice is to include the header file **stdlib.h** in any program that uses the allocation system of Turbo C because the header file declares the allocation functions and ensures proper type-checking.

The following short program provides a simple example of how **malloc( )** and **free( )** work together to allocate enough storage for 40 integers, assign them some values, and then release them back to the system. Here **sizeof** is used to ensure portability to other computer types.

```
#include "stdlib.h"

main()  /* short allocation example */
{
  int *p, t;

  p = (int *) malloc(40*sizeof(int));
  if(!p) {
    printf("out of memory\n");
    exit(0);
  }

  for(t=0; t<40; ++t) *(p+t)=t;
  for(t=0; t<40; ++t) printf("%d ",*(p+t));
  free(p);
}
```

Sparse Array Processing

Numerous examples of applications that require sparse array processing can be cited. Many are scientific and engineering problems that are only easily understood by people in those fields. However, one familiar application that commonly uses sparse arrays is a spreadsheet program. Even though the matrix of the average spreadsheet is large (say 999×999), only a portion of it may actually be used at any one time. Spreadsheets use the matrix to hold formulas, values, and strings associated with each location. In a sparse array, storage for each element is allocated as it is needed from the pool of free memory. Although only a small portion of the elements actually are in use, the array may appear larger than would normally fit in the memory of the computer.

For the remainder of this discussion, the two terms *logical array* and *physical array* are used. The logical array is the array that you think of existing in the system (for example, the spreadsheet matrix). The physical

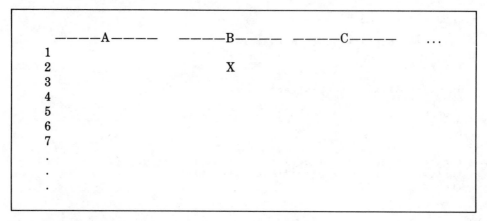

Figure 3-2.   The organization of a sample worksheet

array is the array that actually exists inside the computer. The sparse array support routines are responsible for linking together these two arrays.

Four distinct techniques for creating a sparse array are examined here: the linked list, the binary tree, a pointer array, and hashing. All examples assume that the spreadsheet matrix is organized as shown in Figure 3-2, with **X** in cell B2.

The Linked-List Sparse Array

When implementing a sparse array with a linked list, a structure is used to hold the information for each element, its logical position in the array, and links to the previous and next elements. Each structure is placed in the list with the elements inserted in sorted order based on the array index. The array is accessed by following the links.

For example, you could use the following structure as the basis for a sparse array in a spreadsheet program:

```
struct cell {
  char cell_name[9];  /* cell name e.g., A1, B34 */
  char  formula[128]; /* info e.g.,. 10/B2 */
  struct cell *next;  /* pointer to next entry */
  struct cell *prior;  /* pointer to previous record */
} list_entry;
```

The **cell—name** field holds a string that contains the cell name (such as A1, B34, or Z19). The **formula** string holds the formula assigned to each spreadsheet location.

While an entire spreadsheet program is far too large to use as an example, the key functions that support the linked-list sparse array are examined here. Remember that there are many ways to implement a spreadsheet program, and that the data structure and routines used here serve only as examples of sparse-array techniques. The following global variables point to the beginning and the end of the linked array list:

```
struct cell *start;  /* first element in list */
struct cell *last;   /* last element in list */
```

In most spreadsheets, entering a formula into a cell in effect creates a new element in the sparse array. If the spreadsheet uses a linked list, that new cell is inserted by using a function similar to the **dls—store( )** function developed in Chapter 2. Remember that the list is sorted using the cell name (that is, A12 precedes A13, and so forth).

```
struct cell *dls_store(i)  /* store in sorted order */
struct cell *i;        /* based on cell name   */
{
  struct cell *old, *p;

  if(last==NULL) { /* first element in list */
    i->next = NULL;
    i->prior = NULL;
    last = i;
    return i;
  }

  p = start; /* start at top of list */

  old = NULL;
  while(p) {
    if(strcmp(p->cell_name, i->cell_name)<0){
```

```
      old = p;
      p = p->next;
    }
    else { /* is a middle element */
      if(p->prior) {
        p->prior->next = i;
        i->next = p;
        i->prior = p->prior;
        p->prior = i;
        return start;
      }
      i->next = p; /* new first element */
      i->prior = NULL;
      p->prior = i;
      return   i;
    }
  }
  old->next = i; /* put on end */
  i->next = NULL;
  i->prior = old;
  last = i;
  return start;
}
```

To remove a cell from the spreadsheet, you must remove the proper structure from the list and allow the memory it occupies to be returned to the system by using **free( )**. The **delete( )** function shown here removes a cell from the list when given its cell name:

```
void delete(cell_name)
char *cell_name;
{
  struct cell *info, *find();

  info=find(cell_name);
  if(info) {
    if(start==info) {
      start = info->next;
      if(start) start->prior = NULL;
      else last = NULL;
    }
    else {
      if(info->prior) info->prior->next = info->next;
      if(info!=last)
          info->next->prior = info->prior;
      else
        last = info->prior;
    }
    free(info);  /* return memory to system */
  }
}
```

The **find( )** locates any specific cell. The **find( )** function requires the use of a linear search to locate each item. As shown in Chapter 1, the average number of comparisons in a linear search is $n/2$, where n is the number of elements in the list. In addition, a significant loss of performance occurs because each cell may contain references to other cells in the formula, and each of these cells must be found. The **find( )** function is as follows:

```
struct cell *find(cell_name)
char *cell_name;
{
  struct cell *info;

  info = start;
  while(info) {
    if(!strcmp(cell, info->cell_name)) return info;
    info = info->next;  /* get next cell */
  }
  printf("cell not found\n");
  return NULL;  /* not found */
}
```

Analysis of the Linked-List Approach

The principal advantage of the linked-list method is its memory efficiency. However, one major drawback is that it must use a linear search to access each cell in the list. Without using additional information, which requires additional memory overhead, you cannot perform a binary search to locate a cell. Even the store routine uses a linear search to find the proper location to insert a new cell into the list. You can solve these problems by using a binary tree to support the sparse array.

The Binary Tree
Approach to Sparse Arrays

The binary tree is simply a modified doubly linked list. Its major advantage over a list is that it can be searched quickly, which means that insertions and lookups can be significantly faster. In applications in which you want a linked-list structure, but need fast search times, the binary tree is the solution.

To use a binary tree to support the spreadsheet example, you must change the **cell** structure as follows:

```
struct cell {
  char cell_name[9];  /* cell name e.g., A1, B34 */
  char  formula[128]; /* info e.g., 10/B2 */
  struct cell *left;  /* pointer to left subtree */
  struct cell *right;  /* pointer to right subtree */
} list_entry;
```

You can modify the **stree( )** function from Chapter 2 to build a tree based on the cell name. Notice that the modification assumes the **new** parameter is a pointer to a new entry in the tree.

```
struct cell *stree(root,r,new)
struct cell *root;
struct cell *r;
struct cell *new;
{
  if(r==NULL) {      /* first node in subtree */
    new->left = NULL;
    new->right = NULL;
    if(root) {
        if(strcmp(new->cell_name, root->cell_name)<NULL)
            root->left = new;
      else root->right = new;
    }
    else {  /* first node in tree */
      new->right = NULL;
      new->left = NULL;
    }
    return new;  /* root of tree */
  }

  if(strcmp(new->cell_name, r->cell_name)<=NULL)
    stree(r,r->left, new);
  if(strcmp(new->cell_name, r->cell_name)>NULL)
    stree(r,r->right, new);

  return root;
}
```

The **stree( )** must be called with a pointer to the root node for the first two parameters and a pointer to the new cell for the third parameter. It returns a pointer to the root.

To delete a cell from the spreadsheet, modify the **dtree( )** function to accept the name of the cell as a key, as follows:

```
struct cell *dtree(root, key)
struct cell *root;
char *key;
{
  struct cell *p,*p2;

  if(!strcmp(root->cell_name, key)) { /* delete root */
    /* this means an empty tree */
    if(root->left==root->right){
      free(root);
      return NULL;
    }
    /* or if one subtree is null */
    else if(root->left==NULL) {
      p = root->right;
      free(root);
      return p;
    }
    else if(root->right==NULL) {
      p = root->left;
      free(root);
      return p;
    }
    /* or both tree present */
    else {
      p2 = root->right;
      p = root->right;
      while(p->left) p = p->left;
      p->left = root->left;
      free(root);
      return p2;
    }
  }
  if(strcmp(root->cell_name, key)<NULL)
    root->right = dtree(root->right, key);
  else root->left = dtree(root->left, key);
  return root;
}
```

Finally, you can use a modified **search( )** function to locate any cell in the spreadsheet, given its cell name.

```
struct cell *search_tree(root, key)
struct cell *root;
char *key;
{
  if(!root) return root;  /* empty tree */
  while(strcmp(root->cell_name, key)) {
```

```
    if(strcmp(root->cell_name, key)<0)
      root = root->left;
    else root = root->right;
    if(root==NULL) break;
  }
  return root;
}
```

Analysis of the Binary Tree Approach

The most important advantage of a binary tree over a linked list is that it results in much faster times for inserting and searching. Remember that a sequential search requires, on average, $n/2$ comparisons, where n is the number of elements in the list. A binary search, on the other hand, requires only $\log^2 n$ comparisons. Also, the binary tree is as memory-efficient as a doubly linked list. However, a better alternative may exist in some situations.

The Pointer Array Approach to Sparse Arrays

Suppose that the spreadsheet had the dimensions 26×100 (A1 through Z100), or 2600 total elements. In theory, the following array of structures could hold the spreadsheet entries:

```
struct cell {
  char cell_name[9];
  char  formula[128];
} list_entry[2600];   /* 2,600 cells */
```

However, the problem here is that 2600×137 (the raw size of the structure—some machines will require an even larger amount) requires 356,200 bytes of memory. This is too large for many systems. Also, on processors such as the 8086 that use a segment architecture, memory access to such a large array is slow because 32-bit points will be required. So, this approach often is not practical. Instead, you could create an array of pointers to structures. This method would require significantly less permanent storage than would the creation of an entire array, yet would offer superior performance over the linked-list and binary tree methods. The declaration would be as follows:

```
struct cell {
  char cell_name[9];
  char  formula[128];
} list_entry;

struct cell *sheet[2600]; /* array of 2,600 pointers */
```

You can use this smaller array to hold pointers to the information actually entered in the spreadsheet by the user. As each entry is made, a pointer to the information about the cell is stored in the proper location in the array. Figure 3-3 shows how this might appear in memory, with the pointer array providing support for the sparse array.

Before you can use the pointer array, you must initialize each element

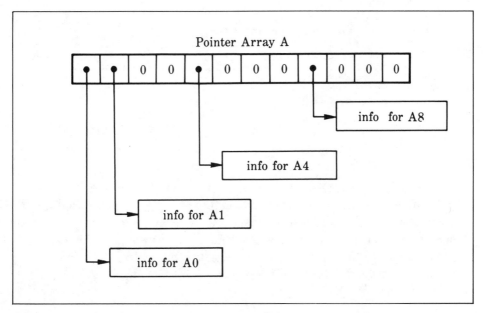

Figure 3-3. A pointer array as support for a sparse array

to null, which indicates that there is no entry in that location. The function to do this is as follows:

```
init_sheet()
{
  register int t;

  for(t=0; t<2600; ++t) sheet[t] = NULL;
}
```

When the user enters a formula for a cell in the spreadsheet, the cell location (defined by its name) produces an index for the **sheet** pointer array. The index is derived from the cell name by converting the name into a number, as shown here in **store()**. When computing the index, **store()** assumes that all cell names begin with a capital letter followed by an integer (for example, B34, C19, and so forth).

```
void store(i)
struct cell *i;
{
  int loc;
  char *p;

  /* compute location given point name */
  loc = (*(i->cell_name)-'A');
  p = &(i->cell_name[1]);
  loc += (atoi(p)-1) * 26;   /* WIDTH columns * num rows */

  if(loc>=2600) {
    printf("cell out of bounds\n");
    return;
  }
  sheet[loc] = i; /* place pointer in the array */
}
```

Because each cell name is unique, each index is also unique. Because the ASCII collating sequence is used, the pointer to each entry is stored into the proper array element. If you compare this procedure to the linked-list or binary tree versions, you will see how much shorter and simpler it is.

The **delete()** function also becomes short. When called with the index of the cell to remove, **delete()** zeros the pointer to the element and returns the memory to the system.

```
void delete(cell_index)
int cell_index;
{
   free(sheet[cell_index]);   /* return memory to system */
   sheet[cell_index] = NULL;
}
```

Again, this code is much faster and simpler than the linked-list version.

The process of locating a cell given its name is trivial because the name itself directly produces the array index. Therefore, the **find( )** function becomes

```
struct cell *find(cell_name)
char *cell_name;
{
   int loc;
   char *p;

   /* compute location given name */
   loc = (*(cell_name)-'A');
   p = &(cell_name[1]);
   loc += (atoi(p)-1) * 26;   /* WIDTH columns * num rows */

   if(loc>=2600 || !sheet[loc]) {  /* no entry in that cell */
     printf("cell not found\n");
     return NULL;  /* not found */
   }
   else return sheet[loc];
}
```

Analysis of the Pointer-Array Approach

The pointer array method of sparse array handling provides much faster access to array elements than either the linked-list or binary tree methods. Unless the array is very sparse, the memory used by the pointer array is generally not a significant drain on the free memory of the system. However, keep in mind that the pointer array itself is using some memory for every location—whether or not the pointers are pointing to actual information. This may be a serious limitation for certain applications, but generally is not a problem.

Hashing

Hashing is the process of extracting the index of an array element directly from the information that is stored there. The generated index is called the *hash*. Traditionally, hashing has generally been applied to disk files as a means of decreasing access time. However, the same general methods can be used as a means of implementing sparse arrays.

The procedure used with the preceding pointer array example used a special form of hashing called *direct indexing* in which each key maps onto one, and only one, array location. That is, each hashed index is unique. (Note that the pointer array approach does not require a direct indexing hash; it was just an obvious approach given the spreadsheet problem.) However, in actual practice, such direct hashing schemes are few and a more flexible method is required. This section shows how hashing can be generalized to allow greater power and flexibility.

It is clear from the spreadsheet example that even in the most rigorous environments, not every cell in the spreadsheet will be used. For the sake of this example, suppose that for all cases no more than 10% of the potential locations will be occupied by actual entries. This means that if the spreadsheet has dimensions 26×100 (2600 locations), then only about 260 actually will ever be used at any one time. Therefore, the largest array normally necessary to hold all the entries will only be 260 elements in size. The problem then becomes how do the logical array locations get mapped onto and accessed from this smaller physical array? What happens when this array is full? The answer is that a *hash chain* is used.

When a formula for a cell is entered in the spreadsheet by the user (the logical array), the cell location (defined by its name) is used to produce an index (a hash) into the smaller physical array (sometimes called the primary array). Assume that the physical array is called **primary**. The index is derived from the cell name by converting the name into a number, as was done in the pointer array example. However, this number is then divided by 10 to produce an initial entry point into the array. (Remember, in this example the physical array is only 10% as big as the logical array.) If the location referenced by this index is free, then the logical index and the value are stored there. However, because ten physical locations actually map onto one logical location, hash collisions can occur. When this happens, a second array (sometimes called the collision array) is used to hold the entry and a linked list of indexes is generated. Figure 3-4 shows this situation.

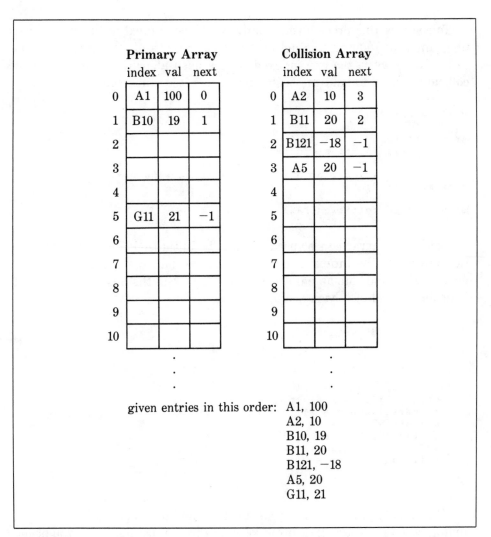

Figure 3-4. A hashing example

To find an element in the physical array given its logical array index, you first transform the logical index into its hash value and check the physical array at the index generated by the hash to see if the logical index stored there matches the one for which you are searching. If it does, return the information. Otherwise, you follow the hash chain until either the proper index is found or the end of the chain is reached.

To see how this procedure actually would be applied to the spreadsheet program first requires the definition of two arrays of structures. The one called **primary** is the one indexed by the hash algorithm. The one called **collision** is used to hold the hash chain generated when collisions occur.

```
#define MAX 260

struct htype {
  int index; /* actual index */
  int val;  /* actual value of the array element */
  int next; /* index of next value with same hash */
} primary[MAX];

struct htype collision[MAX];
```

Before this array can be used, it must be initialized. The following function initializes the **index** field to −1 (a value that by definition cannot be generated) to indicate an empty element. The −1 in the **next** field is used to indicate the end of a hash chain.

```
/* init the hash array */
void init()
{
  register int i;

  for (i=0; i<MAX; i++) {
    primary[i].index = -1;
    primary[i].next = -1;   /* null chain */
    primary[i].val = 0;
    collision[i].index = -1;
    collision[i].next = -1;
    collision[i].val = 0;
  }
}
```

The **store()** procedure converts a cell name into a hashed index into the **primary** array. Notice that if the location directly pointed to by the hashed value is occupied, then it searches for the first free location in the collision array. When a free location is found, the value of the logical index and the value of the array element are stored. It is necessary to store the logical index because it will be needed when that element is accessed again.

```
/* compute hash and store value */
void store(cell_name, v)
char *cell_name;
int v;
{
  int h, c, prior, loc;
```

```
/* produce the hash value */
loc = *cell_name-'A';
loc += (atoi(&cell_name[1])-1) * 26;/* WIDTH columns * num rows */
h = loc/10;

/* store in the location unless full or
     store there if logical indexes agree - i.e., update.
*/
if(primary[h].index==-1 || primary[h].index==loc) {
  primary[h].index = loc;
  primary[h].val = v;
  return;
}
/* place in collision array */
c = primary[h].next; /* see if chain started */
if(c==-1) {
  c = 0; /* start new chain */
  while(collision[c].index!=-1 && c < MAX) c++;
  if(c==MAX) {
    printf("collision array full");
    return;
  }
  primary[h].next = c;
}
else {
  prior = c;
  while(c<MAX) {  /* find a free loc */
    if(collision[c].index == loc ||
      c == -1) break;
    prior = c;
    c = collision[c].next;
  }
  if(c==MAX) {
    printf("hash error or array full\n");
    return;
  }
}
if(c==-1) {  /* not in hash chain so find
                a free spot to put it */
  c = 0;
  while(collision[c].index!=-1 && c<MAX) c++;
  if(c==MAX) {
    printf("hash error or array full\n");
    return;
  }
}
/* store and update hash chain */
collision[c].val = v;
collision[c].index = loc;
collision[c].next = -1;
collision[prior].next = c;
}
```

To find the value of an element, you first compute the physical address and then check to see if the logical index stored in the physical array matches that of the index of the requested logical array. If it does, that value is returned; otherwise, the chain is followed. The **find( )** function, which does this, is shown here:

```
/* compute hash and return value */
int find(cell_name)
char *cell_name;
{
   int h, c, loc;

   /* produce the hash value */
   loc = *cell_name-'A';
   loc += (atoi(&cell_name[1])-1) * 26;/* WIDTH columns * num rows */
   h = loc/10;

   /* return the value if found */
   if(primary[h].index==loc)  return(primary[h].val);
   else { /* look in collision array */
     c = primary[h].next;
     while(c != -1 && c<MAX) {  /* find a loc */
       if(collision[c].index == loc) return collision[c].val;
       c = collision[c].next;
     }
     printf("not in array\n");
     return -1;
   }
}
```

Keep in mind that a simple hashing algorithm is used here. Generally a more complex method is used to provide a more even distribution of indexes in the primary array to avoid the creation of long hash chains. However, the basic principle is the same.

Analysis of Hashing

In its best case (quite rare), each physical index created by the hash is unique and access times approximate that of direct indexing. This means that no hash chains are created and all lookups are essentially direct accesses. However, this will seldom be the case because it requires that the logical indexes be evenly distributed throughout the logical index space. In a worst case (also rare), a hashed scheme degenerates into a linked list. This can happen when the hashed value of the logical indexes are all the same. In the average case (the most likely), the hash method can access any specific element in a time equal to that of using a direct index multiplied by some number that is proportional to the average length of the hash chains. The most critical factor in using hashing to support a sparse array is that the hashing algorithm evenly spreads the physical index so that long hash chains are avoided. Also, hashing is best applied to situations in which you know that the number of required array locations is limited.

Choosing an Approach

Two main considerations are used when deciding whether to use a linked list, a binary tree, a pointer array, or a hashing approach to implement a sparse array. The first is speed and the second is memory efficiency.

When the array is very sparse, the most memory-efficient approaches are the linked-list and binary tree implementations, because only array elements actually in use have memory allocated to them. The links themselves require little additional memory and generally have a negligible effect. The pointer-array design requires that the entire pointer array exist even if some of its elements are not used. Not only must the entire pointer array fit in memory, but there must be enough memory left over for the application to use. This could be a serious problem for certain applications, whereas it may be no problem for others. You can usually decide this issue by calculating the approximate amount of free memory and determining whether that is sufficient for your program.

The hashing method lies somewhere in the middle between the pointer array and the linked-list/binary tree approaches. Although it does require that all of the physical array exists even if it is not all used, it may be that it is still smaller than a pointer array that needs at least one pointer for each logical array location.

When the array is fairly full, however, the situation changes. In this case, the pointer array makes better use of memory because the tree and linked-list implementations need two pointers for each element, whereas the pointer array only has one pointer. For example, if a 1000-element array were full and pointers were two bytes long, then both the binary tree and linked list would use 4000 bytes for pointers, but the pointer array would only need 2000 — a savings of 2000 bytes. In the hashing method, even more memory is "wasted" to support the array.

In terms of execution speed, by far the fastest approach is the pointer array. Often, as in the spreadsheet example, an easy method exists to index the pointer array and link it with the sparse array elements. This method makes accessing the elements of the sparse array nearly as fast as accessing the elements of a normal array. The linked-list version is slow by comparison because it must use a linear search to locate each element. Even if extra information were added to the linked list to allow faster accessing of elements, it still would be slower than the pointer array's direct accessing capability. The binary tree certainly speeds up the search time, but when compared with the pointer array's direct indexing capability, it still seems sluggish. If the hashing algorithm is properly chosen, the access time for the hashing method is faster than that of the binary tree, but it will never be faster than the pointer array approach.

Whenever possible, use a pointer array implementation because it has the fastest access time. If memory usage is critical, you have no choice but to use the linked-list or binary tree approaches.

Reusable Buffers

Dynamic allocation can be used in place of normal variables when memory is scarce. As an example, consider two processes, **A( )** and **B( )**, inside one program. Assume that **A( )** requires 60% of free memory, and that **B( )** needs 55% of free memory. If both **A( )** and **B( )** derive their storage needs from local variables, then **A( )** cannot call **B( )** and **B( )** cannot call **A( )**—more than 100% of memory would be required. If **A( )** never calls **B( )**, then there is no trouble. The problem arises when you want **A( )** to be able to call **B( )**. The only way this can occur is for both to use dynamic storage and to free that memory prior to calling the other. In other words, if both **A( )** and **B( )** require more than one-half of available free memory while executing, and if **A( )** must call **B( )**, then they *must* use dynamic allocation. In this way, both **A( )** and **B( )** will have the memory they need when they need it.

Imagine that there are 10,000 bytes of free memory left in a computer that is running a program with the following two functions in it:

```
A()
{
  char a[6000];
    .
    .
    .
  B();
    .
    .
    .
}
B()
{
  char b[5500];
    .
    .
    .
}
```

Here, **A()** and **B()** both have local variables requiring more than one-half of free memory each. There is no way that **B()** can execute because not enough memory is available to allocate the 5500 bytes needed for the local array **b**.

A situation like this is sometimes insurmountable. But in certain specific instances, you can work around it. If **A()** did not need to preserve the contents of the array **a** while **B()** was executing, then both **A()** and **B()** could share the memory. The way to do this is to dynamically allocate the arrays of **A()** and **B()**. Then **A()** could free the memory prior to the call to **B()** and reallocate it later if needed. Here is the way the code would look:

```
A()
{
    char *a;

    a = (char *) malloc(6000);
    .
    .

    .
    free(a); /* free memory for B() */
    B();
    a=(char *) malloc(6000);
    .
    .

    .
    free(a); /* all done */
```

```
        }
        B()
        {
            char *b;
            b=malloc(5500);
                .

                .

                .
            free(5500);
        }
```

Only the pointer **a** is in existence while **B( )** is executing.

Although you will rarely need to do something like this, the technique is useful to master because it is often the only way around this type of problem.

The "Unknown Memory Dilemma"

If you are a professional programmer, you almost certainly have faced the "unknown memory dilemma." This problem occurs when you write a program that has some aspect of its performance based on the amount of memory inside the computer on which it is running. Examples of programs that exhibit this problem are spreadsheets, in-RAM mailing-list programs, and sorts. For example, an in-memory sort that can handle 10,000 addresses in a 256K machine may only be able to sort 5000 in a 128K computer. If this program were going to be used on computers of unknown memory sizes, then you could not use a fixed-size array to hold the information to be sorted. Either the program would not work on machines with small memory capabilities because the array would not fit, or you would have to create an array for the worst case and not allow users who had more memory to use it. The solution is to use dynamic allocation.

A text editor is a program that illustrates the memory dilemma problem and solution well. Most text editors do not limit the number of characters they can hold and use all of the computer's available memory to store the text you enter. As each line is entered, storage is allocated. When a line is deleted, memory is returned to the system. One way to implement such a text editor would be to use the following structure for each line:

```
struct line {
  char text[81];
  int num;  /* line number of line */
  struct line *next;  /* pointer to next entry */
  struct line *prior;  /* pointer to previous record */
} ;

struct line *start;  /* pointer to first entry in list */
struct line *last;  /* pointer to last entry */
```

For simplicity, the editor always allocates enough memory for each line to be 80 characters long with a null terminator. In reality, an editor should only allocate the exact number of characters present in each line, with additional overhead incurred when the line is altered. The **num** element holds the line number for each line of text. This allows you to use the standard sorted doubly-linked list storage function **dls_store( )** to create and maintain the text file as a linked list.

The entire program for a simple text editor is shown here. It supports only the insertion of lines (at any point based on the specified line number) and the deletion of any line. You may also list the text and store it in a disk file.

The general means of operation for the editor is based on a sorted linked list of lines of text. The sort key is the line number of each line. Not only can you insert text easily at any point by specifying the starting line number, but you can also perform easy deletions. The only function that may not be intuitive is **patchup( )**. It will renumber the **num** element for each line of text when insertions or deletions cause the line number to be changed.

The amount of text the editor can hold is directly based on the amount of free memory in the user's system. Thus, the editor automatically uses additional memory without having to be reprogrammed. This is the most important reason for using dynamic allocation when faced with the memory dilemma.

The program shown is limited, but the basic text-editing support is solid. You may enhance it to create a customized text editor.

```
/* A very simple editor that uses dynamic allocation */

#include "stdio.h"
#include "stdlib.h"

struct line {
  char text[81];
  int num;  /* line number of line */
  struct line *next;  /* pointer to next entry */
  struct line *prior;  /* pointer to previous record */
} ;

struct line *start;  /* pointer to first entry in list */
struct line *last;  /* pointer to last entry */
struct line *dls_store(), *find();

void patchup(), delete(), list(), save(), load();

main(argc, argv)
int argc;
char *argv[];
{
  char s[80], choice, fname[80];
  struct line *info;
  int linenum=1;

  start = NULL; last = NULL; /* zero length list */

  if(argc==2) load(argv[1]); /* read file on command line */

  do {
      choice = menu_select();
      switch(choice) {
        case 1: printf("Enter line number: ");
          gets(s);
          linenum = atoi(s);
          enter(linenum);
          break;
        case 2: delete();
          break;
        case 3: list();
          break;
        case 4: printf("enter filename: ");
          gets(fname);
          save(fname);  /* write to disk */
          break;
        case 5: printf("enter filename: ");
          gets(fname);
          load(fname);  /* read from disk */
          break;
        case 6: exit(0);
      }
  } while(1);
}
/* select a menu option */
menu_select()
{
```

```
   char s[80];
   int c;

   printf("1. Enter text\n");
   printf("2. Delete a line\n");
   printf("3. List the file\n");
   printf("4. Save the file\n");
   printf("5. Load the file\n");
   printf("6. Quit\n");
   do {
     printf("\nEnter your choice: ");
     gets(s);
     c = atoi(s);
   } while(c<0 || c>6);
   return c;
}

enter(linenum)  /* enter text at linenum */
int linenum;
{
   struct line *info;
   char t[81];

   do {
     info = (struct line *) malloc(sizeof(struct line));
     if(!info) {
       printf("\nout of memory");
       return NULL;
     }

     printf("%d : ", linenum);
     gets(info->text);
     info->num = linenum;
     if(*info->text) {
       if(find(linenum)) patchup(linenum, 1); /* fix up
                                         old line nums */
       if(*info->text) start = dls_store(info);
     }
     else break;
     linenum++;

   } while(1); /* entry loop */
   return linenum;
}

/* when text is inserted into middle of file
   line numbers below it must be increased by one
   and those after deleted lines must be decreased
   by 1.
*/
void patchup(n, incr)
int n;
int incr;
{
   struct line *i;

   i = find(n);
```

```
  while(i) {
    i->num = i->num+incr;
    i = i->next;
  }
}

/* store in sorted order by line number */
struct line *dls_store(i)
struct line *i;
{
  struct line *old, *p;

  if(last==NULL) {  /* first element in list */
    i->next = NULL;
    i->prior = NULL;
    last = i;
    return i;
  }

  p = start; /* start at top of list */

  old = NULL;
  while(p) {
    if(p->num < i->num){
      old = p;
      p = p->next;
    }
    else {
      if(p->prior) {
        p->prior->next = i;
        i->next = p;
        p->prior = i;
        return start;
      }
      i->next = p; /* new first element */
      i->prior = NULL;
      p->prior = i;
      return   i;
    }
  }
  old->next = i; /* put on end */
  i->next = NULL;
  i->prior = old;
  last = i;
  return start;
}

/* delete a line */

void delete()
{
  struct line *info;
  char s[80];
  int linenum;

  printf("enter line number ");
  gets(s);
  linenum = atoi(s);
```

```
    info = find(linenum);
    if(info) {
      if(start==info) {
        start = info->next;
        if(start) start->prior = NULL;
        else last = NULL;
      }
      else {
        info->prior->next = info->next;
        if(info!= last)
            info->next->prior = info->prior;
        else
          last = info->prior;
      }
      free(info);  /* return memory to system */
      patchup(linenum+1, -1); /* decrement line numbers */
    }
}

/* find a line of text */
struct line *find(linenum)
int linenum;
{
  struct line *info;

  info = start;
  while(info) {
    if(linenum==info->num) return info;
    info = info->next;  /* get next address */
  }
  return NULL;  /* not found */
}

/* list the text */
void list()
{
  struct line *info;

  info = start;

  while(info) {
    printf("%d: %s\n", info->num, info->text);
    info = info->next;  /* get next address */
  }
  printf("\n\n");
}

/* save the file */
void save(fname)
char *fname;
{
  register int t;
  struct line *info;
  char *p;

  FILE *fp;

  if((fp=fopen(fname, "wb"))==NULL) {
```

```
      printf("cannot open file\n");
      exit(0);
   }
   printf("\nsaving file\n");

   info = start;
   while(info) {
      p = info->text;  /* convert to char pointer */
      while(*p) putc(*p++, fp);  /* save byte at a time */
      putc('\r', fp);  /* terminator */
      putc('\n', fp);  /* terminator */
      info = info->next;  /* get next line */
   }
   fclose(fp);
}

/* load the file */
void load(fname)
char *fname;
{
   register int t, size, lnct;
   struct line *info, *temp;
   char *p;
   FILE *fp;

   if((fp=fopen(fname, "rb"))==NULL) {
      printf("cannot open file\n");
      return;
   }
   while(start) {    /* free any previous edit */
      temp = start;
      start = start->next;
      free(temp);
   }

   printf("\nloading file\n");

   size = sizeof(struct line);
   start = (struct line *) malloc(size);
   if(!start) {
      printf("out of memory\n");
      return;
   }

   info = start;
   p = info->text;  /* convert to char pointer */
   lnct = 1;
   while((*p=getc(fp))!=EOF) {
      p++;
      while((*p=getc(fp))!='\r') p++;
      getc(fp); /* throw away the \n */
      *p = '\0';
      info->num = lnct++;
      info->next = (struct line *) malloc(size); /* get memory for
                                                     next */
      if(!info->next) {
         printf("out of memory\n");
         return;
```

```
   }
   info->prior = temp;
   temp = info;
   info = info->next;
   p = info->text;
  }
  temp->next = NULL;   /* last entry */
  last = temp;
  free(info);
  start->prior = NULL;
  fclose(fp);
}
```

Fragmentation

Because **malloc( )** and **free( )** are not technically part of the C language, but
rather part of the C library, their exact implementation varies from compiler
to compiler. Thankfully, Borland has put a great deal of effort into their
dynamic allocation routines. However, under all implementations of **malloc( )**
and **free( )**, *fragmentation* of memory can occur, which can gradually cause
allocation requests to fail even though enough free memory actually exists.

Fragmentation occurs when pieces of free memory lie between allocated
memory. Although the amount of free memory is usually large enough to fill
allocation requests, a problem develops when the pieces are too small to fill a
request even though there would be sufficient memory if they were added
together. Figure 3-5 shows how a sequence of calls to **malloc( )** and **free( )**
can produce this situation.

You can avoid some types of fragmentation if the dynamic allocation functions combine adjacent regions of memory. For example, in the following
illustration, if memory regions A, B, C, D were allocated, and then regions B
and C were freed, B and C theoretically could be combined because they are
next to each other. However, if B and D were freed, they cannot be combined
because C lies between them and is still in use.

A	B	C	D

At first you might wonder why, since B and D were free while C was
allocated, the allocation routine could not just move the contents of C to D and
combine B and C. The trouble with this is that your program would have no
way of knowing that what was in C had been moved to D.

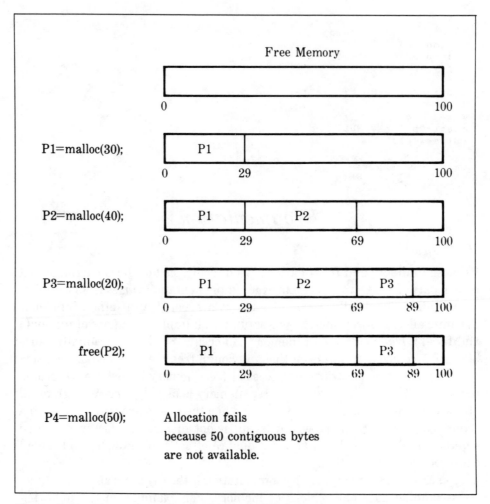

Figure 3-5.   Fragmentation in dynamic allocation

Fragmentation is difficult to eliminate. Sometimes it is possible to pack several small requests into one large request, thus preventing very small fragments from developing. Another solution is, from time to time as the program runs, to write all the information out to a temporary disk file, free all memory, and read back in the information. This works because the dynamic allocation system will then combine all adjacent free memory regions.

Using System
Resources

CHAPTER 4

As powerful as Turbo C is, at times you will want (or need) to access the resources of both the operating system and the host environment directly. To increase performance, you may also need to bypass a standard library routine in favor of directly manipulating a device or operating function yourself.

Each processor, operating system, and environment has its own methods of accessing system resources. This chapter assumes the use of the PC-DOS operating system and the 8086 family of processors. The CPU will be called the 8086, but it is meant to include the entire family. It is beyond the scope of this book to attempt to explain the detailed workings of the 8086 processor. However, the following discussion will give you an overview.

The 8086 Family of Processors

The 8086 family of processors contains 14 registers into which information is placed for processing or program control. The registers fall into the following categories:

- General-purpose registers
- Base pointer and index registers
- Segment registers
- Special-purpose registers

All the registers in the 8086 CPU are 16 bits (2 bytes) wide.

The *general-purpose* registers are the workhorse registers of the CPU. It is in these registers that values are placed for processing. This processing includes arithmetic operations, such as adding or multiplying; comparisons, including equality, less than, greater than, and so forth; and branch (jump) instructions. Each of the general-purpose registers may be accessed in two ways: as a 16-bit register or as two 8-bit registers.

The *base pointer* and *index registers* are used to provide support for such things as relative addressing, the stack pointer, and instructions to move a block.

The *segment registers* are used to support the segmented memory scheme of the 8086. The CS register holds the current code segment, the DS holds the current data segment, the ES holds the extra segment, and the SS holds the stack segment.

Finally, the *special-purpose registers* are the flag register (which holds the state of the CPU) and the instruction pointer (which points to the next instruction for the CPU to execute).

Figure 4-1 shows the layout of the 8086 registers.

The 8086 Interrupts and PC-DOS

An *interrupt* is a special type of instruction that causes the execution of the current program to halt, saves the current state of the system on the stack,

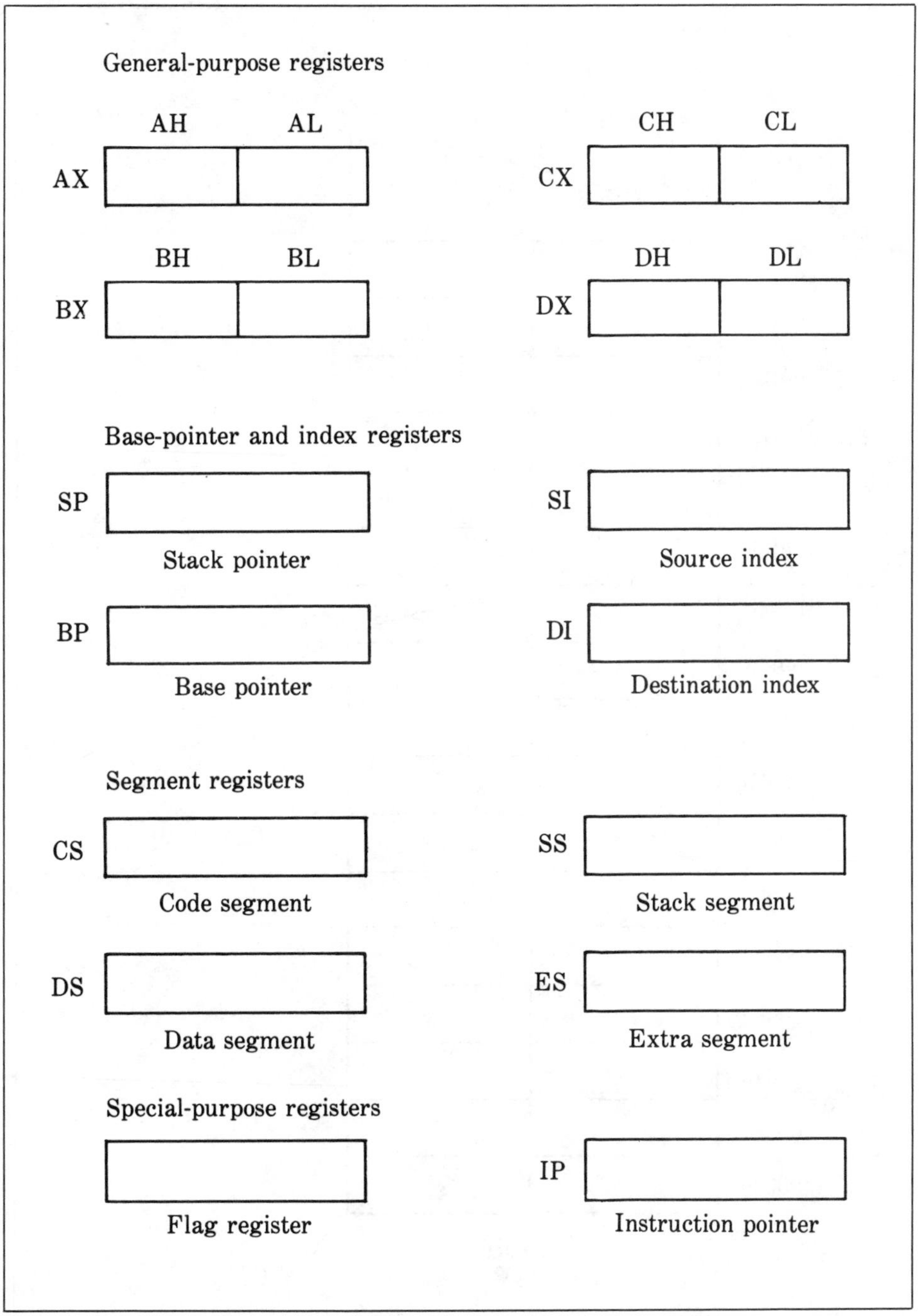

General-purpose registers

AH   AL   CH   CL

AX [|]   CX [|]

BH   BL   DH   DL

BX [|]   DX [|]

Base-pointer and index registers

SP [   ]   SI [   ]

Stack pointer   Source index

BP [   ]   DI [   ]

Base pointer   Destination index

Segment registers

CS [   ]   SS [   ]

Code segment   Stack segment

DS [   ]   ES [   ]

Data segment   Extra segment

Special-purpose registers

[   ]   IP [   ]

Flag register   Instruction pointer

Figure 4-1.   The 8086 CPU registers

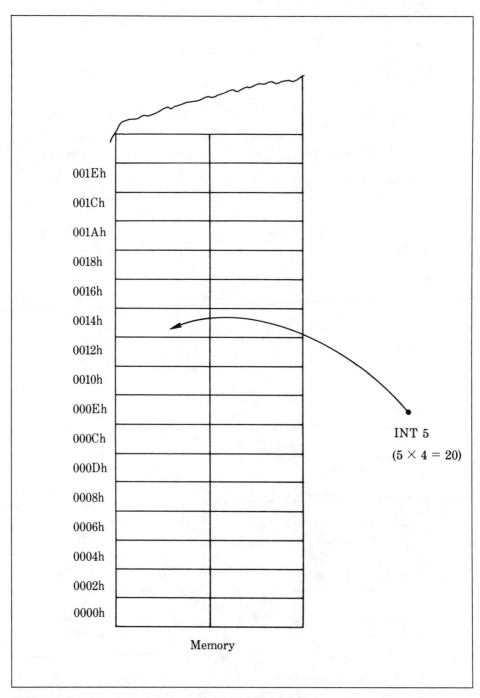

Figure 4-2. The interrupt vector table for the 8086

and then jumps to an interrupt-handling routine that is determined by the number of the interrupt. After the interrupt routine has finished, it performs an *interrupt return*, which causes the previously executing program to resume. There are two basic types of interrupts: those generated by hardware and those caused by software. It is the latter that is of interest at this time.

The 8086 CPU allows a program to execute a *software interrupt* via the **INT** instruction. The number that follows the instruction determines the number of the interrupt. For example, **INT 21h** causes interrupt 21h to be executed. The number of the interrupt is used to find the proper interrupt handler. The 8086 reserves the first 1K bytes in memory for use as an *interrupt vector table*. This table contains the addresses of the interrupt handlers in the form of segment/offset. This means that each address requires 4 bytes. Thus, the 8086 supports 256 interrupt vectors. For example, the **INT 5** instruction tells the CPU to use the address found at the 5×4 byte in memory as the location of the interrupt routine. (By the way, **INT 5** calls the print-screen utility.) This situation is depicted in Figure 4-2.

The PC-DOS operating system has allocated a number of these vectors for use with both ROM-BIOS (Read-Only Memory-Basic I/O System) and DOS (Disk Operating System). The vectors are a means of accessing various functions that are part of the operating system. The way the operating system functions are accessed in PC-DOS is through the use of software interrupts. Each interrupt accesses a specific category of functions, and these functions are determined by the value of the AH register. If additional information is needed, it is passed in the AL, BX, CX, and DX registers.

The PC-DOS operating system separates itself into the ROM-BIOS and DOS. The ROM-BIOS provides the lowest-level routines, which DOS uses to provide the higher-level functions. The two systems overlap, however. Fortunately, for purposes of this discussion, they are accessed in basically the same way—through software interrupts.

This chapter begins with the ROM-BIOS routines and ends with a discussion of the DOS services.

Accessing System Resources in the ROM-BIOS

There are 12 ROM-BIOS interrupts, as shown in Table 4-1.

Each one of the interrupts is associated with a number of options that can

Table 4-1. ROM-BIOS Interrupts

Interrupt	Function
5h	Print screen utility
10h	Video I/O
11h	Equipment list
12h	Memory size
13h	Disk I/O
14h	Serial port I/O
15h	Cassette control
16h	Keyboard I/O
17h	Printer I/O
18h	Execute ROM BASIC
19h	Execute bootstrap loader
1Ah	Time and date

be accessed depending upon the value of the AH register when called. Table 4-2 shows a partial list of the options available for several of the interrupts. For a complete list and explanation, refer to the *IBM Technical Reference Manual* or *DOS: The Complete Reference* by Kris Jamsa (Berkeley: Osborne/McGraw-Hill, 1987).

The Turbo C library routine **int86( )** is used to execute a software interrupt. It is declared as

```
int int86(int intnum, union REGS *in,
          union REGS *out)
```

The number of the interrupt in this routine is **intnum, in** is a union that contains the registers that will be used to pass information to the interrupt handlers, and **out** is a union that will hold the values (if any) returned by the

Table 4-2. Partial List of Interrupt Options

Video I/O Functions—Interrupt 10h

AH Register	Function
0	Sets video mode if AL = 0: 40 × 25 B/W 1: 40 × 25 color 2: 80 × 25 B/W 3: 80 × 25 color 4: 320 × 200 color graphics 5: 320 × 200 B/W graphics 6: 340 × 200 B/W graphics
1	Sets cursor lines CH: bits 0-4 contain start of line bits 5-7 are 0 CL: bits 0-4 contain end of line bits 5-7 are 0
2	Sets cursor position DH: row DL: column BH: video page number
3	Reads cursor position BH: video page number Returns: DH: row DL: column CX: mode
4	Reads light-pen position Returns: if AH = 0: pen not triggered if AH = 1: pen triggered DH: row DL: column CH: raster line (0-199) BX: pixel column (0-319 or 0-639)
5	Sets active video page AL: may be 0-7
6	Scrolls page up AL: number of lines to scroll, 0 for all

Table 4-2. Partial List of Interrupt Options (*continued*)

Video I/O Functions—Interrupt 10h (*continued*)

AH Register	**Function**
	CH: row of upper left corner of scroll CL: column of upper left corner of scroll DH: row of lower right corner of scroll DL: column of lower right corner of scroll BH: attribute to be used on blank line
7	Scrolls page down same as 6
8	Reads character at cursor position BH: video page Returns: AL: character read AH: attribute
9	Writes character and attribute at cursor position BH: video page BL: attribute CX: number of characters to write AL: character
Ah	Writes character at current cursor position BH: video page CX: number of characters to write AL: character
Bh	Sets color palette BH: palette number BL: color
Ch	Writes a pixel DX: row number CX: column number AL: color
Dh	Reads a pixel DX: row number CX: column number Returns: AL: dot read

Table 4-2. Partial List of Interrupt Options (*continued*)

Video I/O Functions—Interrupt 10h (*continued*)

AH Register	Function

Eh — Writes character to screen and advances cursor
    AL: character
    BL: foreground color
    BH: video page

Fh — Reads video state
Returns:
    AL: current mode
    AH: number of columns on screen
    BH: current active video page

Equipment List—Interrupt 11h

Reads equipment list
Returns:
AX: list of equipment installed
    bit 0: one of diskettes present
    bit 1: not used
    bits 2,3: system board RAM, 11 = 64k
    bits 4,5: initial video mode
        10 : 80 column color; 11 = monochrome,
        01 : 40 column
    bits 6,7: number of disk drives, 0 = 1
    bit 8: DMA chip installed, 0 = installed
    bits 9-11: number of RS-232 ports
    bit 12: 1 = game adapter installed
    bit 13: 1 = serial printer (PCjr only)
    bits 14-15: number of printers

Memory Size—Interrupt 12h

Returns the number of kilobytes of RAM that are resident
in the system
Returns:
    AX: number of kilobytes of RAM

Table 4-2. Partial List of Interrupt Options (*continued*)

Disk I/O Functions—Interrupt 13h

AH Register	Function
0	Resets disk system
1	Reads disk status Returns: AL: status (see *IBM Technical Reference* manual)

2	Reads sectors into memory
	    DL: drive number
	    DH: head number
	    CH: track number
	    CL: sector number
	    AL: number of sectors to read
	    ES:BX: address of buffer
	Returns:
	    AL: number of sectors read
	    AH: 0 on success, otherwise status

3	Writes sectors to disk (same as 2 above)
4	Verifies (same as 2 above)

5	Formats a track
	    DL: drive number
	    DH: head number
	    CH: track number
	    ES:BX: sector information

Keyboard I/O Functions—Interrupt 16h

AH Register	Function

0	Reads scan code
	Returns:
	    AH: scan code
	    AL: character code

1	Gets status of buffer
	Returns:
	    ZF: 1 then buffer empty
	        0 then character waiting with
	            next char in AX as described in function 0 above

2	Gets status of keyboard (see *IBM Technical Reference* manual)

Table 4-2. Partial List of Interrupt Options (*continued*)

ROM-BIOS Printer I/O Functions — Interrupt 17h	
AH Register	**Function**
0	Prints a character AL: character DX: printer number Returns: AH: status
1	Initializes printer DX: printer number Returns: AH: status
2	Reads status DX: printer number Returns: AH: status

interrupt routine. However, the value of the AX register will also be returned by **int86( )**. The type **REGS** is supplied in the header **DOS.H**, as shown here:

```
/*
        Copyright (c) Borland International Inc. 1987
        All Rights Reserved.
*/

struct WORDREGS
        {
        unsigned int    ax, bx, cx, dx, si, di, cflag;
        };

struct BYTEREGS
        {
        unsigned char   al, ah, bl, bh, cl, ch, dl, dh;
        };

union   REGS    {
        struct  WORDREGS x;
        struct  BYTEREGS h;
        };
```

Table 4-3. The Screen Modes for IBM PCs

Mode	Type	Dimensions	Adapters
0	Text, B/W	40 × 25	CGA,EGA
1	Text, 16 colors	40 × 25	CGA,EGA
2	Text, B/W	80 × 25	CGA,EGA
3	Text, 16 colors	80 × 25	CGA,EGA
4	Graphics, 4 colors	320 × 200	CGA,EGA
5	Graphics, 4 gray tones	320 × 200	CGA,EGA
6	Graphics, B/W	640 × 200	CGA,EGA
7	Text, B/W	80 × 25	Monochrome
8	Graphics, 16 colors	160 × 200	PCjr
9	Graphics, 16 colors	320 × 200	PCjr
10	Graphics, PCjr, 4 colors EGA, 16 colors	640 × 200	PCjr, EGA
13	Graphics, 16 colors	320 × 200	EGA
14	Graphics, 16 colors	640 × 200	EGA
15	Graphics, 4 colors	640 × 350	EGA

As you can see, **REGS** is a union of two structures. Using the **WORDREGS** structure allows you to access the registers of the CPU as 16-bit quantities. Using **BYTEREGS** gives you access to the individual 8-bit registers.

The **int86( )** function will be used in the examples in this section to access the various ROM-BIOS functions. Although it will not be possible to look at examples of all the ROM-BIOS functions a few of the more interesting ones will be examined. Chapter 6, which deals with graphics, develops several graphics-related routines using the ROM-BIOS.

Changing the Mode of the Screen

Suppose that you wish to change the screen mode during the execution of a program. For PC-DOS there are 16 modes that the screen can display, as shown in Table 4-3.

Using the **int86( )** function, you can create the following function, called **mode( )**, to change the mode of the screen to the specified type.

```
#include "dos.h"

void mode(mode_code)
int mode_code;
{
union REGS r;

  r.h.al = mode_code;
  r.h.ah = 0;
  int86(0x10, &r, &r);
  }
```

Clearing the Screen

It is easy to create a clear-screen function by calling the ROM-BIOS interrupt 10h function 6, as shown here:

```
#include "dos.h"

/* clear the screen */
void cls()
{
  union REGS r;

  r.h.ah=6; /* screen scroll code */
  r.h.al=0; /* clear screen code */
  r.h.ch=0; /* start row */
  r.h.cl=0; /* start column */
  r.h.dh=24; /* end row */
  r.h.dl=79; /* end column */
  r.h.bh=7;  /* blank line is black */
  int86(0x10, &r, &r);
}
```

The value placed in AL determines the number of lines to scroll the screen, given the starting and ending coordinates. However, if AL is 0, then the entire screen is erased. The BH register is used to determine the attribute of a blank line. In this case 7 is used, which means that blank lines will be black.

Cursor Positioning

Another useful function is **goto__xy( )**, which locates the cursor at the specified x and y coordinates. This function uses the ROM-BIOS interrupt 10h, function 2. This interrupt places the cursor at the location specified by the

DL and DH registers. The **goto—xy( )** function is shown here:

```
#include "dos.h"
/* send cursor to x,y */

/* send the cursor to x,y */
void goto_xy(x,y)
int x,y;
{
  union REGS r;

  r.h.ah=2; /* cursor addressing function */
  r.h.dl=y; /* column coordinate */
  r.h.dh=x; /* row coordinate */
  r.h.bh=0; /* video page */
  int86(0x10, &r, &r);
}
```

For the IBM PC, 0,0 is the upper left-hand corner of the screen.

To see how this function works, try the following short program which first clears the screen and then prints Xs diagonally across the screen:

```
#include "dos.h"

void cls(), goto_xy();

/* clear the screen and print Xs */
main()
{
  register int x,y;

  cls();
  for(x=0, y=0; x<25; x++, y+=3) {
    goto_xy(x,y);
    printf("X");
  }
}


/* clear the screen */
void cls()
{
  union REGS r;

  r.h.ah=6; /* screen scroll code */
  r.h.al=0; /* clear screen code */
  r.h.ch=0; /* start row */
  r.h.cl=0; /* start column */
  r.h.dh=24; /* end row */
  r.h.dl=79; /* end column */
  r.h.bh=7;  /* blank line is blank */
```

```
  int86(0x10, &r, &r);
}

/* send the cursor to x,y */
void goto_xy(x,y)
int x,y;
{
  union REGS r;

  r.h.ah=2; /* cursor addressing function */
  r.h.dl=y; /* column coordinate */
  r.h.dh=x; /* row coordinate */
  r.h.bh=0; /* video page */
  int86(0x10, &r, &r);
}
```

Using the Scan Codes from the PC Keyboard

One of the most frustrating experiences you can encounter while working with the IBM PC and its clones is trying to use the arrow keys (as well as the INS, DEL, PGUP, PGDN, END, and HOME keys) and the function keys. The problem is that these keys do not return the normal 8-bit (1-byte) character the way the rest of the keyboard does. When you press a key on the IBM PC, you are actually generating a 2-byte (16-bit) value called a *scan code*. The scan code consists of two pieces: the low-order byte (which, if a normal key, contains the ASCII code for the key) and a high-order byte (which contains the key's position on the keyboard). For most keys on the keyboard, these scan codes are converted into 8-bit ASCII values by the operating system. But for the function keys, arrow keys, and the like, this is not done. The reason is that the character code for a special key is 0. This means that you must use the position code to determine which key was pressed. (The standard character-input routine to read a character from the keyboard supported by DOS function call number 1 does not allow you to read the special keys.) The problem comes in when you want to use these keys in a program.

The easiest way to access the special keys is to write a small function that calls interrupt 16h, which returns the scan code of any key that is pressed. After a call to interrupt 16h, function 0, the position code is in AH and the character code is in AL. The **get—key( )** function, shown here, returns the codes shown on the next page as an integer.

```
#include "dos.h"

/* read the 16-bit scan code of a key */
get_key()
{
  union REGS r;

  r.h.ah = 0;
  return int86(0x16, &r, &r);
}
```

The trick to using **get_key()** is that when a special key is struck, the character code is 0. In this case, you then decode the position code to determine which key was actually typed. To use **get_key()** to do all keyboard input requires that the calling routine make decisions based on the contents of AH and AL. The following is a short program that illustrates one way to do this:

```
#include "dos.h"

main()  /* scan code example */
{
  union scan {
    int c;
    char ch[2];
  } sc;

  do { /* read the keyboard */
    sc.c=get_key();
    if(sc.ch[0]==0)  /* is special key */
      printf("special key number %d",sc.ch[1]);
    else /* regular key */
      printf("%c",sc.ch[0]);
  } while(sc.ch[0]!='q');
}
```

Notice the use of the **union**, which allows you to decode the two halves of the scan code returned by **get_key()**.

There are basically two ways to decode a scan code. The first is to look in the *IBM PC Technical Reference Manual*. The other is to use the preceding program to determine the values experimentally. The latter method is more fun! To help you get started, here are the scan codes for the arrow keys:

LEFT ARROW:	75
RIGHT ARROW:	77
UP ARROW:	72
DOWN ARROW:	80

To fully integrate the special keys with the normal keys requires the writing of special input functions and the bypassing of the normal **gets( )**, **scanf( )**, and **getche( )** type functions found in the library. This is unfortunate, but it is the only way. The reward is that your program will appear very professional and be much easier to use.

Using DOS to Access System Functions

The part of the PC-DOS operating system that is loaded and executed by the ROM-BIOS bootstrap loader is called DOS. It contains various functions that are for the most part of a higher level than the ROM-BIOS routines (although there is some overlap). All the DOS functions are accessed through interrupt 21h, which uses the AH register to pass the requested DOS function number. Table 4-4 shows a partial list of the DOS functions.

Although it is possible to access the DOS functions using **int86( )**, Turbo C includes a specific, more convenient function for this purpose. The function is called **bdos( )**. It is used to perform an interrupt 21h call to access one of the

Table 4-4.   High-Level DOS Function Calls—Interrupt 21h (partial list)

AH Register	Function
1	Reads a character from keyboard Returns: AL: character
2	Displays a character on screen DL: character
3	Reads a character from async port Returns: AL: character
4	Writes a character to async port DL: character

Table 4-4.   High-Level DOS Function Calls—Interrupt 21h (partial list) (*continued*)

AH Register	Function
5	Prints a character to list device
	DL: character
7	Reads a character from keyboard but does not display it
	Returns:
	AL: character
8	Checks keyboard status
	Returns:
	AL: OFFH if key struck; otherwise, returns 0
D	Resets disk
E	Sets default drive
	DL: drive number (0 = A, 1 = B,...)
11	Searches for file name
(4E under 2.x)	DX: Address of FCB
	Returns:
	AL: 0 if found, FFh if not
	with name in disk-transfer address
12	Finds next occurrence of file name
(4F under 2.x)	same as 11 above
1A	Sets disk-transfer address
	DX: disk-transfer address
2A	Gets system date
	Returns:
	CX: year (1980-2099)
	DH: month (1-12)
	DL: day (1-31)
2B	Sets system date
	CX: year (1980-2099)
	DH: month (1-12)
	DL: day (1-31)
2C	Gets system time
	Returns:
	CH: hours (0-23)
	CL: minutes (0-59)
	DH: seconds (0-59)
	DL: hundredths of seconds (0-99)
2D	Sets system time
	CH: hours (0-23)
	CL: minutes (0-59)
	DH: seconds (0-59)
	DL: hundredths of seconds (0-99)

higher-level functions in the operating system. The **bdos( )** function is declared as

$$\text{int bdos(int fnum, unsigned Reg\_DX,}$$
$$\text{unsigned Reg\_AL)}$$

where **fnum** is the number of the DOS function. The values of **Reg__DX** and **Reg__AL** are assigned to the DX and AL registers, respectively. Upon return **bdos( )** returns the value of the AX register.

Checking Keyboard Status

A useful function that uses DOS and the **bdos( )** function is **kbhit( )**, which returns **true** if a key has been struck and **false** otherwise. Although it is found in Turbo C's library, **kbhit( )** can be implemented using **bdos( )** with interrupt 21h number Bh, as shown here:

```
#include "dos.h"

/* return 0 if no key struck, non-zero otherwise */
kbhit()
{
        return((char) bdos(0xB,0,0));
}
```

Notice that zeros were used for all but the first argument because no other information was needed. This is the usual procedure. When a specific register is not used in the call, its value is unimportant. The cast to **char** is necessary because the status is returned in AL and AH is not defined.

A common use of **kbhit( )** is to allow a routine to be interrupted by a user command. For example, a database may be performing a long search that the user wants to stop. The following fragment will give you an idea how this can be done:

```
    .
    .
    .
/* look up something */
while(!found) {
  if(kbhit())
    if(getchar()=='q') return; /* abort the search */
    .
    .
    .
}
```

Using the Printer

You can easily create a function that sends characters to the printer by using the DOS function number 5. The short function **prints( )**, shown here, prints a null-terminated string to the printer:

```
#include "dos.h"

/* send a string to the printer */
prints(s)
char *s;
{
        while(*s) bdos(0x5,*s++,0);
}
```

Reading and Writing the Serial Port

Another function commonly absent from the standard library is one to read or write characters from or to the asynchronous serial port. You would use this port if you wanted to write a modem program, for example. However, it is easy to write two functions to access the serial port using DOS function 3 to read a character and DOS function 4 to write a character. The functions are shown here:

```
#include "dos.h"

/* send a character out the port */
put_async(ch)
char ch;
{
        bdos(0x4,ch,0);
}

/* return a character read from the port */
get_async()
{
        return((char) bdos(0x3,0,0));
}
```

Notice once again the use of the **char** cast to ensure that any value in AH does not confuse any calling routine.

Note that Turbo C's library includes the function **bioscom( )**, which can also be used to access the serial ports.

Final Thoughts on Using
System Resources

This chapter has only scratched the surface of what can be done through the creative use of system resources. To fully integrate your program with the operating system, you must have access to information that describes all the functions in detail.

There are two things that you should remember before using operating-system functions. The first is that they can make your program look very professional. Bypassing some of Turbo C's built-in functions in favor of the operating-system functions can create programs that run faster and use less memory. Also, you have access to functions that are not available in Turbo C's library. The second fact is that without a doubt you are creating more trouble for yourself when you use the operating-system functions instead of Turbo C's standard functions. The reason is that your code is no longer portable. You may also become dependent on specific versions of a given operating system, thus creating compatibility problems for distributing your program. However, only you can decide when or if you should introduce machine and operating-system dependencies into your programs.

Interfacing
to Assembly
Language Routines
CHAPTER 5

Although the subject of assembly language interfacing is covered in significant detail in the Turbo C user manual, it is a sufficiently difficult and confusing subject to merit being examined in this chapter from a different perspective.

As efficient and powerful as Turbo C is, there are times when you must write a routine using assembly language. The three reasons for this are

- To increase speed and efficiency of the routine

- To perform some machine-specific function unavailable in Turbo C

- To use third-party routines

Although Turbo C produces extremely fast and compact object code, no compiler will consistently create code that is as fast or compact as that written by an excellent programmer using assembly language. Frequently the small difference does not matter nor does it warrant the extra time needed to write in assembler. However, special cases exist where a specific function is coded in assembler to decrease execution time. This is true of a function if it will be used frequently and will greatly affect the ultimate execution speed of a program. A good example is a floating-point math package. Also, special hardware devices sometimes need exact timing, and you must code in assembler to meet such a strict timing requirement. In other words, even though Turbo C produces fast, efficient code, you will want to *hand-optimize* various critical sections in situations sensitive to run time. Remember that, as the programmer, you know what the code is actually doing so you can often perform optimizations that the compiler cannot.

Certain instructions cannot be executed by a Turbo C program. For example, it is not possible to change data segments with any C instruction or perform an efficient rotate on a byte or word.

In professional programming environments, subroutine libraries are often purchased for such commonly needed capabilities as graphics and floating-point math. Sometimes you must take these in object format because the developer will not sell the source code. Occasionally, you can simply link these routines with code compiled by Turbo C; at other times you must write an interface module to correct any differences in the interface used by Turbo C and the routines you purchased.

A warning should be noted at this point. The interfacing of Turbo C code with assembly language code is definitely an advanced topic. This chapter is intended for those readers who have some familiarity with assembly language programming. This chapter does not teach how to program in assembler. It assumes you know how. If you do not fall into this category, you will still find the material interesting, but do not try the examples. It is easy to do something slightly wrong and create a disaster such as erasing your hard disk.

Each processor has a different assembly language. In this chapter the examples use the 8086/8088/80286 processor and assume a PC-DOS environment.

To try the examples in this chapter, you must have a copy of Microsoft's MASM macro assembler program version 3.0 (or greater) to assemble the assembly language programs.

There are two ways of combining assembly code routines with Turbo C. The first way involves the creation, assembly, and linkage of separate assembly language routines with C functions. The second method uses the nonstandard extension added to Turbo C, called **asm**, to imbed in-line assembly code instructions directly into C functions.

Calling Conventions

A *calling convention* is the method by which a C compiler passes information to functions and returns values from functions. The usual solutions use either the internal registers of the CPU or the system stack to pass information between functions. Generally, C compilers use the stack to pass arguments to functions, and registers to hold function return values. If an argument is one of the basic data types, then the data's actual value is placed on the stack. If the argument is an array, its address is placed on the stack. When a C function begins execution, it retrieves the argument values from the stack. When a function terminates, it passes a return value back to the calling routine in the register of the CPU. Although theoretically it could pass the return value on the stack, this is seldom done.

In addition to defining the way parameters and return values are handled, the calling convention determines exactly what registers must be preserved and which ones you can use freely. Often a compiler requires that certain processor registers be left intact. You must preserve the contents of the register used by your compiler, generally by pushing the register contents on the stack prior to using them. Any other registers are generally free for your use.

When you write an assembly language module that must interface to code compiled by Turbo C, you must follow all of the conventions that are defined and used by Turbo C. Only by doing this can you have assembly language routines correctly interfaced to your C code.

The Calling Conventions of Turbo C

This section teaches you how Turbo C passes arguments to and returns values from a function. Since it is the most common, only the default C parameter passing method is examined. The optional **pascal** parameter is not discussed. Like most C compilers, Turbo C passes arguments to functions on the stack. The arguments are pushed onto the stack right to left. That is, given the call

func(a,b,c);

c is pushed first, followed by **b**, and **a**. The number of bytes occupied on the stack by each type is shown in Table 5-1.

Table 5-1.   Number of Bytes on Stack by Data Type (Microsoft Version
4.0 Compiler)

Type	Number of Bytes
char	2
short	2
signed char	2
signed short	2
unsigned char	2
unsigned short	2
int	2
signed int	2
unsigned int	2
long	4
unsigned long	4
float	4
double	8
(near) pointer	2 (offset only)
(far) pointer	4 (segment and offset)

Upon entry into an assembly code procedure, the contents of the BP register must be saved on the stack and the current value of the stack pointer (SP)
must be placed into BP. The only other registers that you must preserve are
SI and DI, if your routine uses them.

Prior to returning, your assembly language function must restore the
value of BP, SI, and DI and reset the stack pointer.

If your assembly language function returns a value, it is placed into the
AX register, provided it is a 16-bit value. Otherwise, it is returned according
to Table 5-2.

Creating an Assembly Code Function

Undoubtedly, the simplest way to learn to create assembly language functions is to see how Turbo C generates code by using the −S compiler option.
This option causes an assembly language to output a listing of the code that it

Table 5-2. Register Usage for Return Values

Type	Register(s) and Meaning
char	AX
unsigned char	AX
short	AX
unsigned short	AX
int	AX
unsigned int	AX
long	Low-order word in AX
	High-order word in DX
unsigned long	Low-order word in AX
	High-order word in DX
float	Low-order word in AX
	High-order word in DX
double	Return on 8087 stack or at
	TOS in emulator
struct & union	Address to value
(near) pointer	AX
(far) pointer	Offset in AX, segment in DX

generates. By examining this file you can learn a great deal about not only how to interface to the compiler, but also how Turbo C actually works.

Begin with the following short program:

```
int sum;
main()
{
  sum = add(10, 20);
}

add(a, b)
int a, b;
{
  int t;

  t = a+b;
  return t;
}
```

The variable **sum** is intentionally declared as global so that you can see examples of both local and global data. If this program is called "test," then the following command line causes "test.asm" to be created:

>tcc -S test

The contents of "test.asm" are shown here:

```
        name    test
_text   segment byte public 'code'
dgroup  group   _bss,_data
        assume  cs:_text,ds:dgroup,ss:dgroup
_text   ends
_data   segment word public 'data'
_d@     label   byte
_data   ends
_bss    segment word public 'bss'
_b@     label   byte
_bss    ends
_text   segment byte public 'code'
_main   proc    near
; Line 4
        mov     ax,20
        push    ax
        mov     ax,10
        push    ax
        call    near ptr _add
        pop     cx
        pop     cx
        mov     word ptr dgroup:_sum,ax
; Line 5
@1:
        ret
_main   endp
_add    proc    near
        push    si
        push    bp
        mov     bp,sp
; Line 9
; Line 10
; Line 11
; Line 12
        mov     si,word ptr [bp+6]
        add     si,word ptr [bp+8]
; Line 13
        mov     ax,si
@2:
; Line 14
        pop     bp
        pop     si
        ret
_add    endp
_text   ends
_bss    segment word public 'bss'
        public  _sum
_sum    label   word
        db      2 dup (?)
_bss    ends
```

```
_data     segment word public 'data'
_sa       label   byte
_data     ends
_text     segment byte public 'code'
          public  _add
          public  _main
_text     ends
          end
```

The program begins by establishing the various segments required by a Turbo C program. These will vary with different memory models. (This file was produced by the small-model compiler. All the other examples in this chapter also use the small model.) Notice that two bytes are allocated in the **_bss** segment for the global variable **_sum** near the end of the code. The underscore in front of "sum" is added by the compiler to the front of all function and global variable names to avoid confusion with any internal compiler names. The program begins after this segment. In Turbo C the code segment is called **_text**.

The first thing that happens inside the **_main** procedure is that the two arguments to **_add** are pushed on the stack and **_add** is called. Upon return from the **_add** function, the two **pop cx** instructions restore the stack to its original state. The next line moves the return value from **_add** into **_sum**. Finally, **_main** returns.

The **_add** function begins by saving SI and BP on the stack and then placing the value of SP into BP. At this point the stack looks like this:

```
a       top of stack
b
BP
SI
```

The next three lines of code add the numbers together. Notice that Turbo C is using the register SI to hold the value of the local variable **t**. Even though the program did not specify that **t** should be a **register** type, Turbo C automatically made it one as part of Turbo C's compiler optimizations. If the program had had more than two register variables, space for them would have been made on the stack. Finally, the answer is placed into AX, BP and SI are popped, and **_add** returns.

You can literally assemble this assembly language file using the Microsoft macro-assembler **masm**, link it using the standard **link** utility, and run it. What is more interesting is that you can modify it to make it run faster, but leave the C source code untouched. For example, you could remove the instructions that pushed and popped SI inside the **__add** function (because it is apparent that SI is not used elsewhere in the program), and then assemble the file. Doing this is called *hand optimization.*

Now that you have seen how Turbo C compiles functions, it is just a short step to writing your own assembly language functions. One of the easiest ways to do this is to let the compiler generate an assembly language skeleton for you. Once you have the skeleton, all you have to do is fill in the details. For example, assume that it is necessary to create an assembly routine to multiply two integers. To have the compiler generate a skeleton for this function, first create a file containing only the following function:

```
mul(a, b)
int a, b;
{
}
```

Next, compile it with the −S option so that an assembly language file is produced. The file will look like this:

```
          name      mul
_text     segment   byte public 'code'
dgroup    group     _bss,_data
          assume    cs:_text,ds:dgroup,ss:dgroup
_text     ends
_data     segment   word public 'data'
_d@       label     byte
_data     ends
_bss      segment   word public 'bss'
_b@       label     byte
_bss      ends
_text     segment   byte public 'code'
_mul      proc      near
          push      bp
          mov       bp,sp
@1:
          pop       bp
          ret
_mul      endp
_text     ends
_data     segment   word public 'data'
_s'       label     byte
_data     ends
_text     segment   byte public 'code'
          public    _mul
_text     ends
          end
```

In this skeleton, the compiler has done all the work of defining the proper segments and setting up the stack and registers. All you have to do is fill in the details. The finished **mul( )** function is shown here:

```
          name     mul
_text     segment byte public 'code'
dgroup    group    _bss,_data
          assume   cs:_text,ds:dgroup,ss:dgroup
_text     ends
_data     segment word public 'data'
_d'       label    byte
_data     ends
_bss      segment word public 'bss'
_b'       label    byte
_bss      ends
_text     segment byte public 'code'
_mul      proc     near
          push     bp
          mov      bp,sp
; ********************************************
; here is the code to multiply the numbers
          mov      ax,[bp+4]       ;a
          imul     ax,[bp+6]       ;b
;*********************************************
a1:
          pop      bp
          ret
_mul      endp
_text     ends
_data     segment word public 'data'
_sa       label    byte
_data     ends
_text     segment byte public 'code'
          public   _mul
_text     ends
          end
```

Once this file is assembled it may be linked to any C program that requires it. For example, this program will print the number 10 on the screen (remember to link in **mul( )**):

```
main()
{
  printf("%d ", mul(2, 5));
}
```

You should notice the line of code two lines from the end. It is the line **public _mul**. This statement tells the assembler that the **_mul** identifier should be made available to any routine that needs it. This enables the C program to call **_mul**. Also, if there is data that the C program must know about, it should be made public, too. The rule is very simple: Place the names of procedures that you want public in the **CODE** segment and the names of variables in the **DATA** segment.

The opposite of this is when you want to call a C function or access a variable defined in a C program from an assembly language function. In this case you must declare the objects your assembly language routine needs to be external by using the **extrn** assembler command. The general form of the **extrn** statement is

extrn <object> : <attribute>

If the *object* is a function, then *attribute* can be either **near** or **far**. If you are using a small model, then use **near**; otherwise, use **far**. For variables, *attribute* may be one of the following values:

Value	Size in bytes
byte	1
word	2
dword	4
qword	8
tbyte	10

For example, if your assembler routine needed to access the global integer variable **count** and the function **search( )**, you would place the following statements at the start of the assembly language file:

```
extrn _count : word
extrn _search : near
```

Remember that the name of any assembly language function or external data that will be called by a Turbo C program must have an underscore in front of it.

A little more challenging situation arises when pointers are passed to a function. In this case, you must use indirect accessing methods to access and alter the value of the argument. For example, assume you need to create an assembly language function that negates the integer pointed to by the argument to the function. Assuming that this function is called **neg( )**, the following fragment will print the number −10 on the screen:

```
x = 10;

neg(&x);

printf("%d", x);   /* prints -10 */
```

In C, this function would look like this:

```
neg(a)
int *a;
{
  *a = -*a;
}
```

The **neg( )** function coded in assembler would look like this (remember that this assumes that the small model is used):

```
        name    neg
_text   segment byte public 'code'
dgroup  group   _bss,_data
        assume  cs:_text,ds:dgroup,ss:dgroup
_text   ends
_data   segment word public 'data'
_d@     label   byte
_data   ends
_bss    segment word public 'bss'
_b@     label   byte
_bss    ends
_text   segment byte public 'code'
        public  _neg
_neg    proc    near
        push    bp
        mov     bp,sp
; ******************************************************
; The negate code
        mov     bx, word ptr [bp+4] ; get the address
        mov     ax, word ptr [bx]   ; load the arg
        neg     ax                  ; negate it
        mov     word ptr [bx],ax    ; store it
;
@1:
        pop     bp
        ret
_neg    endp
_text   ends
_data   segment word public 'data'
_s@     label   byte
_data   ends
_text   segment byte public 'code'
        public  _neg
_text   ends
        end
```

The key lines of code are

```
mov     bx, word ptr [bp+4] ; get the address
mov     ax, word ptr[bx]    ; load the arg
neg     ax                  ; negate it
mov     word ptr [bx],ax    ; store it
```

First, the address of the argument is loaded from the stack. Next, the relative addressing mode of the 8086 is used to load the integer to be negated. The **neg** instruction reverses the sign, and the last instruction places the value back at the location pointed to by BX.

The best way to learn more about interfacing assembly language code with your C programs is to write short functions in C that do something similar to what you want the assembly language version to do and create an assembly language file by using the assembly language compiler option. Most of the time all you will have to do is hand-optimize this code instead of actually creating an assembly language routine from scratch.

It is really quite easy to use assembly language functions along with your Turbo C code if you precisely follow the rules.

Using *asm*

Although not supported by the proposed ANSI standard, Turbo C has added the keyword **asm** to allow in-line assembly code to be made part of a C program without using a completely separate assembly language module. The advantage to this is twofold. First, you are not required to write and maintain all the interface code. Second, all the code is in one place, making support a little easier.

To put in-line assembly code in a Turbo C function, you simply place the keyword **asm** at the beginning of each line of assembly code and enter the assembly language statement. All code that follows the **asm** keyword must be correct assembly code for the computer you are using. Turbo C simply passes this code through, untouched, to the assembler phase of the compiler.

A very simple example of in-line assembly code is shown here. It is used to output information to a port, presumably for initialization purposes.

```
init_port1()
{
  printf("Initializing Port\n");
asm       out 26,255
asm       out 26,0
}
```

Here, the C compiler automatically provides the code to save registers and to return from the function. Notice that **asm** statements do not require a semicolon to terminate. Instead, an assembly language statement is terminated by the end of the line.

You could use in-line assembly code to create **mul( )**, from the previous section, without actually creating a separate assembly language file. Using this approach, the code for **mul( )** is shown here:

```
mul(a, b)
int a, b;
{
asm       mov ax,word ptr 8[bp]
asm       imul ax,word ptr 10[bp]
}
```

Remember that Turbo C will provide all customary support for setting up and returning from a function call. You must only provide the body of the function and follow the calling conventions to access the arguments. Although the use of a nonstandard feature certainly reduces portability, the use of assembly code probably reduces it more. So, the use of **asm** can be recommended—especially for short assembly code fragments.

If you wish to place comments in **asm** statements *you must use* the standard C /* and */ method. Do not use the the semicolon convention used by most assemblers as it confuses Turbo C.

Assembly code statements found inside a function are placed in the **CODE** segment. Those found outside any function are placed in the **DATA** segment.

You should keep in mind that whatever method you use, you are creating machine dependencies that make your program difficult to port to a new machine. However, for the demanding situations that require assembly code, it usually will be worth the effort.

When to Code in Assembler

Most programmers only code in assembler when absolutely necessary because such coding is difficult. As a general rule, don't use it—it creates too many problems. However, there are two cases in which coding in assembler makes sense. One case is when there is absolutely no other way to do it—for example, when you need to interface directly to a hardware device that cannot be handled using C.

Another case is when the execution time of a C program must be reduced. In this case, you should carefully choose the functions you code in assembler. If you code the wrong ones, you will see little increase in speed. If you choose the right one, your program will fly! To determine which functions need recoding, you must review the operational flow of your program. The functions inside loops are generally the ones to program in assembler because they are executed repeatedly. Using assembler to code a function that is used only once or twice may not offer significant speed improvements, but using assembler to code a function that is used several times may. For example, consider the following **main( )** function:

```
main()
{
  register int t;

  init();

  ror(t=0;t<1000;++t) {
    phase1();
    phase2();
    if(t==10) phase3();
  }

  byebye();
}
```

Recoding **init( )** and **byebye( )** may not measurably affect the speed of this program, because they execute only once. Both **phase1( )** and **phase2( )** are executed 1000 times, and recoding them is more likely to have a major effect on the run time of this program. The **phase3( )** is only executed once, even though it is inside the loop, so recoding this function into assembler would probably not be worth the effort.

   With careful thought, you can improve the speed of your program by recoding only a few functions in assembler. Remember, however, that the greatest speed increases come from better algorithms, not hand-optimized assembly routines. You should only consider assembly code after you have optimized the underlying algorithm.

Graphics

CHAPTER 6

Graphics rank high on the list of exciting things you can do with a computer. One reason for this is the vast number of different ways that graphics can be used. Computer-aided design/computer-aided manufacturing (CAD/CAM) can present detailed three-dimensional models that can be rotated to provide various views. A statistical package can display business graphics to illustrate a company's sales growth over the past few years. A graphic artist might create a new company logo on the screen of a personal computer. Given the wide range of applications, it may seem like an entire book would be needed to even approach the subject of graphics. (See *Advanced Graphics Using C* by Nelson Johnson and published by Osborne/McGraw-Hill. The functions that Johnson develops are highly efficient, stylistically clear, and easy to understand.) However, what all graphics applications have in common is the ability to draw points, lines, boxes, and circles. It is this ability that will be the concern of this chapter. The main emphasis will not be on how graphics hardware works, but on the creation of a few core graphics routines that you can use, enhance, and evolve.

For the routines developed in this chapter to run correctly, you need an IBM PC/XT/AT or compatible and either a CGA or an EGA graphics board. However, beyond the writing of a pixel, the routines in the chapter are hardware independent and you should have little trouble making them work on other types of systems.

Modes and Palettes

Before any graphics functions can be used, the computer must be placed into the proper video mode. For the IBM PC this means selecting the proper mode and palette.

There are several different video modes available on the IBM PC. (A summary of all the modes appears in Chapter 4.) The functions developed in this chapter require screen mode 4, which is 320×200 four-color graphics. This mode works with both the CGA and the EGA. In Chapter 4, the **mode( )** function was used to set the current video mode through a call to the ROM-BIOS. It is repeated here for your convenience. (Several of the functions developed here will interface to ROM-BIOS, so you may want to read Chapter 4 if you haven't done so yet.)

```
/* set the video mode */
void mode(mode_code)
int mode_code;
{
  union REGS r;

  r.h.al = mode_code;
  r.h.ah = 0;
  int86(0x10, &r, &r);
}
```

Keep in mind that in all modes, the upper left-hand corner is location 0,0.

There are two palettes available in mode 4 graphics. The palette determines which four colors will be displayed. On the IBM PC, palette 0 provides red, green, and yellow; palette 1 provides white, magenta, and cyan. For each the fourth color is the same and is the color of the background, usually black. The function **palette( )**, shown here, selects the palette specified in its argument:

```
/* set the palette */
void palette(pnum)
int pnum;
{
  union REGS r;

  r.h.bh = 1;   /* code for graphics */
  r.h.bl = pnum;
  r.h.ah = 11;  /* set palette function */
  int86(0x10, &r, &r);
}
```

Writing Pixels

The most fundamental of all graphics routines is the one that actually writes
a pixel. Because it is used by higher-level routines, its efficiency is very
important to the overall speed with which the graphics functions operate. On
the IBM PC and compatibles, there are two ways to write information to a
pixel. The first is through the use of a ROM-BIOS routine. This is the easiest,
but is also the slowest. The second and faster method is to place information
directly into the video display RAM. Both methods are examined here.

Writing a Pixel Using ROM-BIOS

The ROM-BIOS interrupt 10h, function 12 writes the specified color in register AL into the pixel at the row value in DX and the column number in CX.
The **writepoint( )** function, shown here, writes the specified color to the specified location. Notice that it also prevents out-of-range locations from being
used.

```
/* write a pixel at x,y specified color */
void writepoint(x, y, color_code)
int x, y, color_code;
{
  union REGS r;

  /* don't display if out-of-range */
  if(x<0 || x>199 || y<0 || y>319) return;
```

```
    r.h.ah = 12; /* set for write */
    r.h.al = color_code; /* color  */
    r.x.dx = x; /* set row */
    r.x.cx = y; /* set column */
    int86(0x10, &r, &r); /* call BIOS */
}
```

To use **writepoint( )**, you simply call it with the coordinates of the pixel and the color you want written there. For example, this program prints three diagonal lines, each of a different color and each 100 pixels long. (In the shorter examples in this chapter, only the **main( )** function is shown, but be sure to include the other necessary functions. In this case the other functions are **mode( )**, **palette( )**, and **writepoint( )**.)

```
#include "dos.h"
#include "stdio.h"

main()
{
    int i,color;

    mode(4);
    palette(0);

    for(i=0;i<100;i++)
        for(color=1;color<4;color++)
            writepoint(i,i+(color*4),color);

    getchar();
    mode(2); /* return to standard text mode
}
```

Figure 6-1 shows output of this program as a result of using the print screen facility after loading PC-DOS's "graphics" print driver.

There is one very interesting feature of the ROM-BIOS function that writes to a pixel. If the seventh bit (the far left bit) of the color code is 1, then the color specified is XORed with the existing color at the specified location; it does not simply overwrite the previous color. The advantage to this is that it guarantees that the pixel will be visible. You will see the value of this feature a little later in this chapter.

Writing Pixels Directly

It is possible to bypass ROM-BIOS and write information directly into the video RAM used by the CGA or EGA in mode 4. The reason you may want to do this is that the graphics routines that directly access the CGA or EGA run much faster than those that use the ROM-BIOS routines.

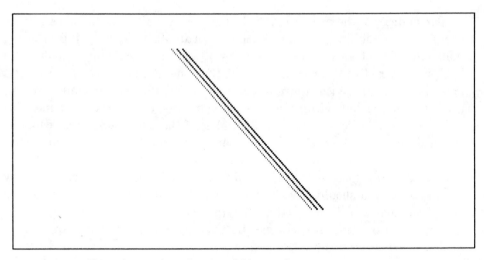

Figure 6-1. Drawing points in graphics mode

In mode 4, both the CGA and the EGA video controllers map the contents of the video-display RAM onto the screen. The CGA video RAM always starts at location B8000h. The EGA uses the same location for those modes that are compatible with the CGA modes. (For information on the video hardware, consult the *IBM Technical Reference* manual.) Each byte holds the color information for four pixels. Because two bits can hold only four different values, there can be only four colors in mode 4. A quirk in the CGA causes the even-numbered pixels to be stored in memory beginning at B8000h, but the odd-numbered pixels are stored 2000h bytes higher at BA000h. Therefore, each row of pixels requires 80 bytes—40 for the even pixels and 40 for the odd. Within each byte the pixels are stored left to right as they appear on the screen. This means that pixel number 0 occupies bits 6 and 7, while pixel number 3 uses bits 0 and 1.

Because there are four pixels encoded into each byte, it is necessary to preserve the value of the other three when changing the value of one pixel. The best way to do this is to create a bit mask that contains all 1's except in the location of the pixel to be changed. This value is ANDed with the original byte, and then this value is ORed with the new information. However, the situation is slightly different if you want to XOR the new value with the old. In this case you simply OR the original byte with 0 and then XOR that result with the new color.

The address of the proper byte is located by first dividing the x coordinate by 40 and then adding the value of the y coordinate divided by 4. By finding the remainder of an integer division by 2, you can determine which video bank is required. If the remainder is 0, then the number is even so the first bank is used; otherwise, the number is odd and the second bank must be used. The proper bits within the byte are computed by performing a modulus division by 4. The remainder is the number of the 2-bit packet that contains the desired pixel. Bit-shift operations are used to arrange the **color_code** byte and the bit mask into their proper positions. Although the bit manipulations that take place in the **mempoint( )** function, shown here, are fairly intimidating, you should have no trouble understanding its operation if you study the code carefully. Notice that the pointer to the video memory is declared as **far**. This is necessary if you are compiling with a small data model. (Turn to Appendix A for an explanation of the differences between the memory models.)

```
/* write a point directly to the CGA */
void mempoint(x,y,color_code)
int x,y,color_code;
{
  union mask {
    char c[2];
    int i;
  } bit_mask;
  int i, index, bit_position;
  unsigned char t;
  char xor; /* xor color in or overwrite */
  char far *ptr = (char far *) 0xB8000000; /* pointer
                                              to CGA memory */

  bit_mask.i=0xFF3F;     /* 11111111 00111111 in binary */

  /* check range for mode 4 */
  if(x<0 || x>199 || y<0 || y>319) return;

  xor=color_code & 128; /* see if xor mode is set */
  color_code=color_code & 127; /* mask off high bit */

  /* set bit_mask and color_code bits to the right location */
  bit_position=y%4;    /* compute the proper location
                          within the byte */
  color_code<<=2*(3-bit_position); /* shift the color_code
                                      into position */
  bit_mask.i>>=2*bit_position; /* shift the bit_mask into
                                  position */


  /* find the correct byte in screen memory */
  index=x*40 +(y/4);
  if(x % 2) index += 8152; /* if odd use 2nd bank */
```

```
/* write the color */
if(!xor) { /* overwrite mode */
  t=*(ptr+index) & bit_mask.c[0];
  *(ptr+index)=t | color_code;
}
else { /* xor mode */
  t=*(ptr+index) | (char)0;
  *(ptr+index)=t ^ color_code;
}
}
```

Notice that the special XOR write mode available in the ROM-BIOS function has been preserved in **mempoint( )**.

The **mempoint( )** function is used in subsequent examples because it is much faster. However, the **writepoint( )** function may be necessary for use with computers that are not 100% IBM compatible.

Drawing Lines

Another fundamental graphics routine is the line-drawing function. It is used to draw a line in the specified color when given the beginning and ending coordinates of the line. Although it is quite easy to draw lines that are either vertical or horizontal, it is a little harder to create a function that can draw lines along any diagonal. For example, to draw a line from 0,0 to 80,120, what are the points in between? Although there are various methods of drawing lines, this chapter examines two.

One approach to creating a line-drawing function uses the ratio between the change in the x and y dimensions. To see how this works, consider a line from 0,0 to 5,10. The change in x is 5 and the change in y is 10. The ratio is 1/2. This ratio is used to determine the rate at which the x and y coordinates change as the line is drawn. In this case it means that the x coordinate will be incremented only half as frequently as the y coordinate. This method is mathematically simple and easy to understand, but if it is to work properly in all situations, floating-point variables and arithmetic must be used to avoid serious round-off errors. This means that the line-drawing function runs quite slowly unless there is a math coprocessor, such as the 8087, installed in the system. The function **slowline( )**, shown here, uses ratios to draw lines on the screen and is presented primarily to illustrate how *not* to implement a line-drawing function.

```
/* Draw a line in specified color using floating point
   ratios.  This function is too slow for most
   applications.

*/
void slowline(startx, starty, endx, endy, color)
int startx, starty, endx, endy, color;
{
  register int t;
  int delta_x, delta_y;
  int incx, incy, run, cx, cy;
  float ratio_x, ratio_y;

  /* compute the increments */
  delta_x=endx-startx;
  delta_y=endy-starty;

  /* Compute the direction of the increment,
     an increment of 0 means either a vertical or horizontal
     line.
  */
  if(delta_x>0) incx=1;
  else if(delta_x==0) incx=0;
  else incx=-1;

  if(delta_y>0) incy=1;
  else if(delta_y==0) incy=0;
  else incy=-1;

  delta_x=abs(delta_x);
  delta_y=abs(delta_y);

  /* determine which coordinates govern the line
  */
  if(delta_x>delta_y)
    run=delta_x;
  else
    run=delta_y;

  /* Draw the line.  This routine uses the ratios
     between between the changes in X and Y to compute
     the next move.
  */
  ratio_x=ratio_y=1.0;
  for (t=0, cx=0, cy=0; t<=run; t++) {
    mempoint(startx, starty, color);
    if(delta_x) ratio_x=(float)cx/(float)delta_x;
    else ratio_x=0;
    if(delta_y) ratio_y=(float)cy/(float)delta_y;
    else ratio_y=0;
    if(run==delta_x) {
      startx+=incx;
      cx++;
```

```
  }
  else if(ratio_x<ratio_y) {
    startx+=incx;
    cx++;
  }

  if(run==delta_y) {
    starty+=incy;
    cy++;
  }
  else if(ratio_y<ratio_x) {
    starty+=incy;
    cy++;
  }
  }
}
```

Notice that **mempoint( )** is used to actually write points to the screen. Much of the code to the routine is used to determine such things as the direction of the line, the magnitude of the change to both the x and y coordinate components, and the appropriate increment. The floating-point calculations in the loop actually draw the line and cause the algorithm to perform poorly. For this reason this approach is seldom used.

By far the most common method used to draw a line employs Bresenham's algorithm. Although still based conceptually upon the ratios between the x and y distances, no divisions or floating-point calculations are required. Instead, the ratio between the change in the x and y directions is handled implicitly through a series of additions and subtractions. The basic idea behind Bresenham's approach is to keep track of how wide the error is between where each point should go and where it must be displayed. The error is introduced by the fact that no display can be totally precise; therefore, the actual location of each dot on the line is the best approximation. In each iteration through the line-drawing loop, two variables called **xerr** and **yerr** are incremented by the changes in magnitude of the x and y coordinates, respectively. When an error value reaches a predetermined limit, it is reset and the appropriate coordinate counter is incremented. This process continues until the entire line is drawn. The **line( )** function, shown here, implements this method. Study it until you understand its operation. Notice that it uses the **mempoint( )** function developed earlier to actually write a dot to the screen.

```
/* Draw a line in specified color
   using Bresenham's integer based algorithm.
*/
void line(startx, starty, endx, endy, color)
int startx, starty, endx, endy, color;
{
  register int t, distance;
  int xerr=0, yerr=0, delta_x, delta_y;
  int incx, incy;

  /* compute the distances in both directions */
  delta_x=endx-startx;
  delta_y=endy-starty;

  /* Compute the direction of the increment,
     an increment of 0 means either a vertical or horizontal
     line.
  */
  if(delta_x>0) incx=1;
  else if(delta_x==0) incx=0;
  else incx=-1;

  if(delta_y>0) incy=1;
  else if(delta_y==0) incy=0;
  else incy=-1;

  /* determine which distance is greater */
  delta_x=abs(delta_x);
  delta_y=abs(delta_y);
  if(delta_x>delta_y) distance=delta_x;
  else distance=delta_y;

  /* draw the line */
  for(t=0; t<=distance+1; t++) {
    mempoint(startx, starty, color);
    xerr+=delta_x;
    yerr+=delta_y;
    if(xerr>distance) {
      xerr-=distance;
      startx+=incx;
    }
    if(yerr>distance) {
      yerr-=distance;
      starty+=incy;
    }
  }
}
```

The following program shows how the **line( )** function can be used to display lines on the screen. Figure 6-2 shows the output of this program by using the print screen facility after loading PC-DOS's "graphics" print driver.

```
#include "dos.h"
#include "stdio.h"

main()
{
  int i,color;

  mode(4);
  palette(0);

  line(0, 0, 100, 100, 1);
  line(50, 90, 180, 300, 2);
  line(10, 10, 20, 200, 3);

  getchar();
  mode(2); /* return to standard text mode */
}
```

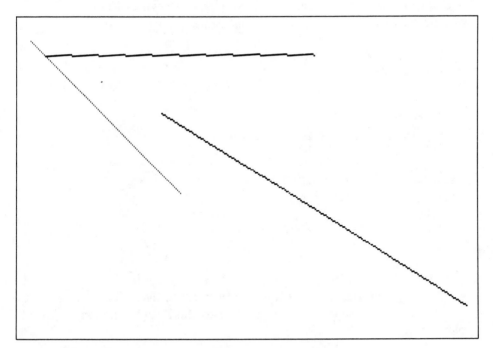

Figure 6-2. Sample output from the **line()** function

Drawing and Filling Boxes

Once you have a line-drawing function, it becomes an easy matter to create a box-drawing function. The one shown here draws the outline of a box in the specified color when given the coordinates of two opposing corners.

```
/* draw a box */
void box(startx,starty, endx, endy, color_code)
int startx,starty,endx,endy,color_code;
{
   line(startx,starty, endx,starty, color_code);
   line(startx,starty, startx,endy, color_code);
   line(startx,endy, endx,endy, color_code);
   line(endx,starty, endx,endy, color_code);
}
```

Using **box( )**, this program draws the boxes shown in Figure 6-3, which were printed by using the print screen utility.

```
#include "dos.h"
#include "stdio.h"

main()
{
   int i,color;

   mode(4);    /* go to graphics mode */
   palette(0);

   box(0, 0, 40, 50, 1);
   box(100, 120, 140, 250, 2);
   box(150, 150, 90, 0, 3);

   getchar();
   mode(2); /* return to standard text mode */
}
```

To fill a box requires that you write to each pixel in the box. The **fill_box( )** routine, shown here, fills a box with the specified color when given the coordinates of two opposing corners. It uses the **line( )** function to actually color in the box.

```
/* fill box with specified color */
void fill_box(startx, starty, endx, endy, color_code)
int startx,starty,endx,endy,color_code;
{
   register int i,begin, end;
```

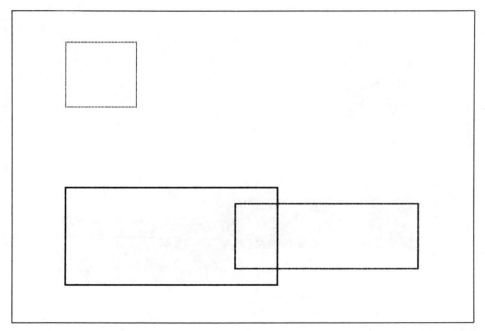

Figure 6-3. Sample output using the **box( )** function

```
  begin = startx<endx ? startx : endx;
  end = startx>endx ? startx : endx;

  for(i=begin; i<=end;i++)
    line(i,starty,i,endy,color_code);
}
```

The following program produced the sample output shown in Figure 6-4, which was printed by using the print screen utility:

```
#include "dos.h"
#include "stdio.h"

main()
{
  int i,color;

  mode(4);  /* go to graphics mode */
  palette(0);
```

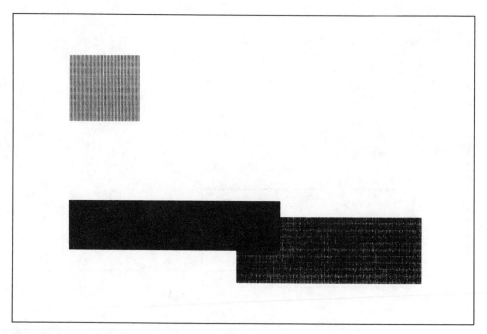

Figure 6-4. Sample output using **fill___box()**

```
fill_box(0, 0, 40, 50, 1);
fill_box(100, 120, 140, 250, 2);
fill_box(150, 150, 90, 0, 3);

getchar();
mode(2); /* return to standard text mode */
}
```

Drawing Circles

The easiest and fastest way to draw a circle is to use Bresenham's circle-drawing algorithm. The basis of its operation is similar to the line-drawing algorithm. Only integers are used, except for the aspect ratio. Essentially, the algorithm works by incrementing the x and y coordinates as needed, based upon the magnitude of the error between them. This value is held in the **delta** variable. The **plot—circle( )** support function actually plots the points. You could place this code in line for extra speed, but it does make the **circle( )** function harder to read and understand. The variable **asp—ratio** is global because it is used by both **circle( )** and **plot—circle( )**. By varying the **asp—ratio** you can draw ellipses. The **circle( )** function is called with the coordinates of the center of the circle, the radius (in pixels) of the circle, and its color. The **circle( )** and **plot—circle( )** functions are shown here:

```
double asp_ratio;
/* Draw a circle using Bresenham's integer based Algorithm. */
void circle(x_center, y_center, radius,  color_code)
int x_center, y_center, radius, color_code;
{
  register int x, y, delta;

  asp_ratio = 1.0;  /* for different aspect ratios, alter
                  this number */

  y = radius;
  delta = 3 - 2 * radius;

  for(x=0; x<y; ) {
    plot_circle(x, y, x_center, y_center, color_code);

    if (delta < 0)
      delta += 4*x+6;
    else {
      delta += 4*(x-y)+10;
      y--;
    }
    x++;
  }
  x=y;
  if(y) plot_circle(x, y, x_center, y_center, color_code);
}

/* plot_circle actually prints the points that
    define the circle */
void plot_circle(x, y, x_center, y_center, color_code)
int x, y, x_center, y_center, color_code;
{
  int startx, endx, x1, starty, endy, y1;

  starty = y*asp_ratio;
  endy = (y+1)*asp_ratio;
  startx = x*asp_ratio;
  endx = (x+1)*asp_ratio;

  for (x1=startx; x1<endx; ++x1)  {
    mempoint(x1+x_center, y+y_center, color_code);
    mempoint(x1+x_center, y_center-y, color_code);
    mempoint(x_center-x1, y_center-y, color_code);
    mempoint(x_center-x1, y+y_center, color_code);
  }
```

```
for (y1=starty; y1<endy; ++y1) {
  mempoint(y1+x_center, x+y_center, color_code);
  mempoint(y1+x_center, y_center-x, color_code);
  mempoint(x_center-y1, y_center-x, color_code);
  mempoint(x_center-y1, x+y_center, color_code);
}
}
```

The following program demonstrates the **circle( )** function. Figure 6-5 shows the output.

```
#include "dos.h"
#include "stdio.h"

main()
{
  int color;

  mode(4);
  palette(0);

  circle(50, 90, 50, 2);
  circle(100, 100, 20, 3);

  getchar();
  mode(2); /* return to standard text mode */
}
```

It is possible to fill a circle by repeatedly calling **circle( )** with increasingly smaller radii. This is the method used by **fill_circle( )** shown here:

```
/* fill a circle by repeatedly calling circle(
   with smaller radiuses
*/
void fill_circle(x, y, r, c)
int x, y, r, c;
{
  while(r) {
    circle(x, y, r, c);
    r--;
  }
}
```

Putting It All Together

To conclude the chapter, a simple "paint" program is created that uses the graphic routines developed in this chapter. You may be familiar with paint programs because they are quite popular. These programs generally use a mouse to allow the user to "brush" lines onto the screen of the computer.

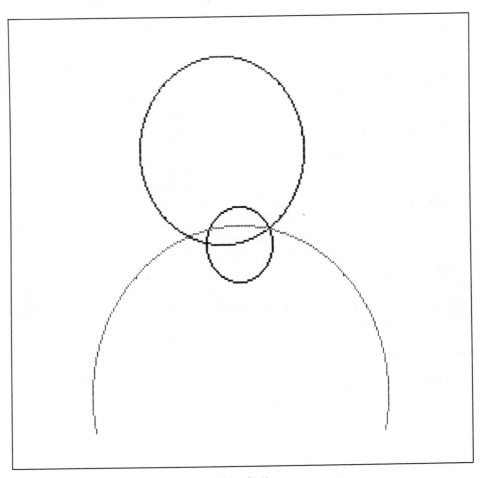

Figure 6-5. Sample output using **circle()**

However, since not everyone has a mouse, the paint program developed here will rely on the cursor keys for operation.

The program requires two additional routines. The first is **get_key()** (developed in Chapter 5) that reads the 16-bit scan code from the keyboard. (The scan codes were discussed in Chapter 4.) The cursor keys and the function keys return 0 for the character code (the low-order 8 bits), meaning that the position code (the high-order 8 bits) must be examined to determine what key was pressed. The **get_key()** function is shown here. It uses **int86()** to access the ROM-BIOS routine that returns the scan code.

```
/* read the scan code */
get_key()
{
  union REGS r;

  r.h.ah = 0;
  return int86(0x16, &r, &r);
}
```

In a paint program you need to be able to see the current x,y positions. (Remember that in graphics mode there is no cursor.) To do this requires the use of a locator, which resembles the cross hairs of a rifle scope. The function **xhairs( )**, shown here, places a small cross hairs on the screen at the current x,y position. Notice that the color code is ORed with 128 causing bit 7 to be set to 1. This tells the **mempoint( )** function to XOR the color onto the screen instead of overwriting the current color. This achieves two very important things. First, the locator always is visible because it will always have a color other than what is around it. Second, it makes it easy to return the pixels occupied by the locator to their former color when the locator is moved—you simply write them a second time. (Recall that two XOR operations always produce the original value.)

```
/* display crosshair locator */
void xhairs(x,y)
int x,y;
{
  line(x-4, y, x+3, y, 1 | 128);
  line(x, y+4, x, y-3, 1 | 128);
}
```

The program allows you to

- Draw lines
- Draw boxes
- Fill boxes
- Draw circles
- Fill circles
- Select color
- Select palette
- Turn the brush on and off
- Set a speed-of-motion parameter

The main loop of the program is shown here:

```
main()
{
  union k{
    char c[2];
    int i;
  } key;

  int x=10, y=10, cc=2, on_flag=1, pal_num=1;
  int startx=0, starty=0, endx=0, endy=0, first_point=1;
  int inc=1;

  mode(4);
  palette(0);

  xhairs(x,y);
  do {
    key.i=get_key();
    xhairs(x,y);  /* draw crosshairs */
    if(!key.c[0]) switch(key.c[1]) {
      case 75: /* left */
        if(on_flag) line(x,y,x,y-inc,cc);
        y-=inc;
        break;
      case 77: /* right */
        if(on_flag) line(x,y,x,y+inc,cc);
        y+=inc;
        break;
      case 72: /* up */
        if(on_flag) line(x,y,x-inc,y,cc);
        x-=inc;
        break;
      case 80: /* down */
        if(on_flag) line(x,y,x+inc,y,cc);
        x+=inc;
        break;
      case 71: /* up left */
        if(on_flag) line(x,y,x-inc,y-inc,cc);
        x-=inc; y-=inc;
        break;
      case 73: /* up right */
        if(on_flag) line(x,y,x-inc,y+inc,cc);
        x-=inc; y+=inc;
        break;
      case 79: /* down left*/
        if(on_flag) line(x,y,x+inc,y-inc,cc);
        x+=inc;y-=inc;
        break;
      case 81: /* down right */
        if(on_flag) line(x,y,x+inc,y+inc,cc);
        x+=inc;y+=inc;
        break;
      case 59: inc=1;  /* F1 - slow speed */
        break;
      case 6U: inc=5;  /* F2 - fast speed */
        break;
    }
    else switch(tolower(key.c[0])) {
```

```
case 'o': on_flag=!on_flag; /* toggle brush */
  break;
case '1': cc=1; /* color 1 */
  break;
case '2': cc=2; /* color 2 */
  break;
case '3': cc=3; /* color 3 */
  break;
case '0': cc=0; /* color 0 */
  break;
case 'b': box(startx, starty, endx, endy, cc);
  break;
case 'f': fill_box(startx, starty, endx, endy, cc);
  break;
case 'l': line(startx, starty, endx, endy, cc);
  break;
case 'c': circle(startx, starty, endy-starty, cc);
  break;
case 'h': fill_circle(startx, starty, endy-starty, cc);
  break;
case '\r': /* set endpoints */
  if(first_point) {
    startx=x, starty=y;
  }
  else {
    endx=x; endy=y;
  }
  first_point = !first_point;
  break;
case 'p': pal_num=pal_num==1 ? 2:1;
  palette(pal_num);
}
xhairs(x,y);
} while (key.c[0]!='q');
getchar();
mode(2);
}
```

The paint program works like this: Upon execution, the screen is set to graphics mode 4. Palette 0 is selected and the locator is displayed in the upper-left corner. The brush is on with a default color of 2 (which is red in palette 0). Therefore, moving the cursor leaves a trail of pixels. This is the way color is brushed onto the screen. Each time a cursor key is struck, the locator moves one pixel in the indicated direction. This can be rather slow at times, so the program allows you to move five pixels at a time by striking the F2 function key. To return to single-pixel moves, strike the F1 function key. Different colors may be selected by typing the numbers 0 through 3 on the keyboard. In palette 0, 0 is blank, 1 is green, 2 is red, and 3 is yellow. The brush may be turned off and on by typing the letter O. The HOME, PGUP, PGDN, and END keys move the locator at 45-degree angles in the expected direction.

The program supports five special commands that draw boxes, fill boxes, draw lines, draw circles, and fill circles. To use these commands you must first define two coordinates. To draw and fill boxes, you must specify the location of two opposing corners. To draw lines, select the beginning and ending points. To draw and fill circles, you specify the center and a point on the circle. The point on the circle must be directly left or right of the center. The selection process is performed by pressing RETURN. Once the locations have been recorded, typing a B draws a box, F draws a filled box, L draws a line, C draws a circle, and H fills a circle. The program is terminated by typing Q.

The entire paint program is shown here. You might find it fun to add other high-level commands or to interface it to a mouse. Or, you could provide the capability to save and load graphics images. Sample output is shown in Figure 6-6.

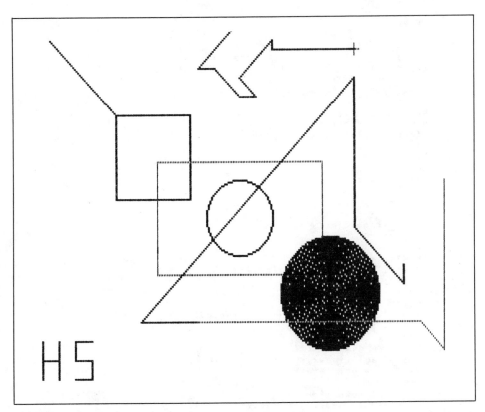

Figure 6-6.   Sample output from the paint program

```
/* A simple paint program for the CGA */

#include "dos.h"
#include "stdio.h"
void mode(), line(), box(),fill_box();
void mempoint(), palette(), xhairs();
void circle(), plot_circle(), fill_circle();

double asp_ratio; /* holds aspect ratio for cirlces */

main()
{
  union k{
    char c[2];
    int i;
  } key;

  int x=10, y=10, cc=2, on_flag=1, pal_num=1;
  int startx=0, starty=0, endx=0, endy=0, first_point=1;
  int inc=1;

  mode(4);
  palette(0);

  xhairs(x,y);
  do {
    key.i=get_key();
    xhairs(x,y);    /* plot the crosshairs */
    if(!key.c[0]) switch(key.c[1]) {
      case 75: /* left */
        if(on_flag) line(x,y,x,y-inc,cc);
        y-=inc;
        break;
      case 77: /* right */
        if(on_flag) line(x,y,x,y+inc,cc);
        y+=inc;
        break;
      case 72: /* up */
        if(on_flag) line(x,y,x-inc,y,cc);
        x-=inc;
        break;
      case 80: /* down */
        if(on_flag) line(x,y,x+inc,y,cc);
        x+=inc;
        break;
      case 71: /* up left */
        if(on_flag) line(x,y,x-inc,y-inc,cc);
        x-=inc; y-=inc;
        break;
      case 73: /* up right */
        if(on_flag) line(x,y,x-inc,y+inc,cc);
        x-=inc; y+=inc;
        break;
      case 79: /* down left*/
        if(on_flag) line(x,y,x+inc,y-inc,cc);
        x+=inc;y-=inc;
        break;
      case 81: /* down right */
        if(on_flag) line(x,y,x+inc,y+inc,cc);
        x+=inc;y+=inc;
        break;
```

```
            case 59: inc=1;  /* F1 - slow speed */
              break;
            case 60: inc=5;  /* F2 - fast speed */
              break;
        }
        else switch(tolower(key.c[0])) {
          case 'o': on_flag=!on_flag; /* toggle brush */
            break;
          case '1': cc=1; /* color 1 */
            break;
          case '2': cc=2; /* color 2 */
            break;
          case '3': cc=3; /* color 3 */
            break;
          case '0': cc=0; /* color 0 */
            break;
          case 'b': box(startx, starty, endx, endy, cc);
            break;
          case 'f': fill_box(startx, starty, endx, endy, cc);
            break;
          case 'l': line(startx, starty, endx, endy, cc);
            break;
          case 'c': circle(startx, starty, endy-starty, cc);
            break;
          case 'h': fill_circle(startx, starty, endy-starty, cc);
            break;
          case '\r': /* set endpoints */
            if(first_point) {
              startx=x, starty=y;
            }
            else {
              endx=x; endy=y;
            }
            first_point = !first_point;
            break;
          case 'p': pal_num=pal_num==1 ? 2:1;
            palette(pal_num);
        }
        xhairs(x,y);
    } while (key.c[0]!='q');
    getchar();
    mode(2);
}

/* set the palette */
void palette(pnum)
int pnum;
{
  union REGS r;

  r.h.bh = 1;   /* code for mode 4 graphics */
  r.h.bl = pnum;
  r.h.ah = 11;  /* set palette function */
  int86(0x10, &r, &r);
}

/* set the video mode */
void mode(mode_code)
int mode_code;
{
  union REGS r;
```

```
  r.h.al = mode_code;
  r.h.ah = 0;
  int86(0x10, &r, &r);
}


/* draw a box */
void box(startx,starty, endx, endy, color_code)
int startx,starty,endx,endy,color_code;
{
  line(startx,starty, endx,starty, color_code);
  line(startx,starty, startx,endy, color_code);
  line(startx,endy, endx,endy, color_code);
  line(endx,starty, endx,endy, color_code);
}


/* Draw a line in specified color
   using Bresenham's integer based algorithm.
*/
void line(startx, starty, endx, endy, color)
int startx, starty, endx, endy, color;
{
  register int t, distance;
  int x=0, y=0, delta_x, delta_y;
  int incx, incy;

  /* compute the distances in both directions */
  delta_x=endx-startx;
  delta_y=endy-starty;

  /* Compute the direction of the increment,
     an increment of 0 means either a vertical or horizontal
     line.
  */
  if(delta_x>0) incx=1;
  else if(delta_x==0) incx=0;
  else incx=-1;

  if(delta_y>0) incy=1;
  else if(delta_y==0) incy=0;
  else incy=-1;

  /* determine which distance is greater */
  delta_x=abs(delta_x);
  delta_y=abs(delta_y);
  if(delta_x>delta_y) distance=delta_x;
  else distance=delta_y;

  /* draw the line */
  for(t=0; t<=distance+1; t++) {
    mempoint(startx, starty, color);
    x+=delta_x;
    y+=delta_y;
    if(x>distance) {
      x-=distance;
      startx+=incx;
```

```
    }
    if(y>distance) {
      y-=distance;
      starty+=incy;
    }
  }
}

/* fill box with specified color */
void fill_box(startx, starty, endx, endy, color_code)
int startx,starty,endx,endy,color_code;
{
  register int i,begin, end;

  begin = startx<endx ? startx : endx;
  end = startx>endx ? startx : endx;

  for(i=begin; i<=end;i++)
    line(i,starty,i,endy,color_code);
}

/* Draw a circle using Bresenham's integer based Algorithm. */
void circle(x_center, y_center, radius,  color_code)
int x_center, y_center, radius, color_code;
{
  register int x, y, delta;

  asp_ratio = 1.0;   /* for different aspect ratios, alter
                         this number */

  y = radius;
  delta = 3 - 2 * radius;

  for(x=0; x<y; ) {
    plot_circle(x, y, x_center, y_center, color_code);

    if (delta < 0)
      delta += 4*x+6;
    else {
      delta += 4*(x-y)+10;
      y--;
    }
    x++;
  }
  x=y;
  if(y) plot_circle(x, y, x_center, y_center, color_code);
}

/* plot_circle actually prints the points that
   define the circle */
void plot_circle(x, y, x_center, y_center, color_code)
int x, y, x_center, y_center, color_code;
{
  int startx, endx, x1, starty, endy, y1;

  starty = y*asp_ratio;
  endy = (y+1)*asp_ratio;
```

```
  startx = x*asp_ratio;
  endx = (x+1)*asp_ratio;

  for (x1=startx; x1<endx; ++x1)  {
    mempoint(x1+x_center, y+y_center, color_code);
    mempoint(x1+x_center, y_center-y, color_code);
    mempoint(x_center-x1, y_center-y, color_code);
    mempoint(x_center-x1, y+y_center, color_code);
  }

  for (y1=starty; y1<endy; ++y1) {
    mempoint(y1+x_center, x+y_center, color_code);
    mempoint(y1+x_center, y_center-x, color_code);
    mempoint(x_center-y1, y_center-x, color_code);
    mempoint(x_center-y1, x+y_center, color_code);
  }
}

/* fill a circle by repeatedly calling circle()
   with smaller radiuses
*/
void fill_circle(x, y, r, c)
int x, y, r, c;
{
  while(r) {
    circle(x, y, r, c);
    r--;
  }
}

/* display crosshair locator */
void xhairs(x,y)
int x,y;
{
  line(x-4, y, x+3, y, 1 | 128);
  line(x, y+4, x, y-3, 1 | 128);
}

/* read the scan code */
get_key()
{
  union REGS r;

  r.h.ah = 0;
  return int86(0x16, &r, &r);
}

/* write a point directly to the CGA */
void mempoint(x,y,color_code)
int x,y,color_code;
{
  union mask {
    char c[2];
    int i;
  } bit_mask;
  int i, index, bit_position;
  unsigned char t;
  char xor; /* xor color in or overwrite */
  char far *ptr = (char far *) 0xB8000000; /* pointer to CGA memory */
```

```
   bit_mask.i=0xFF3F;      /* 11111111 00111111 in binary */

   /* check range for mode 4 */
   if(x<0 || x>199 || y<0 || y>319) return;

   xor=color_code & 128; /* see if xor mode is set */
   color_code=color_code & 127; /* mask off high bit */

   /* set bit_mask and color_code bits to the right location */
   bit_position=y%4;
   color_code<<=2*(3-bit_position);
   bit_mask.i>>=2*bit_position;


 /* find the correct byte in screen memory */
  index=x*40 +(y >> 2);
  if(x % 2) index += 8152; /* if odd use 2nd bank */

  /* write the color */
  if(!xor) { /* overwrite mode */
    t=*(ptr+index) & bit_mask.c[0];
    *(ptr+index)=t | color_code;
  }
  else { /* xor mode */
    t=*(ptr+index) | (char)0;
    *(ptr+index)=t ^ color_code;
  }
}
```

Statistics

CHAPTER 7

Everyone who owns or has frequent access to a computer uses it at some point to perform *statistical analysis*. This analysis could take the form of monitoring or trying to predict the movement of stock prices in a portfolio, performing clinical testing to establish safe limits for a new drug, or even providing batting averages for the Little League team. The branch of mathematics that deals with the condensation, manipulation, and extrapolation of data is called *statistics*.

As a discipline, statistical analysis is quite young. It was born in the 1700s out of studies of games of chance. Indeed, probability and statistics are related. Modern statistical analysis began around the turn of this century when it became possible to sample and handle large sets of data. The computer made it possible to correlate and manipulate even larger amounts of data rapidly and to easily convert this data into a readily usable form. Today, because of the ever-increasing amount of information created and used by the government and the media, every aspect of life is adorned with reams of statistical information. It is difficult to listen to the radio or TV news, or to read a newspaper article, without being informed of some statistic.

Although C was not designed specifically for statistical programming, it adapts to the task well. It even offers some flexibility not found in more common business languages such as COBOL or BASIC. One advantage of C over COBOL is the speed and ease with which C programs can interface to the graphics functions of the system to produce charts and graphs of data.

In this chapter you will study various statistics and procedures, including

- Mean

- Median

- Standard deviation

- Regression equation (line of best fit)

- Coefficient of correlation

It also explores some simple graphing techniques.

Samples, Populations, Distributions, and Variables

Before you use statistics, you must understand a few key concepts. Statistical information is derived first by taking a *sample* of specific data points and then drawing generalizations about them. Each sample comes from the *population*, which consists of all possible outcomes for the situation under study. For example, if you wished to measure the output of a box factory over the period of a year by using only the Wednesday output figures and generalizing from them, then your sample would consist of a year's worth of Wednesday figures taken from the population of each day's output in a year.

It is possible for the sample to equal the population if the sample is exhaustive. In the case of the box factory, your sample would equal the population if you used the actual output figures — five days a week for the entire year. When the sample is less than the population, there is always room for error; however, in many cases you can determine the probability for this error. This chapter assumes that the sample is the same as the population, and hence will not be concerned with the problem of sample error.

For election projections and opinion polls, a proportionately small sample is used to project information about the population as a whole. For example, you might use statistical information about the Dow Jones stocks to make an inference about the stock market in general. Of course, the validity of these conclusions varies widely. In other uses of statistics, a sample that equals or nearly equals the population is used to summarize a large set of numbers for easier handling. For example, a board of education usually reports on the *average grade point* for a class, rather than on each student's individual grade.

Statistics are affected by the way that events are distributed in the population. Of the several common distributions in nature, the most important (and the only one used in this chapter) is the *normal distribution curve*, or the familiar "bell-shaped curve" shown in Figure 7-1. As suggested by the graph in Figure 7-1, the elements in a normal distribution curve are found mostly in the middle. In fact, the curve is completely symmetrical around its peak — which is also the average for all the elements. The further from the middle in either direction of the curve, the fewer elements there are.

In any statistical process there is always an *independent variable*, which is the number under study, and a *dependent variable*, which is the factor that determines the independent variable. This chapter uses *time* — the stepwise

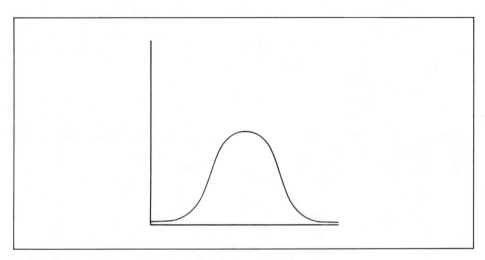

Figure 7-1. The normal distribution curve

incremental passage of events—for the dependent variable. For example, when watching a stock portfolio you may wish to see the movement of the stock on a daily basis. You would therefore be concerned with the movement of stock prices over a given period of time, not with the actual calendar date of each price.

Throughout this chapter, the individual statistical functions will be developed and then assembled into a menu-driven program. You can use this program to perform a wide variety of statistical analyses, as well as to plot information on the screen.

The Basic Statistics

Three important values form the basis of many statistical analyses and are also useful individually. They are the *mean* (arithmetic average), the *median*, and the *mode*.

Throughout this chapter the elements of a sample are discussed. For ease and convenience, those elements are called D, and the index for them is 1 to N, where N is the number of the last element.

Mean

The mean, or arithmetic average, is the most common of all statistics. This single line can be used to represent a set of data—the mean can be called the set's "center of gravity." To compute the mean, elements in the sample are added together and the result is divided by the total number of elements in the sample. For example, the sum of the set

$$1\ 2\ 3\ 4\ 5\ 6\ 7\ 8\ 9\ 10$$

equals 55. When that number is divided by the number of elements in the sample, which is 10, the mean is 5.5.

The general formula for finding the mean is:

$$M = \frac{D_1 + D_2 + D_3 + \ldots + D_N}{N}$$

or

$$M = \frac{1}{N} \sum_{i=1}^{N} D_1$$

Here, the symbol Σ is used to indicate the summation of all elements between 1 and N.

Throughout the statistical functions in this chapter, you should assume that all data is stored in an array of floating-point numbers and that the number of sample elements is known. The following function computes the mean of an array of *num* floating-point numbers and returns the floating-point average:

```
/* compute the average */
float mean(data, num)
float *data;
int num;
{
  int t;
  float avg;

  avg = 0;
  for(t=0; t<num; ++t)
    avg+=data[t];

  avg/=num;

  return avg;
}
```

For example, if you called **mean( )** with a 10-element array that contained the numbers 1 through 10, then **mean( )** would return the result 5.5.

Median

The median of a sample is the middle value based on order of magnitude. For example, in the sample set

1 2 3 4 5 6 7 8 9

5 is the median because it is in the middle. In the set

$$1\ 2\ 3\ 4\ 5\ 6\ 7\ 8\ 9\ 10$$

you could use either 5 or 6 as the median. In a well-ordered sample that has a normal distribution, the median and the mean will be very similar. However, as the sample moves further from the normal distribution curve, the difference between the median and the mean increases. Calculating the mean of a sample is as simple as sorting the sample into ascending order and then selecting the middle element, which is indexed as $N/2$.

The **median( )** function shown here returns the value of the middle element in a sample. Because the data must be sorted in order to compute the median, a modified version of QuickSort, developed in Chapter 1, is used.

```
/* find the median */
float median(data, num)
float *data;
int num;
{
  register int t;
  float dtemp[MAX];

  /* copy data for sorting */
  for(t=0; t<num; ++t) dtemp[t] = data[t];
  quick(dtemp, num);  /* sort data into ascending order */
  return dtemp[num/2];
}

void quick(item, count)  /* quick sort setup */
float *item;
int count;
{
  qs(item, 0, count-1);
}

void qs(item, left, right)  /* quick sort */
float *item;
int left, right;
{

  register int i, j;
  float x, y;

  i = left; j = right;
  x = item[(left+right)/2];

  do {
    while(item[i]<x && i<right) i++;
    while(x<item[j] && j>left) j--;
```

```
     if(i<=j) {
       y=item[i];
       item[i]=item[j];
       item[j]=y;
       i++; j--;
     }
   } while(i<=j);

   if(left<j)  qs(item, left, j);
   if(i<right) qs(item, i, right);
}
```

Mode

The mode of a sample is the value of the most frequently occurring element. For example, in the set

$$1\ 2\ 3\ 3\ 4\ 5\ 6\ 6\ 6\ 7\ 8\ 9$$

the mode would be 6 because it occurs three times. There may be more than one mode; for example, the sample

$$10\ 20\ 30\ 30\ 40\ 50\ 60\ 60\ 70$$

has two modes—30 and 60—because they both occur twice.

The following function, **find_mode( )**, returns the mode of a sample. If there is more than one mode, then it returns the last one found.

```
/* find the mode */
float find_mode(data, num)
float *data;
int num;
{
  register int t, w;
  float md, oldmode;
  int count, oldcount;

  oldmode = 0; oldcount = 0;
  for(t=0; t<num; ++t) {
    md = data[t];
    count = 1;
    for(w=t+1; w<num; ++w)
      if(md==data[w]) count++;
    if(count>oldcount) {
      oldmode = md;
      oldcount = count;
```

```
     }
   }
   return oldmode;
}
```

Using the Mean, Median, and Mode

The mean, median, and mode share the same purpose: to provide one value that is the condensation of all the values in the sample. However, each represents the sample in a different way. Generally speaking, the most useful number is the mean (the arithmetic average) of the sample. Because it uses all values in its computation, the mean partially reflects all elements in the sample. The main disadvantage to the mean is its sensitivity to one extreme value. For example, in Widget, Incorporated (an imaginary business), the owner's salary is $100,000 per year, while the salary of each of the nine employees is $10,000. The average wage at Widget is $19,000, but this figure does not fairly represent the actual situation.

In samples like the salary dispersion at Widget, the mode is sometimes used instead of the mean. The mode of the salaries at Widget is $10,000—a figure that reflects more accurately the actual situation. However, the mode can be misleading. Consider a company that makes cars in five different colors. In a given week they made

- 100 green
- 100 orange
- 150 blue
- 200 black
- 190 white

Here, the mode of the sample is black, because 200 were made, more than any other color. However, it would be misleading to suggest that the car company primarily makes black cars.

The median is interesting because its validity is based on the *hope* that the sample will reflect a normal distribution. For example, if the sample is

1 2 3 4 5 6 7 8 9 10

then the median is 5 or 6, and the mean is 5.5. Hence, in this case the median and mean are similar. However, in the sample

$$1\ 1\ 1\ 1\ 5\ 100\ 100\ 100\ 100$$

the median is still 5, but the mean is about 46.

In certain circumstances, neither the mean, the mode, nor the median can be counted on to give a meaningful value. This leads to two of the most important values in statistics—the *variance* and the *standard deviation*.

Variance and Standard Deviation

Although the one-number summary (such as the mean or median) is convenient, it can be misleading. Giving a little thought to this problem, you can see that the cause of the difficulty is not in the number itself, but rather in the fact that it does not convey any information about the variations of the data. For example, in the sample

$$1\ 1\ 1\ 1\ 9\ 9\ 9\ 9$$

the mean is 5; however, there is no element in the sample that is close to 5. What you would like to know is how close each element in the sample is to the average. If you know how much the data varies, you can better interpret the mean, median, and mode. You can find the variability of a sample by computing its variance and standard deviation.

The variance and its square root, the standard deviation, are numbers that tell you the average deviation from the sample mean. Of the two, the standard deviation is the most important. It can be thought of as the average of the distances between the elements and the mean of the sample. The variance is computed as

$$V = \frac{1}{N} \sum_{i=1}^{N} (D_i - M)^2$$

where N is the number of elements in the sample and M is the sample mean. It is necessary to square the difference of the mean and each element in order to produce only positive numbers. If the numbers were not squared, they would by default always sum to 0.

The variance, produced by this formula, V, is of limited value because it is difficult to understand. However, its square root, the standard deviation, is the number you are really looking for. The standard deviation is derived by first finding the variance and then taking its square root:

$$std = \sqrt{\frac{1}{N} \sum_{i=1}^{N} (D_i - M)^2}$$

where N is the number of elements in the sample and M is the sample mean.

As an example, for the following sample

11 20 40 30 99 30 50

you compute the variance as follows:

	D	D−M	(D−M)²
	11	−29	841
	20	−20	400
	40	0	0
	30	−10	100
	99	59	3481
	30	−10	100
	50	10	100
sum	280	0	5022
mean(M)	40	0	717.42

Here the average of the squared differences is 717.42. To derive the standard deviation, simply take the square root of that number; the result is approximately 26.78. It is easy to understand the standard deviation if you remember that it is the *average distance the elements are from the mean of the sample.*

The standard deviation tells you how nearly the mean represents the entire sample. For example, if you owned a candy bar factory and your plant foreman reported that daily output averaged 2500 bars last month but that the standard deviation was 2000, you would know that the production line needed better supervision!

If your sample follows a standard normal distribution (the "bell curve"), then about 68% of the sample will be within one standard deviation from the mean, and about 95% will be within two standard deviations.

The following function computes and returns the standard deviation of a given sample. Notice that **sqrt( )** requires a **double** type argument and returns **double**.

```
/* compute the standard deviation */
float std_dev(data, num)
float *data;
int num;
{
  register int t;
  float std, avg;
  double temp, sqrt();

  avg = mean(data, num);   /* get average */
  std = 0;
  for(t=0; t<num; ++t)
  {
    std+=((data[t]-avg)*(data[t]-avg));
  }
  std/=num;
  temp = std;
  temp = sqrt(temp);
  std = temp;
  return std;
}
```

Simple Plotting on the Screen

The advantage of using graphs with statistics is that together they can convey the meaning clearly and accurately. A graph shows at a glance how the sample was actually distributed and how variable the data is. The routines developed here are limited to two-dimensional graphs, which use the x-y coordinate system. (Creating three-dimensional graphs is a discipline unto itself and beyond the scope of this book.)

There are two basic forms of two-dimensional graphs: the *bar graph* and the *scatter graph*. The bar graph uses solid bars to represent the magnitude of each element, while the scatter graph uses a single point per element located at its x-y coordinates. Figure 7-2 shows an example of each.

The bar chart is usually used with a relatively small set of information, such as the Gross National Product for the last ten years or the percentage output of a factory on a monthly basis. The scatter graph is generally used to display a large number of data points, such as the daily stock price of a company over a year. Also, a modification of the scatter graph that connects

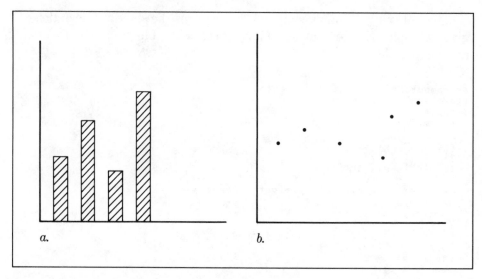

Figure 7-2. Samples of a bar graph (*a*) and a scatter graph (*b*)

the data points with a solid line is useful for plotting projections.

A simple plotting function that creates a bar graph on the IBM PC is shown here. It makes use of some of the graphics functions developed in Chapter 6 and the **goto—xy()** function from Chapter 4.

```
void simple_plot(data,num)  /* bar chart of info */
float *data;
int num;
{
  int a,t;
  mode(4); /* 320x200 graphics mode */

  goto_xy(24,0); printf("%d",0);
  goto_xy(0,0); printf("%d",200);
  goto_xy(24,76); printf("%d",580);
  for(t=0;t<num;++t) {
    a=data[t];
    if(a<0) a=0; /* can't display negative values */
    line((t*10)+20,0,(t*10)+20,a);
  }
  getchar(); /* wait before returning to 25x80
                         character mode */
  mode(3);
}
```

This simple plotting routine has a serious limitation—it assumes that all data will be between 0 and 199 because the only valid numbers that can be used to call the graphic function **line( )** are within the range 0 to 199. This assumption is fine in the unlikely event that your data elements consistently fit in that range. To make the plotting routine handle arbitrary units, you must *normalize* the data before plotting it in order to scale the data values to fit the required range. The process of normalization involves finding a ratio between the actual range of the data and the physical range of the screen resolution. Each data element can be multiplied by this ratio to produce a number that fits the range of the screen. The formula to do this for the y-axis on the PC is

$$Y' = Y * \frac{200}{(max-min)}$$

where Y' is the value used when calling the plotting function. The same function can be used to spread the scale when the data range is very small.

The **barplot( )** function scales the x- and y-axes and plots a bar graph of as many as 280 elements. The x-axis is assumed to be time and is in increments of 1 unit. Generally, the normalizing procedure finds the greatest value and the smallest value in the sample and then calculates their difference. This number, which represents the spread between the minimum and maximum, is used to divide the resolution of the screen. In the case of the IBM PC, the resolution is 200 for the y-axis and 280 for the x-axis, which leaves a little room for the border. This ratio is then used to convert the sample data into the proper scale.

```
/* display a bar chart of num items of data */
void barplot(data, num)
float *data;
int num;
{
  int y, t, max, min, incr;
  float a, norm, spread;
  char s[80];

  mode(4); /* 320x200  graphics mode */
  palette(0);
  /* first find max value to enable normalization */
  max = getmax(data, num);
  min = getmin(data, num);
  if(min>0) min = 0;
  spread = max-min;
  norm = 200/spread;   /* absolute increment/spread */
```

```
  goto_xy(23, 0); printf("%d", min);
  goto_xy(0, 0); printf("%d", max);
  goto_xy(23, 76); printf("%d", num);
  for(t=1; t<23; ++t) {
    goto_xy(t, 0);
    printf("-");
  }
  for(t=0; t<num; ++t) {
    a = data[t];
    a = a-min;
    a*=norm; /* normalize */
    y=a; /* type conversion */
    incr = 280/num;
    line(189, ((t*incr)+20), 189-y, ((t*incr)+20), 1);
  }
  gets(s);
  mode(3);
}
```

This version also prints hash marks along the y-axis that represent 1/24th of the difference between the minimum and the maximum values. Figure 7-3 shows a sample of the output of **barplot( )** with 20 elements. By no means does **barplot( )** provide all the features you may desire, but it will do a good job of displaying a single sample.

Only a slight modification to **barplot( )** is required to make a function that plots a scatter graph. Changing the **line( )** function to **mempoint( )** causes only one point to be plotted. The function **scatterplot( )** is shown here:

```
/* Display scatter chart of num items of data.
   Call with minimum value for Y and max values
   for Y and X.  Also specify color.
*/
void scatterplot(data, num, ymin, ymax, xmax, color)
float *data;
int num, ymin, ymax, xmax, color;
{
  int y, t, incr;
  float norm, a, spread;

  /* first find max value to enable normalization */

  if(ymin>0) ymin = 0;
  spread = ymax-ymin;
  norm = 200/spread;  /* absolute increment/spread */
  goto_xy(23, 0); printf("%d", ymin);
  goto_xy(0, 0); printf("%d", ymax);
  goto_xy(23, 76); printf("%d", xmax);
  for(t=1; t<23; ++t) {
    goto_xy(t, 0);
    printf("-");
  }
  incr = 280/xmax;
  for(t=0; t<num; ++t) {
```

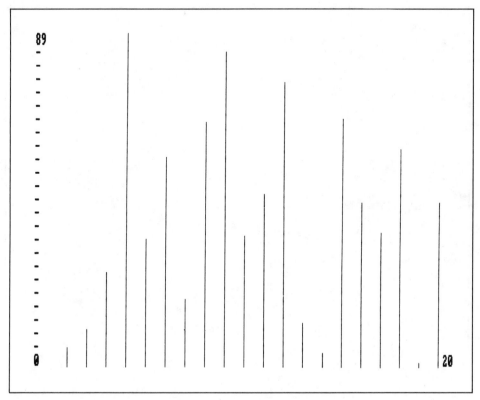

Figure 7-3. A sample bar graph produced by **barplot( )**

```
   a = data[t];
   a = a-ymin;
   a*=norm; /* normalize */
   y = a; /* type conversion */
   mempoint(189-y, ((t*incr)+20), color);
 }

}
```

Notice that in **scatterplot( )**, the minimum and maximum values are passed into the function instead of being computed by the function as they are in **barplot( )**. This allows you to plot multiple data sets on the same screen without changing the scale. Also, **scatterplot( )** includes a color argument so that different data can be plotted in different colors. Figure 7-4 shows a sample scatter graph of 30 data elements produced by this function.

Figure 7-4. Sample scatter graph produced by **scatterplot( )**

Projections and
the Regression Equation

One of the most common uses of statistical information is to make "informed guesses" about the future. Even though everyone knows that the past does not necessarily predict the future and that there are exceptions to every rule, historical data is still used in this way because very often trends do, in fact, continue into the future. When they do, you can try to determine specific values at future points in time. This process is called making a *projection*, or *trend analysis*.

For example, consider a fictitious ten-year study of life spans, which collected the following data:

Year	Lifespan
1970	69
1971	70
1972	72
1973	68
1974	73
1975	71
1976	75
1977	74
1978	78
1979	77

You might first ask whether there is a trend here at all. If there is, you may want to know which way it is going. Finally, if there is indeed a trend, you might wonder what the life expectancy will be in, say, 1985.

First, simply make a bar graph of this data, as shown in Figure 7-5. This graph gives the distinct impression that life spans are getting longer in general. Also, if you placed a ruler on the graph to try to fit the data and drew a line that extended into 1985, you could project that the life span would be about 82 in 1985. Although this intuitive analysis is fairly good, a more formal method would be even better.

Given a set of historical data, the best way to make projections is to find the *line of best fit* in relation to the data. This is what you did with the ruler. A line of best fit most closely represents each point of the data and its trend. Although some or even all of the actual data points may not be on the line, the line best represents them. The validity of the line is based upon how close to the line the sample data points are.

A line in two-dimensional space has the basic equation

$$Y = a + bX$$

where X is the dependent variable, Y is the independent variable, a is y-intercept, and b is the slope of the line. Therefore, to find a line that best fits a sample, you must determine a and b.

Any number of methods can be used to determine the values of a and b, but the most common and generally best is called the *method of least squares*.

Figure 7-5. Bar graph of life expectancy

It attempts to minimize the distance between the actual data points and the line. The method involves two steps: the first computes b (the slope of the line) and the second finds a (the y-intercept). To find b, use the following formula:

$$b = \frac{\sum_{i=1}^{N} (X_i - M_x)(Y_i - M_y)}{\sum_{i=1}^{N} (X_i - M_x)^2}$$

where M_x is the mean of the x coordinate and M_y is the mean of the y coordinate. The derivation of this formula is beyond the scope of this book, but having found b, you can use it to compute a as shown here:

$$a = M_y - bM_x$$

After you have calculated a and b, you can plug in any number for X and find the value of Y. For example, if you use the life expectancy data, you find that the regression equation looks like

$$Y = 67.46 + 0.95 * X$$

Therefore, to find the life expectancy in 1985, which is 15 years from 1970, you have

$$\text{Life expectancy} = 67.46 + 0.95 * 15$$
$$\cong 82$$

At this point it is important to determine how well the line of best fit actually correlates with the data. If the line and data have only a slight correlation, then the regression line is of little use. However, if the line fits the data well, then it is a much more valid indicator. The most common way to determine and represent the correlation of the data to the regression line is to compute the *correlation coefficient*, which is a number between 0 and 1. The correlation coefficient is a percentage that is related to the distance each data point in the sample is from the line. If the correlation coefficient is 1, then the data corresponds perfectly to the line. A coefficient of 0 means that there is no correlation between the line and the points — in fact, any line would be as good (or bad) as the one used. The formula to find the correlation coefficient is

$$Cor = \frac{\dfrac{1}{N} \displaystyle\sum_{i=1}^{N} (X_i - M_x)(Y_i - M_y)}{\sqrt{\dfrac{1}{N} \displaystyle\sum_{i=1}^{N} (X_i - M_x)^2} \; \sqrt{\dfrac{1}{N} \displaystyle\sum_{i=1}^{N} (Y_i - M_y)^2}}$$

where M_x is the mean of X and M_y is the mean of Y. Generally, a value of 0.81 is considered a strong correlation. It means that about 66% of the data fits the regression line. To convert any correlation coefficient into a percentage, you simply square it.

Here is the **regress( )** function, which uses the methods described to find the regression equation, the coefficient of correlation, and to make an optional scatter plot of both the sample data and the line:

```
/* compute the regression equation */
void regress(data, num)
float *data;
int num;
{
  float a, b, x_avg, y_avg, temp, temp2;
  float data2[580], cor;
  float std_dev();
  int t, min, max;
  char s[80];

  /* find mean of y */
  y_avg = 0;
  for(t=0; t<num; ++t)
    y_avg+=data[t];
  y_avg/=num;

  /* find mean of x */
  x_avg = 0;
  for(t=1; t<=num; ++t)
    x_avg+=t;
  x_avg/=num;


  /* now find b */
  temp = 0; temp2 = 0;
  for(t=1; t<=num; ++t) {
    temp+=(data[t-1]-y_avg)*(t-x_avg);
    temp2+=(t-x_avg) * (t-x_avg);
  }

  b = temp/temp2;

  /* now find a */
  a = y_avg-(b*x_avg);

  /* now compute coefficient of correlation */
  for(t=0; t<num; ++t) data2[t]=t+1; /* load x axis */
  cor = temp/(num);
  cor = cor/(std_dev(data, num) * std_dev(data2, num));

  printf("regression equation is: Y = %f + %f * X\n", a, b);
  printf("Correlation Coefficient: %f\n", cor);
  printf("plot data points and regression line? (y/n) ");
  gets(s);
  if(toupper(*s)=='N') return;

  mode(4); /* 320x200  graphics mode */
  palette(0);
```

```
/* now do scatter graph and regression line */
for(t=0; t<num*2; ++t)    /* create plot regression line */
  data2[t] = a+(b*(t+1));
min = getmin(data, num)*2;
max = getmax(data, num)*2;
scatterplot(data, num, min, max, num*2, 1);/* plot the points */
scatterplot(data2, num*2, min, max, num*2, 2);
gets(s);
mode(3);
}
```

A scatter plot of both the sample life-expectancy data and the regression line is shown in Figure 7-6. The important point to remember when using projections like this is that the past does not necessarily predict the future — if it did, life would not be fun!

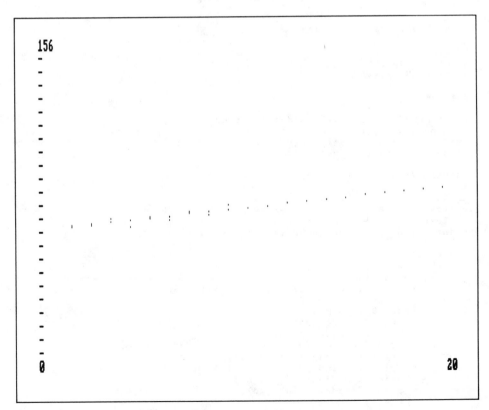

Figure 7-6. Regression line for life expectancy

Making a Complete Statistics Program

So far, this chapter has developed several functions that perform statistical operations on one variable. In this section, you will put them together to form a complete program for analyzing data, printing bar charts or scatter plots, and making projections. Before you can design a complete program, you must define a data structure to hold the variable data information, as well as a few support routines.

First you need an array to hold the sample information. You can use a single-dimension floating-point array, called **data**, of size **MAX**. **MAX** is defined so that it fits the largest sample you will need, which in this case is 100. The **main( )** function, along with the menu selection function **menu( )** and support function **is—in( )**, is shown here:

```
/* A simple statistics program */

#include "stdio.h"
#include "dos.h"
#include "ctype.h"

#define MAX 100

float mean(), std_dev(), median(), find_mode();
void goto_xy(), mempoint(), palette(), mode(), line();
void save(), display(), regress(), barplot();
void scatterplot(), quick(), qs();

main()   /* stats driver */
{
   char ch;
   float data[MAX];   /* this array will hold data */
   float a, m, md, std;
   int num=0; /* number of data items */

   for(;;) {
     ch = menu();
     switch(ch) {
         case 'E': num = enter_data(data);
           break;
         case 'B':a = mean(data, num);
           std = std_dev(data, num);
           m = median(data, num);
           md = find_mode(data, num);
           printf("Average: %f\n", a);
           printf("Standard Deviation: %f\n", std);
           printf("Median: %f\n", m);
           printf("Mode: %f\n", md);
           break;
         case 'R': regress(data, num);
           break;
```

```
        case 'D': display(data, num);
          break;
        case 'L': num = load(data);
          break;
        case 'S': save(data, num);
          break;
        case 'P': barplot(data, num);
          break;
        case 'Q': exit(0);
    }
  }

}

/* get user selection */
menu()
{
  char ch;
  do {
    printf("\nEnter data\n");
    printf("Basic statistics \n");
    printf("Regression line and scatter plot\n");
    printf("Plot a bar graph\n");
    printf("Save\n");
    printf("Load\n");
    printf("Display data\n");
    printf("Quit\n\n");
    printf("chose one (E, B, R, P, S, L, D, Q): ");
    ch = toupper(getche());
  } while(!is_in(ch, "BESLQDPR"));
  printf("\n");
  return ch;
}

is_in(ch, s)
char ch, *s;
{
  while(*s) {
    if(ch==*s) return ch;
    else s++;
  }
  return 0;
}
```

The **is—in( )** function returns TRUE if the character is in and FALSE if it is not.

Besides the statistical functions developed already, you also will need routines to save and load data. The **save( )** routine must also store the number of data elements, and the **load( )** routine must read back that number. These functions are shown here:

```
/* save the data file */
void save(data, num)
float *data;
int num;
{
  FILE *fp;
```

```
  int t;
  char s[80];

  printf("enter filename: ");
  gets(s);

  if((fp=fopen(s, "w"))==0) {
    printf("cannot open file\n");
    exit(1);
  }
  putw(num, fp);  /* write out count */

  for(t=0; t<num; ++t) fprintf(fp, "%f ", data[t]);

  fclose(fp);
}
/* load the data file */
load(data)
float *data;
{
  FILE *fp;
  int t, num;
  char s[80];

  printf("enter filename: ");
  gets(s);
  if((fp=fopen(s, "r"))==0) {
    printf("cannot open file\n");
    exit(1);
  }

  num = getw(fp);
  for(t=0; t<num; ++t) fscanf(fp, "%f", &data[t]);

  fclose(fp);
  return num;
}
```

For your convenience, the entire program is listed here:

```
/* A simple statistics program */

#include "stdio.h"
#include "dos.h"
#include "ctype.h"

#define MAX 100

float mean(), std_dev(), median(), find_mode();
void goto_xy(), mempoint(), palette(), mode(), line();
void save(), display(), regress(), barplot();
void scatterplot(), quick(), qs();

main()  /* stats driver */
{
  char ch;
  float data[MAX];  /* this array will hold data */
```

```
      float a, m, md, std;
      int num=0; /* number of data items */

      for(;;) {
        ch = menu();
        switch(ch) {
            case 'E': num = enter_data(data);
              break;
            case 'B':a = mean(data, num);
              std = std_dev(data, num);
              m = median(data, num);
              md = find_mode(data, num);
              printf("Average: %f\n", a);
              printf("Standard Deviation: %f\n", std);
              printf("Median: %f\n", m);
              printf("Mode: %f\n", md);
              break;
            case 'R': regress(data, num);
              break;
            case 'D': display(data, num);
              break;
            case 'L': num = load(data);
              break;
            case 'S': save(data, num);
              break;
            case 'P': barplot(data, num);
              break;
            case 'Q': exit(0);
        }
      }

}

/* get user selection */
menu()
{
  char ch;
  do {
    printf("\nEnter data\n");
    printf("Basic statistics \n");
    printf("Regression line and scatter plot\n");
    printf("Plot a bar graph\n");
    printf("Save\n");
    printf("Load\n");
    printf("Display data\n");
    printf("Quit\n\n");
    printf("chose one (E, B, R, P, S, L, D, Q): ");
    ch = toupper(getche());
  } while(!is_in(ch, "BESLQDPR"));
  printf("\n");
  return ch;
}

is_in(ch, s)
char ch, *s;
{
  while(*s) {
    if(ch==*s) return ch;
    else s++;
  }
  return 0;
```

```
}

/* display the data */
void display(data, num)
float *data;
int num;
{
  int t;

  for(t=0; t<num; ++t)
    printf("item %d; %f\n", t+1, data[t]);

  printf("\n");
}

/* input the data */
enter_data(data)
float *data;
{

  int t, num;

  printf("number of items?: ");
  scanf("%d", &num);

  for(t=0; t<num; ++t) {
    printf("enter item %d: ", t+1);
    scanf("%f", &data[t]);
  }
  return num;

}

/* compute the average */
float mean(data, num)
float *data;
int num;
{
  int t;
  float avg;

  avg = 0;
  for(t=0; t<num; ++t)
    avg+=data[t];

  avg/=num;

  return avg;
}

/* computer the standard deviation */
float std_dev(data, num)
float *data;
int num;
{
  register int t;
  float std, avg;
  double temp, sqrt();

  avg = mean(data, num);  /* get average */
  std = 0;
```

```
    for(t=0; t<num; ++t)
    {
      std+=((data[t]-avg)*(data[t]-avg));
    }
    std/=num;
    temp = std;
    temp = sqrt(temp);
    std = temp;
    return std;
}

/* find the median */
float median(data, num)
float *data;
int num;
{
  register int t;
  float dtemp[MAX];

  /* copy data for sorting */
  for(t=0; t<num; ++t) dtemp[t] = data[t];
  quick(dtemp, num);  /* sort data into ascending order */
  return dtemp[num/2];
}

/* find the mode */
float find_mode(data, num)
float *data;
int num;
{
  register int t, w;
  float md, oldmode;
  int count, oldcount;

  oldmode = 0; oldcount = 0;
  for(t=0; t<num; ++t) {
    md = data[t];
    count = 1;
    for(w=t+1; w<num; ++w)
      if(md==data[w]) count++;
    if(count>oldcount) {
      oldmode = md;
      oldcount = count;
    }
  }
  return oldmode;
}

/* compute the regression equation */
void regress(data, num)
float *data;
int num;
{
  float a, b, x_avg, y_avg, temp, temp2;
  float data2[580], cor;
  float std_dev();
  int t, min, max;
  char s[80];

  /* find mean of y */
  y_avg = 0;
```

```
  for(t=0; t<num; ++t)
    y_avg+=data[t];
  y_avg/=num;

  /* find mean of x */
  x_avg = 0;
  for(t=1; t<=num; ++t)
    x_avg+=t;
  x_avg/=num;


  /* now find b */
  temp = 0; temp2 = 0;
  for(t=1; t<=num; ++t) {
    temp+=(data[t-1]-y_avg)*(t-x_avg);
    temp2+=(t-x_avg) * (t-x_avg);
  }

  b = temp/temp2;
  /* now find a */
  a = y_avg-(b*x_avg);

  /* now compute coefficient of correlation */
  for(t=0; t<num; ++t) data2[t]=t+1; /* load x axis */
  cor = temp/(num);
  cor = cor/(std_dev(data, num) * std_dev(data2, num));

  printf("regression equation is: Y = %f + %f * X\n", a, b);
  printf("Correlation Coefficient: %f\n", cor);
  printf("plot data points and regression line? (y/n) ");
  gets(s);
  if(toupper(*s)=='N') return;

  mode(4); /* 320x200  graphics mode */
  palette(0);
  /* now do scatter graph and regression line */
  for(t=0; t<num*2; ++t)   /* create plot regression line */
    data2[t] = a+(b*(t+1));
  min = getmin(data, num)*2;
  max = getmax(data, num)*2;
  scatterplot(data, num, min, max, num*2, 1);  /* plot the points */
  scatterplot(data2, num*2, min, max, num*2, 2);
  gets(s);
  mode(3);
}

/* display a bar chart of num items of data */
void barplot(data, num)
float *data;
int num;
{
  int y, t, max, min, incr;
  float a, norm, spread;
  char s[80];

  mode(4); /* 320x200  graphics mode */
  palette(0);
  /* first find max value to enable normalization */
  max = getmax(data, num);
  min = getmin(data, num);
  if(min>0) min = 0;
```

```
      spread = max-min;
      norm = 200/spread;  /* absolute increment/spread */
      goto_xy(23, 0); printf("%d", min);
      goto_xy(0, 0); printf("%d", max);
      goto_xy(23, 76); printf("%d", num);
      for(t=1; t<23; ++t) {
        goto_xy(t, 0);
        printf("-");
      }
      for(t=0; t<num; ++t) {
        a = data[t];
        a = a-min;

        a*=norm; /* normalize */
        y=a; /* type conversion */
        incr = 280/num;
        line(189, ((t*incr)+20), 189-y, ((t*incr)+20), 1);
      }
      gets(s);
      mode(3);
}


/* Display scatter chart of num items of data.
   Call with minimum value for Y and max values
   for Y and X.  Also specify color.
*/
void scatterplot(data, num, ymin, ymax, xmax, color)
float *data;
int num, ymin, ymax, xmax, color;
{
    int y, t, incr;
    float norm, a, spread;

    /* first find max value to enable normalization */

    if(ymin>0) ymin = 0;
    spread = ymax-ymin;
    norm = 200/spread;  /* absolute increment/spread */
    goto_xy(23, 0); printf("%d", ymin);
    goto_xy(0, 0); printf("%d", ymax);
    goto_xy(23, 76); printf("%d", xmax);
    for(t=1; t<23; ++t) {
      goto_xy(t, 0);
      printf("-");
    }
    incr = 280/xmax;
    for(t=0; t<num; ++t) {
      a = data[t];
      a = a-ymin;
      a*=norm; /* normalize */
      y = a; /* type conversion */
      mempoint(189-y, ((t*incr)+20), color);
    }

}


/* returns the maximum value of the data */
getmax(data, num)
float *data;
int num;
{
    int t, max;
```

```
    for(max=data[0],t=1; t<num; ++t)
      if(data[t]>max) max=data[t];
    return max;
}

/* returns the minimum value of the data */
getmin(data, num)
float *data;
int num;
{
  int t, min;

  for(min=data[0],t=1; t<num; ++t)
    if(data[t]<min) min=data[t];
  return min;
}
/* save the data file */
void save(data, num)
float *data;
int num;
{
  FILE *fp;
  int t;
  char s[80];

  printf("enter filename: ");
  gets(s);

  if((fp=fopen(s, "w"))==0) {
    printf("cannot open file\n");
    exit(1);
  }
  putw(num, fp);  /* write out count */

  for(t=0; t<num; ++t) fprintf(fp, "%f ", data[t]);

  fclose(fp);
}

/* load the data file */
load(data)
float *data;
{
  FILE *fp;
  int t, num;
  char s[80];

  printf("enter filename: ");
  gets(s);
  if((fp=fopen(s, "r"))==0) {
    printf("cannot open file\n");
    exit(1);
  }

  num = getw(fp);
  for(t=0; t<num; ++t) fscanf(fp, "%f", &data[t]);

  fclose(fp);
  return num;
```

```
}

void quick(item, count)   /* quick sort setup */
float *item;
int count;
{
  qs(item, 0, count-1);
}

void qs(item, left, right)   /* quick sort */
float *item;
int left, right;
{

  register int i, j;
  float x, y;

  i = left; j = right;
  x = item[(left+right)/2];

  do {
    while(item[i]<x && i<right) i++;
    while(x<item[j] && j>left) j--;

    if(i<=j) {
      y=item[i];
      item[i]=item[j];
      item[j]=y;
      i++; j--;
    }
  } while(i<=j);

  if(left<j)  qs(item, left, j);
  if(i<right) qs(item, i, right);
}

/* set the palette */
void palette(pnum)
int pnum;
{
  union REGS r;

  r.h.bh = 1;   /* code for mode 4 graphics */
  r.h.bl = pnum;
  r.h.ah = 11;  /* set palette function */
  int86(0x10, &r, &r);
}

/* set the video mode */
void mode(mode_code)
int mode_code;
{
  union REGS r;
  r.h.al = mode_code;
  r.h.ah = 0;
  int86(0x10, &r, &r);
}

/* Draw a line in specified color
```

```
     using Bresenham's integer based Algorithm.
*/
void line(startx, starty, endx, endy, color)
int startx, starty, endx, endy, color;
{
  register int t, distance;
  int x=0, y=0, delta_x, delta_y;
  int incx, incy;

  /* compute the distances in both directions */
  delta_x=endx-startx;
  delta_y = endy-starty;

  /* Compute the direction of the increment,
     an increment of 0 means either a vertical or horizontal
     line.
  */
  if(delta_x>0) incx = 1;
  else if(delta_x==0) incx = 0;
  else incx=-1;

  if(delta_y>0) incy = 1;
  else if(delta_y==0) incy = 0;
  else incy=-1;

  /* determine which distance is greater */
  delta_x = abs(delta_x);
  delta_y = abs(delta_y);
  if(delta_x>delta_y) distance = delta_x;
  else distance = delta_y;

  /* draw the line */
  for(t=0; t<=distance+1; t++) {
    mempoint(startx, starty, color);
    x+=delta_x;
    y+=delta_y;
    if(x>distance) {
      x-=distance;
      startx+=incx;
    }
    if(y>distance) {
      y-=distance;
      starty+=incy;
    }
  }
}

/* write a point directly to the CGA */
void mempoint(x, y, color_code)
int x, y, color_code;
{
  union mask {
    char c[2];
    int i;
  } bit_mask;
  int i, index, bit_position;
  unsigned char t;
  char xor; /* xor color in or overwrite */
  char far *ptr = (char far *) 0xB8000000; /* pointer to CGA */

  bit_mask.i=0xFF3F;    /* 11111111 00111111 in binary */
```

```
/* check range for mode 6 */
if(x<0 || x>199 || y<0 || y>639) return;

xor = color_code & 128; /* see if xor mode is set */
color_code = color_code & 127; /* mask off high bit */

/* set bit_mask and color_code bits to the right location */
bit_position = y%4;
color_code<<=2*(3-bit_position);
bit_mask.i>>=2*bit_position;

/* find the correct byte in screen memory */
index = x*40 +(y >> 2);
if(x % 2) index += 8152; /* if odd use 2nd bank */

/* write the color */
if(!xor) { /* overwrite mode */
  t=*(ptr+index) & bit_mask.c[0];
  *(ptr+index)=t | color_code;
}
else { /* xor mode */
  t = *(ptr+index) | (char)0;
  *(ptr+index) = t ^ color_code;
}
}


/* send the cursor to x,y */
void goto_xy(x, y)
int x, y;
{
  union REGS r;

  r.h.ah = 2; /* cursor addressing function */
  r.h.dl = y; /* column coordinate */
  r.h.dh = x; /* row coordinate */
  r.h.bh = 0; /* video page */
  int86(0x10, &r, &r);
}
```

Using the Statistics Program

To give you an idea of how you can use the statistics program developed in this chapter, here is an example of a simple stock-market analysis for Widget, Incorporated. As an investor, you will be trying to decide if it is a good time to invest in Widget by buying stock; if you should sell "short" (the process of selling shares you do not have and hoping for a rapid price drop so that you can buy them later at a cheaper price); or if you should invest elsewhere.

For the past 24 months, Widget's stock price has been as follows:

Month	Stock Price ($)
1	10
2	10
3	11
4	9
5	8
6	8
7	9
8	10
9	10
10	13
11	11
12	11
13	11
14	11
15	12
16	13
17	14
18	16
19	17
20	15
21	15
22	16
23	14
24	16

You should first determine if Widget's stock price has established a trend. After entering the figures you find the following basic statistics:

Mean:	$12.08
Standard deviation:	2.68
Median:	11
Mode:	11

Next, you should plot a bar graph of the stock price as shown in Figure 7-7.
The bar graph looks as if there might be a trend, but it is best to perform a formal regression analysis. The regression equation is

$$Y = 7.90 + 0.33 * X$$

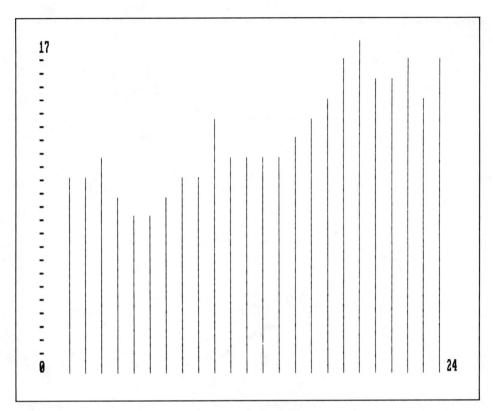

Figure 7-7. Bar chart of Widget's stock price

with a correlation coefficient of 0.86, or about 74%. This is quite good—in fact a definite trend is clear. Printing a scatter graph, as shown in Figure 7-8, makes this strong growth readily apparent. Such results could cause an investor to throw caution to the wind and buy 1000 shares as quickly as possible!

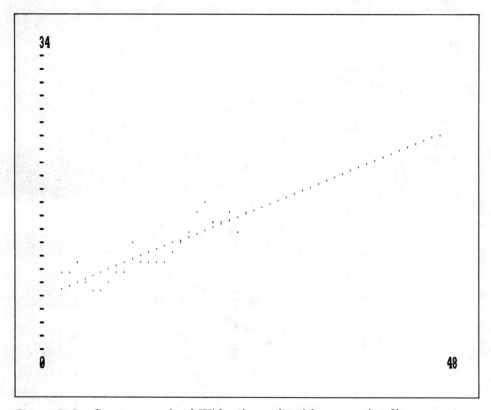

Figure 7-8.   Scatter graph of Widget's stock with regression line

Final Thoughts

The correct use of statistical analysis requires a general understanding of how the results are derived and what they really mean. It is important to remember that past events do not necessarily predict the future (except in some general way, perhaps). Blind reliance on statistical evidence can cause some very disturbing results.

Codes and Data Compression

CHAPTER 8

People who like computers and programming often like to play with codes and ciphers. Perhaps the reason for this is that all codes involve algorithms, just as programs do. Or perhaps these people simply have an affinity for cryptic things that most people cannot understand. All programmers seem to receive a great deal of satisfaction when a nonprogrammer looks at a program listing and says something like, "My God, that sure looks complicated!" After all, the act of writing a program is called "coding."

Closely associated with the topic of cryptography is *data compression*. Data compression is the compacting of information into a smaller space than is usually used. Because data compression can play a role in encryption and uses many of the same principles, it is included in this chapter.

Computer-based cryptography is important for two primary reasons. The most obvious is the need to keep sensitive data on shared systems secure. Although password protection is adequate for many situations, important, confidential files are routinely coded to provide a higher level of protection.

The second reason is that computer-based codes are used in data transmission. Not only are codes used for such things as secret government information, but they are also starting to be used by broadcasters to protect their sky-to-earth station transmissions. Because these types of coding procedures are so complex, they are usually done by a computer.

Data compression is commonly used to increase the storage capacity of various storage devices. Although the cost of storage devices has fallen sharply in the past few years, there can still be a need to fit more information into smaller areas.

A Short History of Cryptography

Although no one knows when secret writing began, one of the earliest examples is a cuneiform tablet made around 1500 BC. It contains a coded formula for making pottery glaze. The Greeks and Spartans used codes as early as 475 BC, and the upper class in Rome frequently used simple ciphers during the time of Julius Caesar. During the Dark Ages, interest in cryptography (as well as many other intellectual pursuits) decreased except among monks who used it occasionally. With the birth of the Italian Renaissance, the art of cryptography flourished. By the time of Louis XIV of France, a code based on 587 randomly selected keys was used for government messages.

In the 1800s two factors helped move cryptography forward. The first was Edgar Allan Poe's stories, such as "The Gold Bug," which featured coded messages and excited the imagination of many readers. The second was the invention of the telegraph and the Morse code. Morse code was the first binary representation (dots and dashes) of the alphabet that received wide use.

By World War I, several nations had constructed "code machines" that permitted easy encoding and decoding of text using sophisticated, complex ciphers. The story of cryptography changes slightly at this point, to the story of code-breaking. Before the use of mechanical devices to encode and decode messages, complex ciphers were used infrequently because of the time and effort required for both encoding and decoding. Hence, most codes could be broken within a relatively short period of time. However, the art of code-breaking became much more difficult when the code machines were used. Although modern computers would have made those codes fairly easy to break, even computers cannot dwarf the incredible talent of Herbert Yardley, still considered the grand master code-breaker of all time. He not only broke the U.S. diplomatic code in 1915 in his spare time, but he also broke the Japanese diplomatic code in 1922—even though he did not know Japanese! He accomplished this by using frequency tables of the Japanese language.

By World War II, the major method used to break codes was to steal the enemy's code machine, thereby foregoing the tedious (if intellectually satisfying) process of code-breaking. In fact, the Allies' possession of a German code machine (unknown to the Germans) contributed greatly to the outcome of the war.

With the advent of computers—especially multiuser computers—secure and unbreakable codes have become even more important. Not only do computer files occasionally need to be kept secret, but access to the computer itself must also be managed and regulated. Numerous methods of encrypting a data file have been developed and the DES (Data Encryption Standard) algorithm, accepted by the National Bureau of Standards, is generally considered to be secure from code-breaking efforts. However, DES is very difficult to implement and may not be suitable for all situations.

The Three Basic Types of Ciphers

Of the more traditional coding methods, there are two basic types: *transposition* and *substitution*. A transposition cipher essentially scrambles the characters of a message according to some rule. A substitution cipher replaces one character with another, but leaves the message in the proper order. These types of codes can be used at whatever level of complexity is desired and even intermixed. The digital computer adds a third basic encryption technique, called *bit manipulation*, which alters the computerized representation of data by some algorithm.

All three methods may make use of a *key*. A key is a string of characters that is needed to decode a message. Do not confuse the key with the method, however, because the key itself is never sufficient to decode—the encryption algorithm must also be known. The key "personalizes" a coded message so that only the people who know the key can decode it, at least easily, even though the method used to encode the message may be accessible.

Two terms that you should become familiar with are *plaintext* and *ciphertext*. The plaintext of a message is text you can read; the ciphertext is the encoded version.

This chapter presents various computerized methods that use each of the three basic methods to code text files. You will see several short programs that encode and decode text files. With one exception, all of these programs have both a **code( )** and a **decode( )** function. The **decode( )** function always reverses the **code( )** process used to create the ciphertext.

Substitution Ciphers

A *substitution cipher* is a method of encrypting a message by substituting, on a regular basis, one character for another. One of the simplest forms of substitution ciphers involves offsetting the alphabet by a specified amount. For example, if each letter were offset by three, then

abcdefghijklmnopqrstuvwxyz

becomes

defghijklmnopqrstuvwxyzabc

Notice the letters "abc" that were shifted off the front were added to the end. To encode a message using this method, you simply substitute the shifted alphabet for the real one. For example, the message

meet me at sunset

becomes

phhw ph dw vxqvhw

The program shown here enables you to code any text message using any offset after you specify which letter of the alphabet to begin with.

```
#include "ctype.h"
#include "stdio.h"

void code(), decode();

main(argc, argv)  /* simple substitution cipher */
int argc;
char *argv[];
{
  if(argc!=5) {
    printf("usage: input output encode/decode offset\n");
    exit(1);
  }
  if(!isalpha(*argv[4])){
    printf("start letter must be alphabetical character\n");
    exit(1);
  }

  if(toupper(*argv[3])=='E') code(argv[1], argv[2], *argv[4]);
  else decode(argv[1], argv[2], *argv[4]);
}

void code(input, output, start)
char *input, *output;
char start;
{
  int ch;
  FILE *fp1, *fp2;

  if((fp1=fopen(input, "r"))==NULL) {
    printf("cannot open input file\n");
    exit(1);
  }

  if((fp2=fopen(output, "w"))==NULL) {
    printf("cannot open output file\n");
    exit(1);
  }

  start = tolower(start);
  start = start-'a';
  do {
    ch = getc(fp1);
    ch = tolower(ch);
    if(isalpha(ch)) {
      ch+=start; /* shift the letter */
      if(ch>'z') ch-=26; /* wrap around */
    }
    putc(ch, fp2);
    if(feof(fp1)) break;
  } while(!ferror(fp1) && !ferror(fp2));
  fclose(fp1); fclose(fp2);
```

```
}
void decode(input, output, start)
char *input, *output;
char start;
{
  int ch;
  FILE *fp1, *fp2;

  if((fp1=fopen(input, "r"))==NULL) {
    printf("cannot open input file\n");
    exit(1);
  }

  if((fp2=fopen(output, "w"))==NULL) {
    printf("cannot open output file\n");
    exit(1);
  }

  start = tolower(start);
  start = start-'a';
  do {
    ch = getc(fp1);
    ch = tolower(ch);
    if(isalpha(ch)) {
      ch-=start; /* shift letter back to original */
      if(ch<'a') ch+=26;  /* wrap around */
    }
    putc(ch, fp2);
    if(feof(fp1)) break;
  } while(!ferror(fp1) && !ferror(fp2));
  fclose(fp1); fclose(fp2);
}
```

As an example, to code a file called "message," putting the coded version into a file called "cmess," and offsetting the alphabet by two places, you would type from the command line:

>code message cmess encode c

To decode, you would then type

>code cmess message decode c

Although a substitution cipher based on a constant offset will generally fool grade-schoolers, it is not suitable because it is too easy to crack. After all, there are only 26 possible offsets, and it is easy to try all of them within a short period of time. An improvement on the substitution cipher is to use a scrambled alphabet instead of a simple offset.

A second failing of the simple substitution cipher is that it preserves the spaces between words, which makes it doubly easy for a code-breaker to crack. Another improvement would be to encode spaces. (Actually, all punctuation should be encoded, but for simplicity the examples will not do this.) For example, you could map this random string containing every letter of the alphabet and a space

abcdefghijklmnopqrstuvwxyz<space>

into the string

qazwsxedcrfvtgbyhnujm ikolp

You may wonder if there is a significant improvement in the security of a message encoded by using a randomized version of the alphabet compared to a simple offset version. The answer is *yes* —there are 26 factorial (26!) ways to arrange the alphabet; with the space that number becomes 27 factorial (27!) ways. The factorial of a number is that number times every whole number smaller than it down to 1. For example, 6! is 6*5*4*3*2*1 = 720. Therefore, 26! is a very large number.

The program shown here is an improved substitution cipher that uses the randomized alphabet shown earlier. If you encoded the message:

meet me at sunset

by using the improved substitution cipher program, it would look like

tssjptspqjpumgusj

which is definitely a harder code to break.

```
#include "ctype.h"
#include "stdio.h"

void code(), decode();

char sub[28]=    "qazwsxedcrfvtgbyhnujm ikolp";
char alphabet[28]="abcdefghijklmnopqrstuvwxyz ";

main(argc, argv)  /* improved substitution cipher */
int argc;
char *argv[];
```

```
{
  if(argc!=4) {
    printf("usage: input output encode/decode\n");
    exit();
  }
  if(toupper(*argv[3])=='E') code(argv[1], argv[2]);
  else decode(argv[1], argv[2]);
}

void code(input, output)
char *input, *output;
{
  int ch;
  FILE *fp1, *fp2;

  if((fp1=fopen(input, "r"))==NULL) {
    printf("cannot open input file\n");
    exit();
  }

  if((fp2=fopen(output, "w"))==NULL) {
    printf("cannot open output file\n");
    exit();
  }

  do {
    ch = getc(fp1);
    ch = tolower(ch);
    if(isalpha(ch) || ch==' ')
      ch = sub[find(alphabet, ch)];
    putc(ch, fp2);
    if(feof(fp1)) break;
  } while(!ferror(fp1) && !ferror(fp2));
  fclose(fp1); fclose(fp2);
}

void decode(input, output)
char *input, *output;
{
  int ch;
  FILE *fp1, *fp2;

if((fp1=fopen(input, "r"))==NULL) {
  printf("cannot open input file\n");
  exit();
}

if((fp2=fopen(output, "w"))==NULL) {
  printf("cannot open output file\n");
  exit();
}

do {
  ch = getc(fp1);
  ch = tolower(ch);
```

```
    if(isalpha(ch) || ch==' ')
      ch = alphabet[find(sub, ch)];
    putc(ch, fp2);
    if(feof(fp1)) break;
  } while(!ferror(fp1) && !ferror(fp2));

  fclose(fp1); fclose(fp2);
}

/* Find the correct index. */
find(s, ch)
char *s;
char ch;
{
  register int t;
  for(t=0;t<28;t++) if(ch==s[t]) return t;
  return -1;
}
```

Although code-breaking is examined later in this chapter, you should know that even this improved substitution code can be broken easily by using a frequency table of the English language, in which the statistical information of the use of each letter of the alphabet is recorded. By looking at the coded message of the example, you can probably deduce that "s" represents "e," the most common letter in the English language, and that "p" represents the space. You can probably decode the rest. (You use the same process to solve the "cryptogram" which is next to the crossword puzzle in your newspaper.) Furthermore, the larger the coded message is, the easier it is to crack with a frequency table.

To impede the progress of a code-breaker who applies frequency tables to a coded message, you can use a *multiple substitution cipher* in which the same letter in the plaintext message will not necessarily have the same letter in the coded form. You can do this by adding a second randomized alphabet, and switching between it and the first alphabet each time a space is encountered. For example, the program can be rewritten to use this second string:

poi uytrewqasdfghjklmnbvcxz

The multiple substitution ciper shown here will work only with letters of the alphabet, switching randomized alphabets after a space is encountered. Hence, spaces are not encoded. Using the cipher to code the message

meet me at sunset

results in the coded form

tssj su qj kmdkul

To see how this works, set up the ordered alphabet and the two randomized alphabets (called R1 and R2) over one another.

```
alphabet: abcdefghijklmnopqrstuvwxyz<space>
R1:       qazwsxedcrfvtgbyhnujm ikolp
R2:       poi uytrewqasdfghjklmnbvcxz
```

Here is how the program operates: at the start, R1 is used. This randomized alphabet is used for the word "meet," producing the ciphertext "tssj." The spaces following "meet" cause R2 to be used for the word "me." This produces the ciphertext "su." Next the space causes R1 to be selected. This process of alternating alphabets continues until the message ends.

Using multiple substitution ciphers makes it much harder to break a code by using frequency tables because, at different times, different letters stand for the same thing. It would be possible to use several different randomized alphabets and a more complex switch routine to have all letters in the coded text occur equally. In this case a frequency table would be useless in breaking the code. The multiple substitution cipher shown here will work only with the letters of the alphabet:

```
#include "ctype.h"
#include "stdio.h"

void code(), decode();

char sub[28]=    "qazwsxedcrfvtgbyhnujm ikolp";
char sub2[28]=   "poi uytrewqasdfghjklmnbvcxz";
char alphabet[28]="abcdefghijklmnopqrstuvwxyz ";

main(argc,argv)  /* multiple substitution cipher */
int argc;
char *argv[];
{
  register int t;

  if(argc!=4) {
    printf("usage: input output encode/decode\n");
    exit();
  }
  if(toupper(*argv[3])=='E') code(argv[1],argv[2]);
  else decode(argv[1],argv[2]);
}
```

```
void code(input,output)
char *input,*output;
{
  int ch,change,t;
  FILE *fp1,*fp2;

  if((fp1=fopen(input,"r"))==NULL) {
    printf("cannot open input file\n");
    exit();
  }

  if((fp2=fopen(output,"w"))==NULL) {
    printf("cannot open output file\n");
    exit();
  }

  change=1;
  do {
    ch=getc(fp1);
    ch=tolower(ch);
    if(isalpha(ch))
      if(change)
        ch=sub[find(alphabet,ch)];
      else
        ch=sub2[find(alphabet,ch)];
    putc(ch,fp2);
    if(feof(fp1)) break;
    if(ch==' ') change=!change;
  } while(!ferror(fp1) && !ferror(fp2));
  fclose(fp1); fclose(fp2);

}

void decode(input,output)
char *input,*output;
{
  int ch,change;
  FILE *fp1,*fp2;

  if((fp1=fopen(input,"r"))==NULL) {
    printf("cannot open input file\n");
    exit();
  }

  if((fp2=fopen(output,"w"))==NULL) {
    printf("cannot open output file\n");
    exit();
  }
  change=1;
  do {
    ch=getc(fp1);
    ch=tolower(ch);
    if(isalpha(ch))
      if(change)
        ch=alphabet[find(sub,ch)];
      else
        ch=alphabet[find(sub2,ch)];
```

```
   putc(ch,fp2);
   if(feof(fp1)) break;
   if(ch==' ')  change=!change;
  } while(!ferror(fp1) && !ferror(fp2));
  fclose(fp1); fclose(fp2);
}

/* Find an element */
find(s,ch)
char *s;
char ch;
{
  register int t;

  for(t=0;t<28;t++) if(ch==s[t]) return t;
  return -1;
}
```

Transposition Ciphers

A *transposition cipher* is one in which the actual characters of the message are rearranged, according to some algorithm, in such a way as to conceal the content of the text. One of the earliest known uses of a transposition code was designed by the Spartans around 475 BC. It used a device call a *skytale*. A skytale is basically a strap upon which a message is written crossways. When the strap is wrapped around a cylinder the message can be read. The strap is then unwound and delivered to the recipient of the message, who also has a cylinder of equal size. Theoretically, it is impossible to read the strap without the cylinder because the letters are out of order. In actual practice, however, this method leaves something to be desired because different cylinder sizes can be tried until the message begins to make sense.

You can create a computerized version of a skytale by placing your message into an array a certain way and writing it out a different way. For example, if the following **union**

```
union message {
  char s[100];
  char s2[20][5];
} skytale;
```

is initialized to nulls, and if you then placed the message

meet me at sunset

into **skytale.s** but viewed it as the two-dimensional array **skytale.s2**, it would look like this:

m	e	e	t	
m	e		a	t
	s	u	n	s
e	t	0	0	0
0	0	0	0	0

⋮

If you then wrote the array out by column, the message would look like this:

mm e...eest...e u...tan... ts...

where the periods indicate the null padding. To decode the message, columns in **skytale.s** are fed into **skytale.s2**. Then the array **skytale.s** can be displayed in normal order. The **skytale.s** array can be printed as a string because the message will be null-terminated. The Skytale Cipher program uses this method to code and decode messages.

```
#include "ctype.h"
#include "stdio.h"
union message {
   char s[100];
   char s2[20][5];
} skytale;

void code(), decode();
```

```
main(argc, argv)   /* skytale cypher */
int argc;
char *argv[];
{
  int t;

  for(t=0; t<100; ++t) skytale.s[t]='\0';   /* load array */

  if(argc!=4) {
    printf("usage: input output encode/decode\n");
    exit();
  }

  if(toupper(*argv[3])=='E') code(argv[1], argv[2]);
  else decode(argv[1], argv[2]);
}

void code(input, output)
char *input, *output;
{
  int t, t2;
  FILE *fp1, *fp2;

  if((fp1=fopen(input, "r"))==NULL) {
    printf("cannot open input file\n");
    exit();
  }

  if((fp2=fopen(output, "w"))==NULL) {
    printf("cannot open output file\n");
    exit();
  }
  for(t=0;  t<100;  ++t) {
    skytale.s[t] = getc(fp1);
    if(feof(fp1))  break;
  }
  for(t=0;  t<5;  ++t)
    for(t2=0;  t2<20;  ++t2)
      putc(skytale.s2[t2][t], fp2);

  fclose(fp1);  fclose(fp2);
}

void decode(input, output)
char *input, *output;
{
  int t, t2;
  FILE *fp1, *fp2;

  if((fp1=fopen(input, "r"))==NULL) {
    printf("cannot open input file\n");
    exit();
  }
```

```
    if((fp2=fopen(output, "w"))==NULL) {
      printf("cannot open output file\n");
      exit();
    }
    for(t=0;  t<5 && !feof(fp1);  ++t)
      for(t2=0;  t2<20 && !feof(fp1);  ++t2)
        skytale.s2[t2][t] = getc(fp1);

    for(t=0;  t<100;  ++t)
      putc(skytale.s[t], fp2);

    fclose(fp1);  fclose(fp2);
}
```

Of course, there are other methods of obtaining transposed messages. One method particularly suited for computer use swaps letters within the message as defined by some algorithm. For example, here is a program that transposes letters up to a user-specified distance, starting from the front of the array and alternating its exchange with the end of the array:

```
#include "ctype.h"
#include "stdio.h"

void code(), decode();

main(argc, argv)  /* transposition cipher */
int argc;
char *argv[];
{
  int dist;

  if(argc!=5) {
      printf("usage: input output encode/decode distance\n");
      exit();
  }

  dist=atoi(argv[4]);
  if(toupper(*argv[3])=='E') code(argv[1], argv[2], dist);
  else decode(argv[1], argv[2], dist);
}

void code(input, output, dist)
char *input, *output;
int dist;
{
  char done, temp;
  int t;
  char s[256];
  FILE *fp1, *fp2;
```

```
  if((fp1=fopen(input, "r"))==0) {
    printf("cannot open input file\n");
    exit();
  }

  if((fp2=fopen(output, "w"))==0) {
    printf("cannot open output file\n");
    exit();
  }

  done=0;
  do {
    for(t=0; t<(dist*2); ++t) {
      s[t]=getc(fp1);
      if(feof(fp1)) {
        s[t]='\0';  /* if eof then null */
        done=1;
      }
    }
    for(t=0; t<dist; t++) {
      temp=s[t];
      s[t]=s[t+dist];
      s[t+dist]=temp;
      t++;
      temp=s[t];
      s[t]=s[dist*2-t];
      s[dist*2-t]=temp;
    }
    for(t=0; t<dist*2; t++) putc(s[t], fp2);
  } while(!done);
  fclose(fp1);  fclose(fp2);
}

void decode(input, output, dist)
char *input, *output;
int dist;
{
  char done, temp;
  int t;
  char s[256];
  FILE *fp1, *fp2;

  if((fp1=fopen(input, "r"))==0) {
    printf("cannot open input file\n");
    exit();
  }

  if((fp2=fopen(output, "w"))==0) {
    printf("cannot open output file\n");
    exit();
  }

  done=0;
  do {
    for(t=0; t<(dist*2); ++t) {
      s[t]=getc(fp1);
      if(feof(fp1)) {
```

```
      s[t]=0;   /* if eof then null */
      done=1;
    }
  }
  for(t=0; t<dist; t++) {
    t++;
    temp=s[t];
    s[t]=s[dist*2-t];
    s[dist*2-t]=temp;
    t--;
    temp=s[t];
    s[t]=s[t+dist];
    s[t+dist]=temp;
    t++;
  }
  for(t=0; t<dist*2; t++) putc(s[t], fp2);
} while(!done);
fclose(fp1);  fclose(fp2);
}
```

If you use this method with a distance of 10, the message

meet me at sunset

will look something like

<space>usetn smte metae

Used by themselves, transposition ciphers can accidentally create "clues" in the transposition process. In the sample text just given, the partial words "set" and "me" are suspiciously suggestive.

Bit-Manipulation Ciphers

The digital computer has given rise to a new method of encoding: manipulating the bits that compose the actual characters of the plaintext. This method of encryption is called a bit-manipulation cipher. Although the real purist would claim that bit manipulation (or *alteration*, as it is sometimes called) is really just a variation on the substitution cipher, the concepts, methods, and options differ so significantly that it must be considered a cipher method in its own right.

Bit-manipulation ciphers are well-suited for computer use because they employ operations easily performed by the system. Also, the cipher text tends to look completely unintelligible, which adds to the security of the message by making the data look like unused or crashed files and thereby confusing anyone who tries to gain access to the file.

Generally, bit-manipulation ciphers are only applicable to computer-based files and cannot be used to create hardcopy messages because the bit manipulations tend to produce nonprinting characters. For this reason, you should assume that any file coded by bit-manipulation methods will remain in a computer file.

Bit-manipulation ciphers convert plaintext into ciphertext by altering the actual bit pattern of each character through the use of one or more of the following logical operators:

AND
OR
NOT
XOR
1's Complement

C is perhaps the best language for creating bit-manipulation ciphers because it supports the following bitwise operators:

Operator	Meaning
|	OR
&	AND
^	XOR
~	1's Complement

The simplest and least secure bit-manipulation cipher uses only the 1's complement operator. (Remember that the ~ operator causes each bit within a byte to be inverted: a 1 becomes a 0, and a 0 becomes a 1. Therefore, a byte complemented twice is the same as the original.) The 1's Complement Cipher program presented here codes any text file:

```
#include "stdio.h"

void code(), decode();

main(argc, argv)  /* 1's complement cipher */
int argc;
char *argv[];
{
```

```
   if(argc!=4) {
     printf("usage: input output encode/decode\n");
     exit();
   }
   if(toupper(*argv[3])=='E') code(argv[1], argv[2]);
   else decode(argv[1], argv[2]);
}

void code(input, output)
char *input, *output;
{
   int ch;
   FILE *fp1, *fp2;

   if((fp1=fopen(input, "r"))==NULL) {
     printf("cannot open input file\n");
     exit();
   }

   if((fp2=fopen(output, "w"))==NULL) {
     printf("cannot open output file\n");
     exit();
   }

   do {
     ch = getc(fp1);
     ch = ~ch;
     putc(ch, fp2);
     if(feof(fp1)) break;
   } while(!ferror(fp1) && !ferror(fp2));
   fclose(fp1); fclose(fp2);
}

void decode(input, output)
char *input, *output;
{
   int ch;
   FILE *fp1, *fp2;

   if((fp1=fopen(input, "r"))==NULL) {
     printf("cannot open input file\n");
     exit();
   }

   if((fp2=fopen(output, "w"))==NULL) {
   printf("cannot open output file\n");
   exit();
   }

  do {
    ch = getc(fp1);
    ch = ~ch;
    putc(ch, fp2);
    if(feof(fp1)) break;
  } while(!ferror(fp1) && !ferror(fp2));
  fclose(fp1); fclose(fp2);
}
```

It is not easily possible to show what the ciphertext of a message would look like, because the bit manipulation used here generally creates nonprinting characters. Try it on your computer and examine the file—it will look quite cryptic, indeed!

There are two problems with this simple coding scheme. First, the encryption program does not use a key to decode, so anyone with access to the program can decode an encoded file. Second, and perhaps more important, this method would easily be spotted by any experienced computer programmer.

An improved method of bit-manipulation coding uses the XOR operator. The XOR operator has the following truth table:

XOR	0	1
0	0	1
1	1	0

The outcome of the XOR operation is TRUE if and only if one operand is TRUE and the other is FALSE. This gives the XOR a unique property: if you XOR a byte with another byte called the *key*, and then take the outcome of that operation and XOR it again with the key, the result will be the original byte, as shown here:

```
          1 1 0 1    1 0 0 1  ─┐
XOR       0 1 0 1    0 0 1 1 (key)
          ───────    ───────    │
          1 0 0 0    1 0 1 0     │
                                 ├─same
          1 0 0 0    1 0 1 0     │
XOR       0 1 0 1    0 0 1 1 (key)
          ───────    ───────    │
          1 1 0 1    1 0 0 1  ─┘
```

When used to code a file, this process solves the two inherent problems of the method that uses the 1's complement. First of all, because it uses a key, the encryption program alone cannot decode a file; second, because using a key makes each file unique, what has been done to the file is not obvious to someone schooled only in computer science.

The key does not have to be just one byte long. For example, you could use a key of several characters and alternate the characters through the file. However, a single-character key is used here to keep the program uncluttered.

```c
#include "stdio.h"

void code(),  decode();

main(argc, argv) /* XOR cipher with key */
int argc;
char *argv[];
{
  if(argc!=5) {
    printf("usage: input output decode/encode key\n");
    exit();
  }
  if(toupper(*argv[3])=='E')
    code(argv[1], argv[2], *argv[4]);
  else
    decode(argv[1], argv[2], *argv[4]);

}

void code(input, output, key)
char *input, *output;
char key;
{
  int ch;
  FILE *fp1, *fp2;

  if((fp1=fopen(input, "r"))==NULL) {
    printf("cannot open input file\n");
    exit();
  }

  if((fp2=fopen(output, "w"))==NULL) {
    printf("cannot open output file\n");
    exit();
  }

  do {
    ch = getc(fp1);
    ch = ch^key;
    putc(ch, fp2);
    if(feof(fp1)) break;
  } while(!ferror(fp1) && !ferror(fp2));
  fclose(fp1);  fclose(fp2);
}

void decode(input, output, key)
char *input, *output;
char key;
{
  int ch;
```

```
    FILE *fp1, *fp2;

    if((fp1=fopen(input, "r"))==NULL) {
    printf("cannot open input file\n");
    exit();
  }

  if((fp2=fopen(output, "w"))==NULL) {
    printf("cannot open output file\n");
    exit();
  }

  do {
    ch = getc(fp1);
    ch = ch^key;
    putc(ch, fp2);
    if(feof(fp1)) break;
  } while(!ferror(fp1) && !ferror(fp2));
  fclose(fp1);  fclose(fp2);
}
```

Try this program and you will find the file is not only unintelligible, but also can only be decoded through the use of the key.

Data Compression

Data compression essentially squeezes a given amount of information into a smaller area. Data compression is often used in computer systems to increase the storage (by reducing the storage needs of the computer user), to save transfer time (especially over phone lines), and to provide a level of security. Although there are many data-compression schemes available, this chapter examines only two of them. The first is *bit compression*, where more than one character is stored in a single byte, and the second is *character deletion*, in which actual characters from the file are deleted.

Eight into Seven

The uppercase and lowercase letters and punctuation only require about 63 different codes needing only 6 bits to represent a byte. (A 6-bit byte could have values of 0 through 63.) However, most computers use an 8-bit byte; thus, 25% of the byte's storage is wasted in simple text files. You could, therefore, actually compact 4 characters into 3 bytes if you could use the last 2 bits in each byte.

The only problem is the way in which the ASCII codes are organized—there are more than 63 different ASCII character codes, and the uppercase and lowercase alphabet falls more or less in the middle. This means that some of the characters will require at least 7 bits. It is possible to use a non-ASCII representation (which, on rare occasions, is done), but it is not generally advisable. An easier option is to compact 8 characters into 7 bytes, exploiting the fact that no letter or common punctuation mark uses the eighth bit of a byte. Therefore, you can use the eighth bit of each of the 7 bytes to store the eighth character. However, you should realize that many computers—including the IBM PC—do use 8-bit characters to represent special characters or graphics characters. Also, some word processors use the eighth bit to indicate text-processing instructions. Therefore, the use of this type of data compaction will only work on "straight" ASCII files that do not use the eighth bit for anything.

To visualize how this would work, consider the following 8 characters represented as 8-bit bytes:

byte 1	0 1 1 1	0 1 0 1
byte 2	0 1 1 1	1 1 0 1
byte 3	0 0 1 0	0 0 1 1
byte 4	0 1 0 1	0 1 1 0
byte 5	0 0 0 1	0 0 0 0
byte 6	0 1 1 0	1 1 0 1
byte 7	0 0 1 0	1 0 1 0
byte 8	0 1 1 1	1 0 0 1

As you can see, the eighth bit is always 0. This is always the case unless the eighth bit is used for parity checking. The easiest way to compress 8 characters into 7 bytes is to distribute the 7 significant bits of byte 1 into the 7 unused eighth-bit positions of bytes 2 through 8. The 7 remaining bytes then appear as shown on the next page.

```
                 ┌───────────────────────── byte 1 — read down
     byte 2     1  1  1  1    1  1  0  1
     byte 3     1  0  1  0    0  0  1  1
     byte 4     1  1  0  1    0  1  1  0
     byte 5     0  0  0  1    0  0  0  0
     byte 6     1  1  1  0    1  1  0  1
     byte 7     0  0  1  0    1  0  1  0
     byte 8     1  1  1  1    1  0  0  1
```

To reconstruct byte 1, you must put it back together again by taking the eighth bit off of each of the 7 bytes.

This compression technique compresses any text file by 1/8, or 12.5%. This is quite a substantial savings. For example, if you were transmitting the source code for your favorite program to a friend over long-distance phone lines, you would be saving 12.5% of the expense of transmission. (Remember, the object code, or executable version of the program, needs the full 8 bits.)

The following program compresses a text file using the method just described. Be aware that in order for the algorithm to work correctly at the end of the file, up to 7 extra bytes may be appended to the output file. Thus, on extremely short files (less than 56 bytes), it is possible that the compressed file can be longer than the noncompressed file. However, these bytes are insignificant in longer files. You may find it interesting to try to alter the algorithm so this is not the case.

```c
#include "stdio.h"

void compress(), decompress();

main(argc, argv)
int argc;
char *argv[];
{
  if(argc!=4) {
    printf("usage: input output compress/decompress\n");
    exit();
  }
  if(toupper(*argv[3])=='C')
    compress(argv[1], argv[2]);
  else
    decompress(argv[1], argv[2]);
```

```
}

void compress(input, output)
char *input, *output;
{
  char ch, ch2, done, t;
  FILE *fp1, *fp2;

  if((fp1=fopen(input, "r"))==NULL) {
    printf("cannot open input file\n");
    exit();
  }

  if((fp2=fopen(output, "w"))==NULL) {
    printf("cannot open output file\n");
    exit();
  }

  done = 0;
  do {
      ch = getc(fp1);
      ch = ch << 1;
      for(t=0; t<7; ++t) {
        ch2 = getc(fp1);
        if(feof(fp1)) {
          ch2 = 0;
          done = 1;
        }
        ch2 = ch2 & 127;    /* turn off top bit */
        ch2 = ch2 | ((ch<<t) & 128);
        putc(ch2, fp2);
      }
      if(feof(fp1)) break;
  } while(!done && !ferror(fp1) && !ferror(fp2));
  fclose(fp1);  fclose(fp2);
}

void decompress(input, output)
char *input, *output;
{
  unsigned char ch, ch2, t;
  char s[7], temp;
  FILE *fp1, *fp2;

  if((fp1=fopen(input, "r"))==NULL) {
    printf("cannot open input file\n");
    exit();
  }

  if((fp2=fopen(output, "w"))==NULL) {
    printf("cannot open output file\n");
    exit();
  }

  do {
    ch = 0;
```

```
  for(t=0;  t<7;  ++t) {
    temp = getc(fp1);
    ch2 = temp;  /* type conversion */
    s[t] = ch2 & 127;  /* turn off top bit */
    ch2 = ch2 & 128;   /* turn off all but top bit */
    ch2 = ch2 >> t+1;
    ch = ch | ch2;
  }
  putc(ch, fp2);
  for(t=0; t<7; ++t) putc(s[t], fp2);
  if(feof(fp1)) break;
} while(!ferror(fp1) && !ferror(fp2));
fclose(fp1);  fclose(fp2);
}
```

This program's code is fairly complex because the bits that make up the first byte must be shifted into their proper positions.

The 16-Character Language

Although unsuitable for most situations, an interesting method of data compression deletes unnecessary letters from words, in essence making most words into abbreviations. Data compression is accomplished because the unused characters are not stored. The use of abbreviations to save space is very common: for example, "Mr." is commonly used instead of "Mister." Instead of using actual abbreviations, the method presented in this section automatically removes certain letters from a message. To do this, a *minimal alphabet* will be needed. A minimal alphabet is one in which several seldom-used letters have been removed, leaving only those necessary to form most words or avoid ambiguity. Therefore, any character not in the minimal alphabet will be extracted from any word in which it appears. Exactly how many characters there are in a minimal alphabet is a matter of choice. However, this section uses the 14 most common, plus spaces and newlines.

Automating the abbreviation process requires that you know what letters in the alphabet are used most frequently so that you can create a minimal alphabet. In theory, you could count the letters in each word in a dictionary; however, different writers use a different frequency mix than others, so a frequency chart based just on the words that make up the English language

may not reflect the actual usage frequency of letters. (It would also take a
long time to count the letters!) As an alternative, you can count the frequency
of the letters in this chapter and use them as a basis for your minimal
alphabet. To do this, you could use the following simple program. The program skips all punctuation except periods, commas, and spaces.

```c
#include "stdio.h"
#include "ctype.h"


main(argc, argv) /* character frequency program */
int argc;
char *argv[];
{
  FILE *fp1;
  int alpha[26], t;
  int space=0, period=0, comma=0;
  char ch;

  if(argc!=2) {
    printf("Please specify text file.\n");
    exit(1);
  }

  if((fp1=fopen(argv[1], "r"))==NULL) {
    printf("cannot open input file\n");
    exit(1);
  }

  for(t=0; t<26; t++) alpha[t]=0;

  do {
    ch=getc(fp1);
    if(isalpha(ch))
      alpha[toupper(ch)-'A']++;
    else switch(ch) {
      case ' ': space++;
        break;
      case '.': period++;
        break;
      case ',': comma++;
        break;
    }
  } while(!feof(fp1));

  for(t=0; t<26; ++t)
    printf("%c: %d\n", 'A'+t, alpha[t]);

  printf("period: %d\n", period);
  printf("space: %d\n", space);
  printf("comma: %d\n", comma);
  fclose(fp1);
}
```

By running this program on the text of this chapter, you get the following
frequency:

A	2525
B	532
C	838
D	1145
E	3326
F	828
G	529
H	1086
I	2242
J	39
K	94
L	1103
M	1140
N	2164
O	1767
P	697
Q	62
R	1656
S	1672
T	3082
U	869
V	376
W	370
X	178
Y	356
Z	20
Space	5710
Period	234
Comma	513

The frequency of letters in this chapter compares well with the standard
English mix and is offset only slightly by the repeated use of the C keywords
in the programs.

To achieve significant data compression, you need to cut the alphabet
substantially by removing the letters used least frequently. Although there
are different ideas about what a workable minimum alphabet is, the 14 most
common letters and the space account for about 85% of all characters used in
this chapter. Because the newline character is also necessary to preserve
word breaks, it must be included. Therefore, the minimal alphabet used in
this section consists of the following:

$$A\ C\ D\ E\ H\ I\ L\ M\ N\ O\ R\ S\ T\ U\ \text{<space> <newline>}$$

Here is a program that removes all characters other than these:

```c
#include "stdio.h"

void comp2();

main(argc,argv)  /*  Character deletion compression program */
int argc;
char *argv[];
{
  if(argc!=3) {
    printf("usage: input output\n");
    exit();
  }
  comp2(argv[1],argv[2]);
}

void comp2(input,output)
char *input,*output;
{
  char ch;
  FILE *fp1,*fp2;

  if((fp1=fopen(input,"r"))==NULL) {
    printf("cannot open input file\n");
    exit();
  }

  if((fp2=fopen(output,"w"))==NULL) {
    printf("cannot open output file\n");
    exit();
  }

  do {
    ch=getc(fp1);
    if(feof(fp1)) break;
    if(is_in(toupper(ch),"ACDEJILMNORSTU '\n'")) {
      if(ch=='\n') putc('\r',fp2);
      putc(ch,fp2);
    }
  } while(!ferror(fp1) && !ferror(fp2));
  fclose(fp1); fclose(fp2);
}

is_in(ch,s)
char ch,*s;
{
  while(*s) {
    if(ch==*s) return 1;
    s++;
  }
  return 0;
}
```

If you use this program on the following message:

> Attention High Command:
> Attack successful. Please send additional supplies and
> fresh troops. This is essential to maintain our foothold.
> General Frashier

the compressed message would look like this:

> Attention i Command
> Attac successul lease send additional sulies and res troos
> Tis is essential to maintain our ootold   eneral rasier

As you can see, the message is largely readable, although some ambiguity is present. Ambiguity is the chief drawback of this method of data compression. However, if you were familiar with the vocabulary of the writer of the message, you could probably select a better minimal alphabet that would remove some of this ambiguity. In spite of the potential for ambiguity, quite a bit of space was saved. The original message was 168 bytes long and the compacted message was 142 bytes long—a savings of about 16%.

If both character deletion and bit compression were applied to the message, then about 28% less storage space would have been needed, which could be very important. For example, if you were a submarine captain and wanted to send a message to headquarters but did not want to give away your position, you might want to compress the message by using both methods so that it was as short as possible.

Both the bit-compression and character-deletion methods of data compression have uses in encryption. Bit compression further encrypts the information and makes decoding more difficult. If used before encryption, the character-deletion method has one wonderful advantage: it disguises the character frequency of the source language.

Code-Breaking

No chapter on encryption methods is complete without a brief look at code-breaking. The art of code-breaking is essentially one of trial and error. With the use of digital computers, relatively simple ciphers can easily be broken through exhaustive trial and error. However, the more complex codes either cannot be broken or require techniques and resources not commonly available. For simplicity, this section focuses on breaking the more straightforward codes.

If you wish to break a message that was ciphered using the simple substitution method, and only an offset alphabet, then all you need to do is try all 26 possible offsets to see which one fits. A program to do this is shown here:

```
#include "ctype.h"
#include "stdio.h"
main(argc, argv)  /* code breaker for simple substitution
         cipher */
int argc;
char *argv[];
{
  if(argc!=2) {
    printf("usage: input\n");
    exit();
  }
  bc(argv[1]);
}

/* try to break a simple substitution cipher */
bc(input)
char *input;
{
  register int t, t2;
  char ch, s[1000], q[10];
  FILE *fp1;

  if((fp1=fopen(input, "r"))==NULL) {
    printf("cannot open input file\n");
    exit();
  }

  for(t=0; t<1000; ++t) {
    s[t]=getc(fp1);
    if(s[t]==EOF) break;
  }
  s[t] = '\0';
  fclose(fp1);
  for(t=0; t<26; ++t) {
    for(t2=0; s[t2]; t2++) {
      ch = s[t2];
      if(isalpha(ch)) {
        ch = tolower(ch)-t;
        if(ch>'z') ch-=26;
      }
      printf("%c", ch);
    }
    printf("\n");
    printf("decoded? (y/n): ");
    gets(q);
```

```
    if(*q=='y') break;
  }
  printf("\noffset is: %d", t);

}
```

With only a slight variation, you could use the same program to break ciphers that use a random alphabet. In this case, substitute manually entered alphabets as shown in the following program:

```
#include "ctype.h"
#include "stdio.h"
char sub[28];
char alphabet[28]="abcdefghijklmnopqrstuvwxyz ";

void bc2();

main(argc, argv)  /* code-breaker for random substitution */
int argc;
char *argv[];
{
  char s[80];

  if(argc!=2) {
    printf("usage: input");
    exit();
  }

  do {
    printf("enter test alphabet:\n");
    gets(sub);
    bc2(argv[1]);
    printf("\nIs this right?: (y/n) ");
    gets(s);
  } while(tolower(*s)!='y');

}

/* break a random substitution cipher */
void bc2(input)
char *input;
{
  char ch;
  FILE *fp1;

  if((fp1=fopen(input, "r"))==NULL) {
    printf("cannot open input file\n");
    exit();
  }

  do {
    ch=getc(fp1);
    if(feof(fp1)) break;
```

```
      if(isalpha(ch) || ch==' ') {
        printf("%c", alphabet[find(sub, ch)]);
      }
  } while(!ferror(fp1));
  fclose(fp1);
}

/* find the corresponding character */
find(s, ch)
char *s;
char ch;
{
  register int t;

  for(t=0; t<28; t++) if(ch==s[t]) return t;
}
```

Unlike the substitution ciphers, transposition and bit-manipulation ciphers are harder to break using the trial-and-error methods. If you have to break such complex codes, good luck!

Oh and by the way: hsaovbno wlymljapvu pz haahpuhisl, pa vjjbyz vusf hz hu hjjpklua.

Random Number
Generators and
Simulations

C H A P T E R   9

Random number sequences are used in a variety of programming situations that range from simulations, which are the most common, to games and other recreational software. The ANSI standard defines the **rand( )** function, which returns a pseudo-random integer between 0 and 32,767. This function is part of Turbo C's standard library. Although this function is quite good, you will sometimes want to create your own random number generator functions. For example, you may want to use multiple random number generators to allow the independent control of various facets of your program. Or, you may want a generator that skews its random numbers about some value when you are working with abnormal distributions. Whatever the case, the study and creation of random number generators has captivated computer scientists since the beginning of the use of computers.

In this chapter you will study the way various random number generating functions are written and learn how to evaluate them. You will also look at two interesting simulations that use the random number generators developed in the chapter. The first is a grocery store check-out simulation and the second is a random-walk stock portfolio manager.

Random Number Generators

Technically, the term *random number generator* is absurd because numbers, in and of themselves, are not random! For example, is 100 a random number? Is 25? Of course not. What is really meant by "random number generator" is something that creates a *sequence* of numbers that appears to be in random order. This raises the more complex question: What is a random sequence of numbers? The only correct answer is that a random sequence of numbers is one in which all elements are completely unrelated. This definition leads to the paradox that any sequence can be both random and nonrandom, depending on the way the sequence was obtained. For example, this list of numbers

$$1\ 2\ 3\ 4\ 5\ 6\ 7\ 8\ 9\ 0$$

was created by typing the top keys on the typewriter keyboard in order, so the sequence certainly cannot be construed as random. But what if you happen to pull out exactly that sequence from a barrel full of ping-pong balls that had numbers on them? That *would* be a random sequence. This discussion shows that the randomness of a sequence depends on *how it was generated*, not on what the actual sequence is.

Keep in mind that sequences of numbers generated by a computer are *deterministic:* each number other than the first depends on the number that precedes it. Technically, this means that only a *quasi-random* sequence of numbers can be created by a computer. However, this is sufficient for most problems and, for the purposes of this book, the sequences will simply be called random.

Generally, it is best if the numbers in a random sequence are *uniformly distributed.* (Do not confuse this with the normal distribution, or bell-shaped curve.) In a uniform distribution, all events are equally probable, so that a graph of a uniform distribution tends to be a flat line rather than a curve.

Before the widespread use of computers, whenever random numbers were needed they were produced by either throwing dice or pulling numbered balls from a jar. In 1955, the RAND Corporation published a table of 1 million random digits obtained with help from a computer-like machine. In the early days of computer science, although many methods were devised to generate random numbers, most were discarded.

One particularly interesting method that almost worked was developed by none other than John von Neumann—the father of the modern computer. Often referred to as the *middle-square method*, it squares the previous random number, and then extracts the middle digits. For example, if you were creating three-digit numbers and the previous value was 121, then you would square 121 to make 14641. Extracting the middle three digits would give you 464 as the next number. The problem with this method is that it tends to lead to a very short repeating pattern called a *cycle*, especially after a 0 has entered the pattern. For this reason, this method is not presently used.

Today, the most common way to generate random numbers is by using the following equation:

$$R_{n+1} = (aR_n + c) \bmod m$$

where

$$R > = 0$$
$$a > = 0$$
$$c > = 0$$
$$m > R_0, \ m > a, \ m > c$$

This method is sometimes referred to as the *linear congruential method*. Looking at this equation, you probably think random number generation is simple. There is a catch, though—how well this equation performs depends heavily on the values of a, c, and m. Choosing these values is sometimes more of an art than a science. There are complex rules that can help you choose those values; however, this discussion will cover only a few simple rules and experiments.

The modulus (m) should be fairly large because it determines the range of the random numbers. The modulus operation yields the remainder of a division. Hence,

$$10 \ \% \ 4 \ \text{is} \ 2$$

because 4 goes into 10 twice with a remainder of 2. Therefore, if the modulus is 12, then only the numbers 0 through 11 can be produced by the randomizing equation, whereas if a modulus is 21,425, the numbers 0 through 21,424 can be generated. Remember, a small modulus does not actually affect randomness, only range. The choice of the multiplier, *a*, and the increment, *c*, is much harder. Usually, the increment can be fairly small and the multiplier can be fairly large. A lot of testing is needed to confirm that a good generator has been created.

As a first example, here is a common random number generator. The equation shown in **ran1( )** has been used as the basis for the random number generator in a number of popular languages.

```
float ran1()
{
  static long int a=100001;

  a = (a*125) % 2796203;
  return (float) a/2796203;
}
```

This function has three important features. First, the random number is actually an integer—**long int** in this case—even though the function returns a **float**. The integers are necessary for the linear congruential method, but random number generators, by convention, are expected to return a number between 0 and 1, which means it is a floating point.

Second, the *seed*, or starting value, is hard-coded into the function by using the **static long int a**. This method provides seed value to the next call. Although this feature is fine for most situations, it is possible to let the user specify the initial value to try to make the sequence more random. If a user-specified seed value is used, the function is as follows:

```
float ran1(seed)
float seed;
{
  static long int a;
  static char once=1;

  if(once){
    a=seed*1000;   /* get a first value */
    once=0;
  }

  a = (a*125) % 2796203;
  return (float) a/2796203;
}
```

However, for the rest of this chapter, the seed will be hard-coded into the functions for the sake of simplicity.

Third, the random number is divided by the modulus prior to the return.

This obtains a number between 0 and 1. Although the random number generator **rand( )** specified by ANSI and used by Turbo C returns a number between 0 and 32,767, traditionally random number generators have returned values between 0 and 1. (This is the format followed by BASIC, Turbo Pascal, FORTRAN, and others.) This is because random numbers are frequently used in probabilistic simulations that require values in this range. For the sake of tradition, this chapter also creates generators that return the values 0 through 1. If you study this, you will see that the value of **a** prior to the return line must be a value between 0 and 2796202. Therefore, when **a** is divided by 2796203, a number equal to or greater than 0 but less than 1 is obtained. By the same reasoning, you can convert the output of the **rand( )** function to a value between 0 and 1 by dividing it by 32,767.

Many random number generators are not useful because they produce nonuniform distributions or have short, repeating sequences. Even when they are very slight, these problems can produce biased results if the same random number generator is used over and over again. The solution is to create several different generators and use them either individually or jointly to obtain more random numbers.

The following generator, called **ran2( )**, produces a good distribution:

```
float ran2()
{
   static long int a=1;

   a = (a * 32719+3) % 32749;
   return (float) a / 32749;
}
```

Each of the random number generators presented here produces a good sequence of random numbers. Yet the questions remain: How "random" are the numbers? How good are these generators?

Determining the Quality
of a Generator

You can apply a number of different tests to determine the randomness of a sequence of numbers. None of these tests will tell you if a sequence is random, but they will tell you if it is not. The tests can identify a nonrandom sequence, but just because a specific test does not find a problem does not mean that a given sequence is indeed random. A test does, however, raise your confidence in the random number generator that produced the sequence. For the purposes of this chapter, most of these tests are either too complicated or time-consuming in their most rigorous forms. Therefore, you will look briefly at some of the ways a sequence can be tested and how it can fail.

To begin, it is important to know how closely the distribution of the numbers in a sequence conforms to what you would expect a random distribution to be. For example, say that you are attempting to generate random sequences of the digits 0 through 9. Therefore, the probability of each digit occurring is 1/10, because there are ten possibilities for each number in the sequence, all of which are equally possible. Assume that the sequence

$$9\ 1\ 8\ 2\ 4\ 6\ 3\ 7\ 5\ 8\ 2\ 9\ 0\ 4\ 2\ 4\ 7\ 8\ 6\ 2$$

was actually generated. If you count the number of times each digit occurs, the result is

Digit	Occurrences
0	1
1	1
2	4
3	1
4	3
5	1
6	2
7	2
8	3
9	2

The question you should ask is if this distribution is sufficiently similar to the expected distribution.

Remember, if a random number generator is good, it generates sequences randomly. In a truly random state, all sequences are possible. This seems to imply that any sequence generated should qualify as a valid random sequence. So how can you tell if this sequence is random? In fact, how could any sequence of the ten digits be nonrandom, since any sequence is possible? The answer is that some sequences are *less likely* to be random than others. You can determine the *probability* of a given sequence being random by using the *chi-square test*. The chi-square test basically subtracts the expected number of occurrences from the observed number of occurrences for all pos-

	p=99%	p=95%	p=75%	p=50%	p=25%	p=5%
n=5	0.5543	1.1455	2.675	4.351	6.626	11.07
n=10	2.558	3.940	6.737	9.342	12.55	18.31
n=15	5.229	7.261	11.04	14.34	18.25	25.00
n=20	8.260	10.85	15.45	19.34	23.83	31.41
n=30	14.95	18.49	24.48	29.34	34.80	43.77

Figure 9-1. Selected chi-square values

sible outcomes and produces a number, generally called V. You then look up this number in a table of chi-square values to find the likelihood that the sequence is random in distribution. A small chi-square table appears in Figure 9-1. Complete tables can be found in most books on statistics.

The formula to obtain V is

$$V = \sum_{1 \leq i \leq N} \frac{(O_i - E_i)^2}{E_i}$$

where O_i is the observed occurrences, E_i is the expected occurrences, and N is the number of discrete elements. The value for E_i is determined by multiplying the probablity of that element occurring by the number of observations. In this case, because each digit is expected to occur 1/10th of the time, if 20 samples are taken, the value for E will be 2 for all digits. N is 10 because there are 10 possible elements, the digits 0-9. Therefore,

$$V = \frac{(1-2)^2}{2} + \frac{(1-2)^2}{2} + \frac{(4-2)^2}{2} + \frac{(1-2)^2}{2} + \frac{(3-2)^2}{2} + \frac{(1-2)^2}{2} +$$

$$\frac{(2-2)^2}{2} + \frac{(2-2)^2}{2} + \frac{(3-2)^2}{2} + \frac{(2-2)^2}{2} = 5$$

To determine the likelihood that the sequence is not random, find the row in the table in Figure 9-1 that equals the number of observations; in this case it is 20. Then read across until you find a number that is greater than V. In this case, it is column 1. This means that that there is a 99% likelihood that a sample of 20 elements will have a V greater than 8.260. Therefore, there is only a 1% probability that the sequence is random. To "pass" the chi-square test, the probability of V must fall between 75% and 25%. (This range is derived from mathematics beyond the scope of this book.)

You might, however, counter this conclusion with the following question: Since all sequences are possible, how can this sequence have only a 1% chance of being legitimate? The answer is that it is just a probability—the chi-square test is actually not a test at all, only a confidence builder. In fact, if you use the chi-square test, you should obtain several different sequences and average the results to avoid rejecting a good random number generator. Any single sequence might be rejected, but averaging several sequences should provide a good test.

On the other hand, a sequence can pass the chi-square test and still not be random. For example:

$$1\ 3\ 5\ 7\ 9\ 7\ 5\ 3\ 1$$

would pass the chi-square test but does not appear very random. In this case, a *run* was produced. A run is a sequence of strictly ascending or descending numbers that are at evenly spaced intervals. Each group of four digits on either side of the 9 is in strictly ascending or descending order, and as such (assuming it continued) would not be a random sequence. Runs can be separated by "noise" digits as well: the digits that comprise the run can be interspersed throughout an otherwise random sequence. It is possible to design tests to detect these situations, but they are beyond the scope of this book.

Another feature to test for is the length of the *period;* that is, how many numbers can be generated before the sequence begins to repeat—or worse, degenerate into a short cycle. All computer-based random number generators eventually repeat a sequence. The longer the period, the better the generator. Even though the frequency of the numbers within the period is uniformly distributed, the numbers do not constitute a random series, because a truly random series will not repeat itself consistently. Generally, a period of several thousand numbers is sufficient for most applications. (Again, a test for this can be performed, but it is beyond the scope of this book.)

Several other tests can be applied to determine the quality of a random number generator. In fact, there has probably been more code written to test random number generators than has been written to construct them. Here is yet another test that allows you to test random number generators "visually" using a graph to show how the sequence is generated.

Ideally, the graph should be based on the frequency of each number. However, since a random number generator can produce thousands of different numbers, this is impractical. Instead, you will create a graph grouped by the tenths digit of each number; for example, the number 0.9365783 is grouped under 9, and 0.34523445 is grouped under 3. This means that the graph of the output of the Random Number Generator Display program has ten lines, with each line representing the number of times a particular number in that group occurs. The program also prints the mean of each sequence, which can be used to detect a bias in the numbers. Like other graphic programs in this chapter, this program runs only on an IBM PC that is equipped with a color-graphics display adapter and makes use of the graphics functions developed in Chapter 6.

```
#include "dos.h"

int freq1[10]={0, 0, 0, 0, 0, 0, 0, 0, 0, 0};
int freq2[10]={0, 0, 0, 0, 0, 0, 0, 0, 0, 0};
int freq3[10]={0, 0, 0, 0, 0, 0, 0, 0, 0, 0};

float ran1(), ran2();
void mempoint(), palette(), mode(), goto_xy();
void line(), display();

main()  /* random number generator display program */
{
    int x, y;
    float f, f2, f3, r, r2, r3;
    char s[80];

    mode(4);
    palette(1);
    f=0; f2=0; f3=0;

    goto_xy(0, 6);
    printf("Comparison of Random Number");
    goto_xy(2, 15);
    printf("Generators");
    line(180, 0, 180, 90, 1);
    line(180, 110, 180, 200, 1);
    line(180, 220, 180, 310, 1);
    goto_xy(23, 3);
    printf("ran1()        ran2()        rand()");

    for(x=0; x<1000; ++x) {
```

```
    r = ran1();
    f+=r;
    y = r*10;
    freq1[y]++;

    r2 = ran2();
    f2+=r2;
    y = r2*10;
    freq2[y]++;

    /* normalize the rand() function */
    r3 = (float) rand() / 32767;
    f3+=r3;
    y = r3*10;
    freq3[y]++;

    display();
  }
  gets(s);
  mode(3);
  printf("mean of rand1() function 1: %f\n", f/1000);
  printf("mean of rand2() function 2: %f\n", f2/1000);
  printf("mean of rand() function 3: %f\n", f3/1000);
}

/* display the graph of the random numbers */
void display()
{
  register int t;
  for(t=0; t<10; ++t) {
    line(180, t*10, 180-freq1[t], t*10, 2);
    line(180, t*10+110, 180-freq2[t], t*10+110, 2);
    line(180, t*10+220, 180-freq3[t], t*10+220, 2);
  }
}

float ran1()
{
  static long int a=100001;

  a = (a*125) % 2796203;
  return (float) a/2796203;
}

float ran2()
{
  static long int a=1;

  a = (a * 32719+3) % 32749;
  return (float) a/32749;
}


/* set the palette */
void palette(pnum)
int pnum;
```

```
{
  union REGS r;

  r.h.bh = 1;    /* code for mode 4 graphics */
  r.h.bl = pnum;
  r.h.ah = 11;  /* set palette function */
  int86(0x10, &r, &r);
}

/* set the video mode */
void mode(mode_code)
int mode_code;
{
  union REGS r;

  r.h.al = mode_code;
  r.h.ah = 0;
  int86(0x10, &r, &r);
}

/* Draw a line in specified color
   using Bresenham's integer based algorithm.
*/
void line(startx, starty, endx, endy, color)
int startx, starty, endx, endy, color;
{
  register int t, distance;
  int x=0, y=0, delta_x, delta_y;
  int incx, incy;

  /* compute the distances in both directions */
  delta_x=endx-startx;
  delta_y=endy-starty;

  /* Compute the direction of the increment,
     an increment of 0 means either a vertical or horizontal
     line.
  */
  if(delta_x>0) incx=1;
  else if(delta_x==0) incx=0;
  else incx=-1;

  if(delta_y>0) incy=1;
  else if(delta_y==0) incy=0;
  else incy=-1;

  /* determine which distance is greater */
  delta_x=abs(delta_x);
  delta_y=abs(delta_y);
  if(delta_x>delta_y) distance=delta_x;
  else distance=delta_y;

  /* draw the line */
  for(t=0; t<=distance+1; t++) {
    mempoint(startx, starty, color);
    x+=delta_x;
```

```
      y+=delta_y;
      if(x>distance) {
        x-=distance;
        startx+=incx;
      }
      if(y>distance) {
        y-=distance;
        starty+=incy;
      }
    }
  }
}


/* write a point directly to the CGA */
void mempoint(x,y,color_code)
int x,y,color_code;
{
  union mask {
    char c[2];
    int i;
  } bit_mask;
  int i, index, bit_position;
  unsigned char t;
  char xor; /* xor color in or overwrite */
  char far *ptr = (char far *) 0xB8000000; /* pointer to CGA */

  bit_mask.i=0xFF3F;   /* 11111111 00111111 in binary */

  /* check range for mode 4 */
  if(x<0 || x>199 || y<0 || y>319) return;

  xor=color_code & 128; /* see if xor mode is set */
  color_code=color_code & 127; /* mask off high bit */

  /* set bit_mask and color_code bits to the right location */
  bit_position=y%4;
  color_code<<=2*(3-bit_position);
  bit_mask.i>>=2*bit_position;


  /* find the correct byte in screen memory */
  index=x*40 +(y >> 2);
  if(x % 2) index += 8152; /* if odd use 2nd bank */

  /* write the color */
  if(!xor) { /* overwrite mode */
    t=*(ptr+index) & bit_mask.c[0];
    *(ptr+index)=t | color_code;
  }
  else { /* xor mode */
    t=*(ptr+index) | (char)0;
    *(ptr+index)=t ^ color_code;
  }
}


/* send the cursor to x,y */
void goto_xy(x, y)
```

```
int x, y;
{
  union REGS r;

  r.h.ah = 2; /* cursor addressing function */
  r.h.dl = y; /* column coordinate */
  r.h.dh = x; /* row coordinate */
  r.h.bh = 0; /* video page */
  int86(0x10, &r, &r);
}
```

In this program, the **ran1()**, **ran2()**, and **rand()** functions are tested to create a side-by-side comparison. Each function generates 1000 numbers and, based on the digit in the tenths position, the appropriate frequency array is updated. Notice that the output of the **rand()** function is manually converted into a number between 0 and 1. The **display()** function plots all three frequency arrays on the screen after each number is generated, so you can actually watch the display grow. Figure 9-2 shows the output from each of the random number generators at the end of the 1000 numbers. The mean

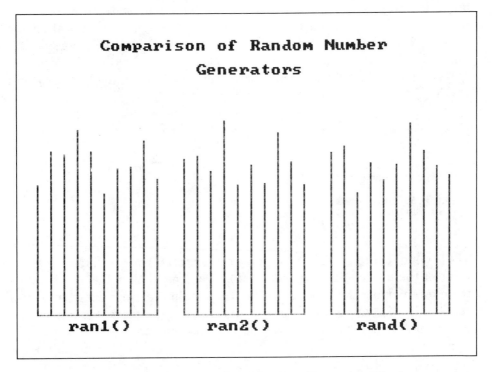

Figure 9-2. Output from the Random Number Generator Display program

is 0.496960 for **ran1()**, 0.490550 for **ran2()**, and 0.500417 for **rand()**. These are all quite acceptable.

To use the display program effectively, you should watch both the shape of the graph and the way that it grows to check for any short, repeating cycles. This "test" is, of course, not conclusive, but it does give you insight into the way a generator produces its numbers, and it can speed up the testing process by allowing obviously poor generators to be rejected quickly. (It also makes a great program to run when someone asks you to show them your computer!)

Using Multiple Generators

One simple technique that improves the randomness of the sequences produced by the three generators is to combine them under the control of one master function. This function selects between two of them, based on the result of the third. With this method you can obtain very long periods and diminish the effects of any cycle.

The function called **random()** shown here combines **ran1()**, **ran2()**, and **rand()**:

```
float random()   /* random selection of generators */
{
   float f;

   f=(float) rand() /32767;

   if(f>.5) return ran1();
   else return ran2();
}
```

The result of **rand()** is used to decide whether **ran1()** or **ran2()** becomes the value of the master function **random()**. Feel free to alter the mix between them by changing the constant in the **if** to obtain the exact distribution you require. Here is a program to display the graph of **random()** and its mean. Figure 9-3 shows the final graph after 1000 random numbers have been computed.

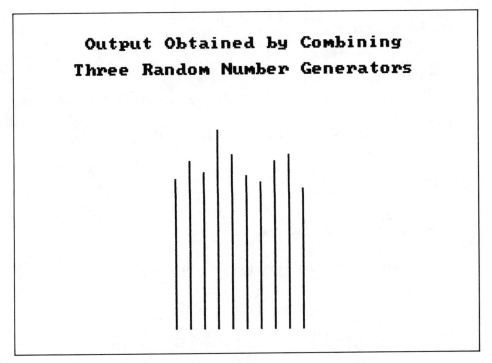

Figure 9-3. The final graph of **random( )**

```
#include "dos.h"

int freq1[10]={0,0,0,0,0,0,0,0,0,0};

float ran1(), ran2(), random();
void mempoint(), palette(), mode(), goto_xy();
void line(), display();

main()  /* using random numbers to further randomize */
{  /* the output from random number generators  */

    int x, y;
    float   f=0.0, r;
    char s[80];

    mode(4);
    palette(1);
    goto_xy(0, 6);
    printf("Output Obtained by Combining");
    goto_xy(2, 5);
    printf("Three Random Number Generators");
```

```
    line(180, 110, 180, 200, 1);
    for(x=0; x<1000; ++x) {
      r=random();
      f+=r;
      y=r*10;
      freq1[y]++;
      display();
    }
    gets(s);
    mode(3);
    printf("mean of random number function 1: %f\n", f/1000);

}

void display()
{
  register int t;
  for(t=0; t<10; ++t)
    line(180, t*10+110, 180-freq1[t], t*10+110, 2);
}

float random()  /* random selection of generators */
{
  float f;

  f=(float) rand() /32767;

  if(f>.5) return ran1();
  else return ran2();
}

float ran1()
{
  static long int a=100001;

  a = (a*125) % 2796203;
  return (float) a/2796203;
}

float ran2()
{
  static long int a=1;

  a = (a * 32719+3) % 32749;
  return (float) a/32749;
}

/* set the palette */
void palette(pnum)
int pnum;
{
  union REGS r;

  r.h.bh = 1;    /* code for mode 4 graphics */
  r.h.bl = pnum;
  r.h.ah = 11;  /* set palette function */
  int86(0x10, &r, &r);
}
```

```
/* set the video mode */
void mode(mode_code)
int mode_code;
{
  union REGS r;

  r.h.al = mode_code;
  r.h.ah = 0;
  int86(0x10, &r, &r);
}

/* Draw a line in specified color
   using Bresenham's integer based algorithm.
*/
void line(startx, starty, endx, endy, color)
int startx, starty, endx, endy, color;
{
  register int t, distance;
  int x=0, y=0, delta_x, delta_y;
  int incx, incy;

  /* compute the distances in both directions */
  delta_x=endx-startx;
  delta_y=endy-starty;

  /* Compute the direction of the increment,
     an increment of 0 means either a vertical or horizontal
     line.
  */
  if(delta_x>0) incx=1;
  else if(delta_x==0) incx=0;
  else incx=-1;

  if(delta_y>0) incy=1;
  else if(delta_y==0) incy=0;
  else incy=-1;

  /* determine which distance is greater */
  delta_x=abs(delta_x);
  delta_y=abs(delta_y);
  if(delta_x>delta_y) distance=delta_x;
  else distance=delta_y;

  /* draw the line */
  for(t=0; t<=distance+1; t++) {
    mempoint(startx, starty, color);
    x+=delta_x;
    y+=delta_y;
    if(x>distance) {
      x-=distance;
      startx+=incx;
    }
    if(y>distance) {
      y-=distance;
      starty+=incy;
    }
  }
}
```

```
/* write a point directly to the CGA */
void mempoint(x,y,color_code)
int x,y,color_code;
{
  union mask {
    char c[2];
    int i;
  } bit_mask;
  int i, index, bit_position;
  unsigned char t;
  char xor; /* xor color in or overwrite */
  char far *ptr = (char far *) 0xB8000000; /* pointer to CGA */

  bit_mask.i=0xFF3F;  /* 11111111 00111111 in binary */

  /* check range for mode 4 */
  if(x<0 || x>199 || y<0 || y>319) return;

  xor=color_code & 128; /* see if xor mode is set */
  color_code=color_code & 127; /* mask off high bit */

  /* set bit_mask and color_code bits to the right location */
  bit_position=y%4;
  color_code<<=2*(3-bit_position);
  bit_mask.i>>=2*bit_position;


  /* find the correct byte in screen memory */
  index=x*40 +(y >> 2);
  if(x % 2) index += 8152; /* if odd use 2nd bank */

  /* write the color */
  if(!xor) { /* overwrite mode */
    t=*(ptr+index) & bit_mask.c[0];
    *(ptr+index)=t | color_code;
  }
  else { /* xor mode */
    t=*(ptr+index) | (char)0;
    *(ptr+index)=t ^ color_code;
  }
}


/* send the cursor to x,y */
void goto_xy(x, y)
int x, y;
{
  union REGS r;

  r.h.ah = 2; /* cursor addressing function */
  r.h.dl = y; /* column coordinate */
  r.h.dh = x; /* row coordinate */
  r.h.bh = 0; /* video page */
  int86(0x10, &r, &r);
}
```

The mean of **random()** is 0.495913.

Simulations

For the remainder of this chapter, the application of random number generators will be examined for computer *simulations*. A simulation is a computerized model of some real-world situation. Anything can be simulated, and the success of the simulation is based primarily upon how well the programmer understands the event being simulated. Because real-world situations often have thousands of variables, many things are difficult to simulate effectively. However, there are several events that lend themselves very well to simulations.

Simulations are important for two reasons. First, they let you alter the parameters of a situation to observe the possible results, even though in real life such experimentation might be either too costly or dangerous. For example, a simulation of a nuclear power plant can be used to test the effects of certain types of failures without danger. Second, simulation allows you to create situations that cannot occur in the real world. For example, a psychologist might want to study the effects of gradually increasing the intelligence of a mouse to that of a human to see at what point the mouse runs a maze the fastest. Although this cannot be done in real life, a simulation may provide insight into the nature of intelligence versus instinct.

Simulating a Check-out Line

The first simulation example in this discussion is of a check-out line in a grocery store. Assume the store is open ten hours a day, with peak hours being from 12 to 1 P.M. and from 5 to 6 P.M. The 12 to 1 P.M. slot is twice as busy as normal and the 5 to 6 P.M. slot is three times as busy. As the simulation runs, one random number generator "creates" customers, another generator determines how long it will take one customer to check out, and a third generator decides to which of the open lines the customers will go. The goal of the simulation is to help management find the minimal number of check-out lines that need to be available on a typical shopping day, while limiting the number of people in line at any time to ten.

The key to this type of simulation is the creation of multiple processes. Although C does not support simultaneity directly, you can simulate multiprocessing by having each function inside of a main program loop do some work and return—in essence time-slicing the function. For example, the function that simulated the check-out only checks out a part of each order each time it is called. In this way, each function inside the main loop continues to execute. The **main( )** function to the Check-out program, along with its global data, is shown here.

```
#include "dos.h"

float ran1(), ran2();

void mempoint(), palette(), mode(), goto_xy();
void line(), display(), add_cust();
void check_out(), add_queue(), circle(), plot_circle();

char queues[10];
char qopen[10];
int   cust;    /* total number of customers */
int time=0;

double asp_ratio=1.0;

main()  /* check-out line simulation */
{
  int x, y;
  char s[80];

  mode(4);
  palette(1);
  for(x=0; x<10; ++x) {
    queues[x]=0;
    qopen[x]=0;    /* all closed at start of day */
  }
  goto_xy(24, 20);  printf("1            10");
  goto_xy(24, 0);  printf("Check-out lines:");
  qopen[0]=1; /* open up number 1 */
  do {
    add_cust();  /* add customers */
    add_queue(); /* add another check out line */
    display();   /* show state of system */
    check_out(); /* check the customer out */
    display();
    if(time>30 && time<50) add_cust();
    if(time>70 && time < 80) {
       add_cust();
       add_cust();
    }
    time++;
  } while (!kbhit() && time<100);
  gets(s);
  mode(3);
}
```

The main loop

```
do {
  add_cust();   /* add customers */
  add_queue();  /* add another check out line */
  display();    /* show state of system */
  check_out();  /* check the customer out */
  display();
  if(time>30 && time<50) add_cust();
  if(time>70 && time < 80) {
    add_cust();
    add_cust();
  }
  time++;
} while (!kbhit() && time<100);
```

is used to drive the entire simulation. The **add—cust( )** function uses either **ran1( )** or **rand( )** to generate the number of customers arriving at the check-out lines at each request. The **add—queue( )** function is used to place the customers into an open check-out line, according to the results of **ran2( )**, and it also opens a new line if all currently open lines are full. The **display( )** function shows a graphic representation of the simulation. The **check-out( )** function uses **ran2( )** to assign each customer a check-out count, and each call decrements that count by 1. When a customer's count is 0, the customer leaves the check-out line.

The variable **time** alters the rate at which customers are generated in order to match the peak hours of the store. In essence, each pass through the loop is one-tenth of an hour.

Figures 9-4, 9-5, and 9-6 show the state of the check-out lines when **time** = 28, **time** = 60, and **time** = 88, corresponding to normal, the end of first peak, and the end of second peak, respectively. Notice that at the end of the second peak, a maximum of six check-out lines is needed. This means that if the simulation was completed correctly, the grocery store does not need to operate the remaining four lines.

You can directly control several variables in the program. First, you can alter the way customers arrive and the number of customers that arrive. You can also change **add—cust( )** to return gradually more or fewer customers as the peak hours approach and wane. The program assumes that customers will randomly choose which line to stand in. Although this may be true of some customers, others will obviously choose the shortest line. You can

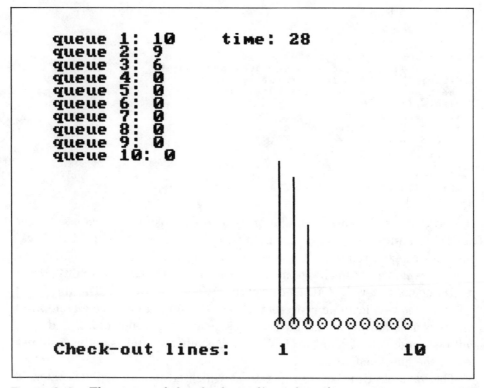

Figure 9-4. The status of the check-out line when **time** = 28

account for this by altering the **add—queue( )** function to put customers into the shortest line at some times and to place customers randomly at other times. The simulation does not account for the occasional accident—such as a dropped ketchup bottle, or an unruly customer at the check-out counter, both of which would cause a line to stall temporarily.

The entire program is shown here:

```
#include "dos.h"

float ran1(), ran2();

void mempoint(), palette(), mode(), goto_xy();
void line(), display(), add_cust();
void check_out(), add_queue(), circle(), plot_circle();
```

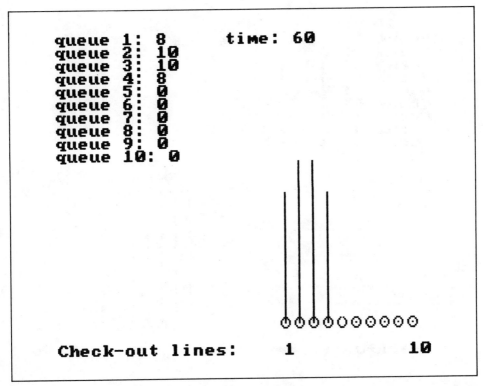

Figure 9-5. The status of the check-out line when **time** = 60

```
char queues[10];
char qopen[10];
int  cust;   /* total number of customers */
int time=0;

double asp_ratio=1.0;

main()  /* check-out line simulation */
{

  int x, y;
  char s[80];

  mode(4);
  palette(1);
  for(x=0; x<10; ++x) {
    queues[x]=0;
    qopen[x]=0;   /* all closed at start of day */
```

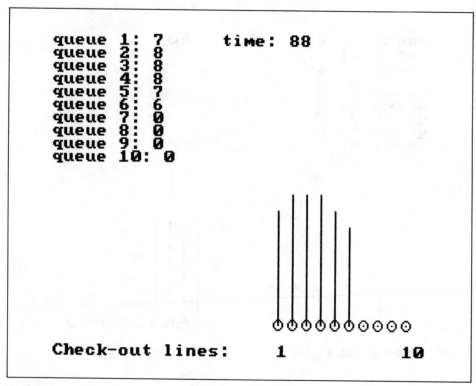

Figure 9-6.   The status of the check-out line when **time** = 88

```
}
goto_xy(24, 20);  printf("1            10");
goto_xy(24, 0);  printf("Check-out lines:");
qopen[0]=1;  /* open up number 1 */
do {
  add_cust();  /* add customers */
  add_queue(); /* add another check out line */
  display();   /* show state of system */
  check_out(); /* check the customer out */
  display();
  if(time>30 && time<50) add_cust();
  if(time>70 && time < 80) {
     add_cust();
     add_cust();
  }
  time++;
} while (!kbhit() && time<100);
gets(s);
mode(3);
}
```

```
/* add a customer to a line */
void add_cust()
{

  float f, r;
  static char swap=0;

  /* use two different number generators */
  if(swap) f=ran1();   /* to get a random number */
  else f=(float) rand() / 32767;
  swap=!swap;

  if(f<.5) return;   /* no customers */
  else if(f<.6) {
    cust++;   /* add one customer */
    return;
  }
  else if(f<.7) {
    cust+=2;   /* add two customers */
    return;
  }
  else if(f<.8) {
    cust+=3;
    return;
  }
  else cust+=4;
}

/* check out the customer */
void check_out()
{
  static char count[10]={0, 0, 0, 0, 0, 0, 0, 0, 0, 0};
  register int t;

  for(t=0; t<10; ++t) {
    if(queues[t]) {
      /* get check out time */
      while(count[t]==0) count[t]=ran2()*5;
      count[t]--;
      if(count[t]==0) queues[t]--;
    }
    if(!queues[t]) qopen[t]=0;   /* close the line */
  }
}

/* add another check out line */
void add_queue()
{
  register int t;
  int line;

  while(cust) {
    if(allfull())
      for(t=0; t<10; t++) if(!qopen[t]) {
        qopen[t]=1;
        break;
      }
```

```
      line=((float) rand()/32767)*10;
      if(qopen[line] && queues[line]<10) {
        queues[line]++;
        cust--;
      }
      if(t==10) return;    /* all queues full */
  }
}

/* return 1 if all lines are full; 0 otherwise */
allfull()
{
  register int t;

  for(t=0; t<10; t++) if(queues[t]<10 && qopen[t]) return 0;
  return 1;
}

/* show the current state of the system */
void display()
{
  register int t;

  goto_xy(0, 15);
  printf("time: %d", time);
  for(t=0; t<10; ++t) {
    /* first, erase the old line by printing in 0 color */
    line(180, (t*10)+160, 80, (t*10)+160, 0);
    /* now, draw the circle */
    circle(180, (t*10)+160, 3, 1);
    /* now draw current state of the queue */
    line(180, (t*10)+160, 180-queues[t]*10, (t*10)+160, 2);
    goto_xy(0+t, 0);  printf("queue %d: %d  ", t+1, queues[t]);
  }
}

float ran1()
{
  static long int a=100001;

  a = (a*125) % 2796203;
  return (float) a/2796203;
}

float ran2()
{
  static long int a=1;

  a = (a * 32719+3) % 32749;
  return (float) a/32749;
}


/* set the palette */
void palette(pnum)
int pnum;
{
```

```
  union REGS r;
  r.h.bh = 1;    /* code for mode 4 graphics */
  r.h.bl = pnum;
  r.h.ah = 11;   /* set palette function */
  int86(0x10, &r, &r);
}

/* set the video mode */
void mode(mode_code)
int mode_code;
{
  union REGS r;

  r.h.al = mode_code;
  r.h.ah = 0;
  int86(0x10, &r, &r);
}

/* Draw a line in specified color
   using Bresenham's integer based algorithm.
*/
void line(startx, starty, endx, endy, color)
int startx, starty, endx, endy, color;
{
  register int t, distance;
  int x=0, y=0, delta_x, delta_y;
  int incx, incy;

  /* compute the distances in both directions */
  delta_x=endx-startx;
  delta_y=endy-starty;

  /* Compute the direction of the increment,
     an increment of 0 means either a vertical or horizontal
     line.
  */
  if(delta_x>0) incx=1;
  else if(delta_x==0) incx=0;
  else incx=-1;

  if(delta_y>0) incy=1;
  else if(delta_y==0) incy=0;
  else incy=-1;

  /* determine which distance is greater */
  delta_x=abs(delta_x);
  delta_y=abs(delta_y);
  if(delta_x>delta_y) distance=delta_x;
  else distance=delta_y;

  /* draw the line */
  for(t=0; t<=distance+1; t++) {
    mempoint(startx, starty, color);
    x+=delta_x;
    y+=delta_y;
    if(x>distance) {
    x-=distance;
```

```
      startx+=incx;
    }
    if(y>distance) {
      y-=distance;
      starty+=incy;
    }
  }
}


/* write a point directly to the CGA */
void mempoint(x,y,color_code)
int x,y,color_code;
{
  union mask {
    char c[2];
    int i;
  } bit_mask;
  int i, index, bit_position;
  unsigned char t;
  char xor; /* xor color in or overwrite */
  char far *ptr = (char far *) 0xB8000000; /* pointer to CGA */

  bit_mask.i=0xFF3F;   /* 11111111 00111111 in binary */

  /* check range for mode 4 */
  if(x<0 || x>199 || y<0 || y>319) return;

  xor=color_code & 128; /* see if xor mode is set */
  color_code=color_code & 127; /* mask off high bit */

  /* set bit_mask and color_code bits to the right location */
  bit_position=y%4;
  color_code<<=2*(3-bit_position);
  bit_mask.i>>=2*bit_position;


  /* find the correct byte in screen memory */
  index=x*40 +(y >> 2);
  if(x % 2) index += 8152; /* if odd use 2nd bank */

  /* write the color */
  if(!xor) { /* overwrite mode */
    t=*(ptr+index) & bit_mask.c[0];
    *(ptr+index)=t | color_code;
  }
  else { /* xor mode */
    t=*(ptr+index) | (char)0;
    *(ptr+index)=t ^ color_code;
  }
}


/* send the cursor to x,y */
void goto_xy(x, y)
```

```
int x, y;
{
  union REGS r;

  r.h.ah = 2; /* cursor addressing function */
  r.h.dl = y; /* column coordinate */
  r.h.dh = x; /* row coordinate */
  r.h.bh = 0; /* video page */
  int86(0x10, &r, &r);
}

/* Draw a circle using Bresenham's integer based Algorithm. */
void circle(x_center, y_center, radius,  color_code)
int x_center, y_center, radius, color_code;
{
  register int x, y, delta;

  asp_ratio = 1.0;  /* for different aspect ratios, alter
                       this number */

  y = radius;
  delta = 3 - 2 * radius;

  for(x=0; x<y; ) {
    plot_circle(x, y, x_center, y_center, color_code);

    if (delta < 0)
      delta += 4*x+6;
    else {
      delta += 4*(x-y)+10;
      y--;
    }
    x++;
  }
  x=y;
  if(y) plot_circle(x, y, x_center, y_center, color_code);
}


/* plot_circle actually prints the points that
   define the circle */
void plot_circle(x, y, x_center, y_center, color_code)
int x, y, x_center, y_center, color_code;
{
  int startx, endx, x1, starty, endy, y1;

  starty = y*asp_ratio;
  endy = (y+1)*asp_ratio;
  startx = x*asp_ratio;
  endx = (x+1)*asp_ratio;

  for (x1=startx; x1<endx; ++x1)  {
    mempoint(x1+x_center, y+y_center, color_code);
    mempoint(x1+x_center, y_center-y, color_code);
    mempoint(x_center-x1, y_center-y, color_code);
```

```
    mempoint(x_center-x1, y+y_center, color_code);
  }

  for (y1=starty; y1<endy; ++y1) {
    mempoint(y1+x_center, x+y_center, color_code);
    mempoint(y1+x_center, y_center-x, color_code);
    mempoint(x_center-y1, y_center-x, color_code);
    mempoint(x_center-y1, x+y_center, color_code);
  }
}
```

Random-Walk
Portfolio Management

The art of stock portfolio management is generally based on various theories
and assumptions about many factors, some of which cannot be easily known
unless you are an insider. There are buy/sell strategies based on statistical
analyses of stock prices and PE ratios; there are correlations with the price
of gold, the GNP, and even the cycles of the moon. The computer scientist's
revenge is to use the computer to simulate the free marketplace—the stock
exchange—without all the theoretical worry.

You may think that the stock exchange is simply too hard to simulate; that
it has too many variables and too many unknowns; and that it swings wildly
at times and coasts smoothly at others. However, the problem itself is the
solution: because the marketplace is so complex, it can be thought of as *randomly occurring events*. This means that you can simulate the stock exchange
as a series of disconnected random occurrences. This is affectionately
referred to as the *random-walk method* of portfolio management. The term is
derived from the classic experiment that involves a drunk wandering a
street, randomly weaving from lamppost to lamppost. In the random-walk
theory, you let chance be your guide because it is as good as any other
method.

Before you continue, be warned: the random-walk method is generally
discredited by professional money managers; it is presented here for fun and
your enjoyment, not for actual investing.

To implement the random-walk method, first select ten companies from
the *Wall Street Journal*, by some chance method. After you have selected ten
companies, feed their names into the Random-Walk Simulation program so
that it can tell you what to do with them.

Basically, the program can tell you five things to do with the stock of each company:

- Sell
- Buy
- Sell short
- Buy on margin
- Hold (do nothing)

The operations of buying, selling, and holding stock are obvious. When you *sell short*, you sell stock that you do not own in the hopes that soon you can buy it cheaper and deliver it to the person you sold it to. Selling short is a way to make money when the market is going down. When you *buy on margin*, you use, for a small fee, the money of the brokerage house to finance part of the cost of the stock that you purchased. The idea behind buying on margin is that if the stock increases enough, then you make more money than you could if you only bought a smaller amount of stock with cash. This makes money only in a bull (rising) market.

The Random-Walk Simulation program is shown here. Notice that the program waits until you strike a key. This allows you to use the sequence produced by the random number generator at a random point. Otherwise, you would always get the same advice.

```
{
  register int t;

  for(t=0;t<10;t++) {
    printf("enter company name: ");
    gets(stock[t]);
  }
}

/* return advice */
char *action()
{
  register int x;
  float f;

  f=ran1();
  x=f*10;

  switch(x) {
    case 0: return "sell";
    case 1: return "buy";
```

```
   case 3: return "sell short";
   case 4: return "buy on margin";
   default: return "hold";
  }
}

float ran1()
{
  static long int a=100001;

  a = (a*125) % 2796203;
  return (float) a/2796203;
}
```

The program requires that you interpret the instructions in the following way:

Instruction	Interpretation
Buy	Buy as much of the specified stock as you can afford without borrowing.
Sell	Sell all of the stock if any is owned. Then randomly select a new company to take its place.
Sell short	Sell 100 shares of the specified company even though you don't own it in the hopes that you can buy it cheaper in the future.
Buy on margin	Borrow money to buy shares of the specified stock.
Hold	Do nothing.

For example, if you were to run this program using the fictitious company names of Com1 through Com10, the first day's advice would look like this:

Com1:	sell
Com2:	buy
Com3:	buy on margin
Com4:	sell short
Com5:	hold
Com6:	hold
Com7:	hold
Com8:	buy
Com9:	hold
Com10:	sell short

The second day's advice might be

Com1:	hold
Com2:	hold
Com3:	sell
Com4:	sell short
Com5:	hold
Com6:	hold
Com7:	buy
Com8:	buy on margin
Com9:	hold
Com10:	sell

If you prefer, you can run the program weekly instead of daily.

Feel free to alter the program in any way. For example, you could change the program to give you amounts of stock to buy and sell. Again, remember that this program is only for fun and is not recommended as a way to make actual investments in the market. However, it is interesting to create a portfolio on paper and track its performance.

Expression Parsing and Evaluation

C H A P T E R   1 0

How do you write a program that will take as input a string containing a numeric expression, such as (10−5)*3, and return the answer, in this case 15? If a "high priesthood" still exists among programmers, then it must be made up of those few who know how to do this. Almost everyone who uses a computer is mystified by the way a high-level language converts complex expressions, such as 10*3−(4+count/12), into instructions that a computer can execute. This procedure is called *expression parsing*. It forms the backbone of all language compilers and interpreters, spreadsheet programs, and anything else that converts those numeric expressions understood by humans into forms that a computer can use. Few programmers know how to write an expression parser; this realm of programming is generally thought of as "off limits," except to those enlightened few.

However, this is not the case. Expression parsing is actually very straightforward and similar to other programming tasks. In some ways it is easier, because it works with the strict rules of algebra. This chapter develops what is commonly referred to as a *recursive descent parser*, as well as all the necessary support routines to enable you to evaluate complex numeric expressions.

After you have mastered the parser, you can enhance and modify it to suit your needs—and join the "high priesthood" yourself.

Expressions

Although expressions can be made up of all types of information, you will be studying only one type: *numeric expressions*. For the purposes of this chapter, assume that numeric expressions can be made up of the following:

- Numbers
- The operators +, −, /, *, ^, %, and =
- Parentheses
- Variables

The ^ symbol indicates exponentiation, as in BASIC, and the = symbol represents the assignment operator. These items can be combined in expressions according to the rules of algebra. Here are some examples:

```
10−8
(100−5) * 14/6
a+b−c
10^5
a=10−b
```

Assume the following precedence for each operator:

```
highest:   ^
           * / %
           + −
lowest:    =
```

Operators of equal precedence evaluate from left to right.

For the examples in this chapter, the following assumptions will be made. All variables are single letters, which means that 26 variables—the letters A through Z—are available for use. The variables will not be case-sensitive, which means "a" and "A" will be treated as the same variable. All numbers are **float**, although you could easily write the routines to handle other types of numbers. Finally, only a minimal amount of error checking is included in the routines to keep the logic clear and easy to understand.

Take a look at this sample expression:

$$10-2*3$$

This expression has the value 4. Although you could easily create a program that would compute that specific expression, you may wonder how to create a computer program that will give you the correct answer for any arbitrary expression of this type. At first you might think that you could use a routine like this:

a = *get first operand*
while(*operands present*) {
    op = *get operator*
    b = *get second operand*
    a = *a op b*
}

According to this routine, you could get the first operand, the operator, and the second operand; perform the operation; then get the next operator and operand, if any; perform that operation; and so on. If you use this basic method, the expression 10−2*3 evaluates to 24 (that is, 8*3) instead of the correct answer of 4, because this procedure neglects the precedence of the operators. You cannot take the operands and operators in order from left to right, because the multiplication must be done prior to the subtraction. A beginner may think that this could be easily overcome—and sometimes, in very restrictive cases, it can—but the problem only gets worse when parentheses, exponentiation, variables, function calls, and the like are added.

Although there are a few ways to write functions that evaluate expressions of this sort, you will study the one that is most easily written and is also the most common. (Some other methods used to write parsers employ complex tables that require another computer program to generate them. These are sometimes called *table-driven parsers*.) The method used here is called a recursive descent parser, and you will see how it got its name.

Dissecting an Expression

Before it is possible to develop a parser for evaluating expressions, you must break an expression into its components. For example, the expression

$$A*B-(W+10)$$

has the components A, B, W, the parentheses, and the operators *, #, and $-$. Each component represents an indivisible unit of the expression. In general, you need a routine that will return each item in the expression individually. The routine needs to be able to skip over spaces and tabs, and it must know when the end of the expression has been reached.

Formally, each component of an expression is called a *token*. Therefore, the function that returns the next token in the expression is often called **get—token( )**. A global character pointer is needed to point into the expression string. This pointer is called **prog**. The variable **prog** is global because it must maintain its value between calls to **get—token( )** and allow other functions to use it. You also need to know what *type* of token you are getting. For the parser developed in this chapter, you only need three types: VARIABLE, NUMBER, and DELIMITER, where DELIMITER is used for both operators and parentheses. Here is **get—token( )** with its necessary globals, #**define** statements, and support functions:

```
#define DELIMITER  1
#define VARIABLE   2
#define NUMBER     3

extern char *prog;   /* holds expression to be analyzed */
char token[80];
char tok_type;


void get_token()
{

  register char *temp;

  tok_type = 0;
  temp = token;

  while(isspace(*prog)) ++prog;    /* skip over white space */
```

```
    if(is_in(*prog, "+-*/^%()")){
       tok_type = DELIMITER;
       *temp++ = *prog++;
       /* advance to next position */
    }
    else if(isalpha(*prog))
       serror(0);  /* not a number - abort */

    else if(isdigit(*prog)) {
       while(!isdelim(*prog)) *temp++ = *prog++;
       tok_type = NUMBER;
    }

    *temp = '\0';
}

/* return true if c is a delimiter */
isdelim(c)
char c;
{
    if(is_in(c, " +-/*^%()") || c==9 || c=='\r' || c==0)
       return 1;
    return 0;
}

is_in(ch, s)
char ch, *s;
{
    while(*s) if(*s++==ch) return 1;
    return 0;
}
```

Because people like to put spaces into expressions to add clarity but not
meaning, leading spaces are skipped over using the library function
isspace( ), which returns true if its argument is any of the white-space
characters.

After the spaces have been skipped, **prog** will be pointing to either a
number, a variable, an operator, or a null, if trailing spaces end the expression. If the next character is an operator, the character is returned as a
string in the global variable **token**, and the type of DELIMITER is placed in
tok_type. If the next character is a letter instead, it will be assumed to be
one of the variables and will be returned as a string in **token**; **tok_type** is
assigned the value VARIABLE. If the next character is a number, then the
integer is read and placed in the string **token** with a type of NUMBER.
Finally, if the next character is none of these, you can then assume that the
end of the expression has been reached and **token** is null.

As stated earlier, to keep the code clean in this function, a certain amount
of error checking has been omitted and some assumptions have been made.

For example, any unrecognized character may end an expression. Also, in this version, variables may be any length, but only the first letter is significant. However, you can fill in these and other details according to your specific application. You can modify or enhance **get—token( )** easily to enable character strings, other types of numbers, or whatever you want to be returned from an input-string token.

To understand how **get—token( )** works, study what it returns for each token and type for the expression A+100−(B∗C)/2:

Token	Token type
A	VARIABLE
+	DELIMITER
100	NUMBER
−	DELIMITER
(	DELIMITER
B	VARIABLE
∗	DELIMITER
C	VARIABLE
)	DELIMITER
/	DELIMITER
2	NUMBER
null	null

Remember that **token** always holds a null-terminated string, even if that string is just a single character.

Expression Parsing

There are a number of possible ways to parse and evaluate an expression. For use with a recursive descent parser, think of expressions as *recursive data structures*, that are defined in terms of themselves. If, for the moment, you restrict expressions to using only +, −, ∗, /, and parentheses, you could say that expressions can be defined by using the following rules:

Expression => Term [+ Term] [− Term]
Term => Factor [∗ Factor] [/ Factor]
Factor => Variable, Number or (Expression)

where any part of the above can be null. The square brackets mean optional, and the => means "produces." In fact, the rules are usually called the *production rules* of the expression. Therefore, you could read the second rule as, "Term produces factor times factor, or factor divided by factor." The precedence of the operators is implicit in the way an expression is defined.

The expression

$$10+5*B$$

has two terms: 10 and 5*B. However, it has three factors: 10, 5, and B. These factors consist of two numbers and one variable.

On the other hand, the expression

$$14*(7-C)$$

has two terms, 14 and (7−C), which is one number and one parenthesized expression. The parenthesized expression evaluates to one number and one variable.

This process forms the basis for a recursive descent parser, which is basically a set of mutually recursive functions that work in a chain-like fashion. At each appropriate step, the parser can perform the specified operations in the algebraically correct sequence. To see how this process works, follow the parsing of the following input expression:

$$9/3-(100+56)$$

and perform the arithmetic operations at the right time:

Step 1.   Get first term: 9/3.

Step 2.   Get each factor and divide integers. That value is 3.

Step 3.   Get second term: (100+56). At this point, you must analyze the second expression recursively.

Step 4.   Get each factor and add. That value is 156.

Step 5.   Return from recursive call and subtract 156 from 3, which yields an answer of −153.

If you are a little confused at this point, don't worry. This is a complex concept that takes getting used to. There are two things to remember about this recursive view of expressions: first, the precedence of the operators is *implicit* in the way the production rules are defined; second, this method of parsing and evaluating expressions is similar to the way you would parse and evaluate without a computer.

A Simple Expression Parser

In the remainder of this chapter, two parsers are developed. The first one parses and evaluates only constant expressions—that is, expressions with no variables. This is the parser in its simplest form. The second parser includes the 26 variables A through Z.

Here is the entire simple version of the recursive descent parser for floating-point expressions:

```c
#include "stdlib.h"
#include "ctype.h"

#define DELIMITER  1
#define VARIABLE   2
#define NUMBER     3

extern char *prog;   /* holds expression to be analyzed */
char token[80];
char tok_type;

void get_exp(), level2(), level3(), level4(), level5();
void level6(), primitive(), get_token(), arith(), unary();
void serror(), putback();

/* entry point into the parser */
void get_exp(result)
float *result;
{
  get_token();
  if(!*token) {
    serror(2);
    return;
  }
  level2(result);

}

/* add or subtract two terms */
void level2(result)
float *result;
{
  register char  op;
  float hold;
```

```
  level3(result);
  while((op = *token) == '+' || op == '-') {
    get_token();
    level3(&hold);
    arith(op, result, &hold);
  }
}

/* multiply or divide two factors */
void level3(result)
float *result;
{
  register char  op;
  float hold;

  level4(result);
  while((op = *token) == '*' || op == '/' || op == '%') {
    get_token();
    level4(&hold);
    arith(op, result, &hold);
  }
}

/* process an exponent */
void level4(result)
float *result;
{
  float hold;

  level5(result);
  if(*token== '^') {
    get_token();
    level4(&hold);
    arith('^', result, &hold);
  }
}

/* unary + or - */
void level5(result)
float *result;
{
  register char  op;

  op = 0;
  if((tok_type == DELIMITER) && *token=='+' || *token == '-') {
    op = *token;
    get_token();
  }
  level6(result);
  if(op)
    unary(op, result);
}

/* parenthesized expression */
void level6(result)
float *result;
{
  if((*token == '(') && (tok_type == DELIMITER)) {
    get_token();
```

```
    level2(result);
    if(*token != ')')
      serror(1);
    get_token();
  }
  else
    primitive(result);
}

/* get actual value of a number */
void primitive(result)
float *result;
{

  if(tok_type==NUMBER) {
    *result=atof(token);
    get_token();
    return;
  }
  serror(0);  /* otherwise syntax error in expression */
}

/* perform the indicated arithmetic */
void arith(o, r, h)
char o;
float *r, *h;
{
  register float t, ex;

  switch(o) {
    case '-':
      *r = *r-*h;
      break;
    case '+':
      *r = *r+*h;
      break;
    case '*':
      *r = *r * *h;
      break;
    case '/':
      *r = (*r)/(*h);
      break;
    case '%':
      t = (*r)/(*h);
      *r = *r-(t*(*h));
      break;
    case '^':
      ex = *r;
      if(*h==0) {
        *r = 1;
        break;
      }
      for(t=*h-1; t>0; --t) *r=(*r) * ex;
      break;
  }
}

void unary(o, r)
char o;
float *r;
{
  if(o=='-') *r = -(*r);
}
```

```
/* return a token to its resting place */
void putback()
{
  char *t;
  t = token;
  for(; *t; t++) prog--;
}

/* display a syntax error */
void serror(error)
int error;
{
  static char *e[]= {
      "syntax error",
      "unbalanced parentheses",
      "no expression present"
        };
  printf("%s\n", e[error]);
}

void get_token()
{

  register char *temp;

  tok_type = 0;
  temp = token;

  while(isspace(*prog)) ++prog;   /* skip over white space */

  if(is_in(*prog, "+-*/%^=()")){
    tok_type = DELIMITER;
    *temp++ = *prog++;
    /* advance to next position */
  }
  else if(isalpha(*prog)) {
    while(!isdelim(*prog)) *temp++ = *prog++;
    tok_type = VARIABLE;
  }
  else if(isdigit(*prog)) {
    while(!isdelim(*prog)) *temp++ = *prog++;
    tok_type = NUMBER;
  }

  *temp = '\0';

}

/* return true if c is a delimiter */
isdelim(c)
char c;
{
  if(is_in(c, " +-/*%^=()") || c==9 || c=='\r' || c==0)
    return 1;
  return 0;
}

is_in(ch, s)
char ch, *s;
{
  while(*s) if(*s++==ch) return 1;
  return 0;
}
```

The parser as it is shown can accept the operators +, −, *, /, and %, as well as integer exponentiation (^), the unary minus, and parentheses. It has six levels and the **primitive( )** function, which returns the value of a number. Also included are routines **arith( )** and **unary( )** for performing the various arithmetic operations, as well as **get_token( )**. As discussed previously, the two globals **token** and **tok_type** return the next token and its type from the expression string. The **extern prog** is a pointer to the expression string.

A simple **main( )** function that demonstrates the use of the parser is shown here:

```
char *prog;
void get_exp();

main()   /* Parser driver program */
{
  float answer;
  char *p;

  p = (char *) malloc(100);
  if(!p) {
    printf("allocation failure\n");
    exit(1);
  }

   /* Process expressions until a blank line
      is entered.
   */
  do {
    prog = p;
    printf("enter expression: ");
    gets(prog);
    if(!*prog) break;
    get_exp(&answer);
    printf("answer is: %.2f\n", answer);
  } while(*p);
}
```

To understand exactly how the parser evaluates an expression, work through the following expression, which you can assume is pointed to by **prog**.

$$10-3*2$$

When **get_exp( )** (the entry routine into the parser) is called, it gets the first token and, if it is null, it prints the message **no expression present** and returns. If a token is present, then **level2( )** is called. (A **level1( )** will be added to the parser when the assignment operator is added, but it is not needed here.)

Now the token contains the number 10. The **level2()** function calls **level3()**, and **level3()** calls **level4()**, which in turn calls **level5()**. The **level5()** function checks to see if the token is a unary + or −; in this case it is not, so **level6()** is called. The **level6()** function either recursively calls **level2()** in the case of a parenthesized expression, or calls **primitive()** to find the value of the number.

Finally, when **primitive()** is executed and **result** contains the number 10, another token is retrieved, and the functions begin to return up the chain. The token is now the operator − and the functions return up to **level2()**.

The next step is very important. Because the token is −, it is saved, the parser gets the new token 3, and the descent down the chain begins again. Again, **primitive()** is entered, the number 3 is returned in **result**, and the token * is read. This causes a return back up the chain to **level3()**, where the final token 2 is read. At this point, the first arithmetic operation occurs with the multiplication of 2 and 3. This result is then returned to **level2()** and the subtraction is performed to yield an answer of 4. Although the process may seem complicated at first, you should work through some other examples to verify for yourself that it functions correctly every time.

You could use this parser as a desktop calculator, as illustrated by the sample driver program. You could also use it in a limited database. Before it could be used in a language or a sophisticated calculator, the parser would have to be able to handle variables, which is the subject of the next section.

Adding Variables to the Parser

All programming languages, many calculators, and spreadsheets use variables to store values for later use. The simple parser in the preceding section must be expanded to include variables before you can use it for this purpose. First, you need the variables themselves. The parser will only recognize the variables A through Z, although you could expand that if you wanted to. Each variable uses one array location in a 26-element array of **floats**. Therefore, you should add the following:

```
float vars[26]= {    /* 26 user variables, A-Z */
  0.0, 0.0, 0.0, 0.0, 0.0, 0.0, 0.0, 0.0, 0.0, 0.0,
  0.0, 0.0, 0.0, 0.0, 0.0, 0.0, 0.0, 0.0, 0.0, 0.0,
  0.0, 0.0, 0.0, 0.0, 0.0, 0.0
};
```

As you can see, the variables are initialized to 0 as a courtesy to the user.

You also need a routine to look up the value of a given variable. Because you are using the letters A through Z, you can easily index the array **vars** by subtracting the ASCII value for "A" from the variable name. The **find_var()** function is shown here:

```
float find_var(s)
char *s;
{
  if(!isalpha(*s)){
    serror(1);
    return 0;
  }
  return vars[toupper(*token)-'A'];
}
```

As written, this function actually accepts long variable names, but only the first letter is significant. You may modify this feature to fit your needs.

You must also modify the **primitive()** function to handle both numbers and variables. The new version is shown here:

```
void primitive(result)
float *result;
{

  switch(tok_type) {
  case VARIABLE:
    *result=find_var(token);
    get_token();
    return;
  case NUMBER:
    *result=atof(token);
    get_token();
    return;
  default:
    serror(0);
  }
}
```

Technically, this is all you need for the parser to use variables correctly; however, there is no way for these variables to be assigned values. Often you can assign variables outside the parser, but since it is possible to treat the = as an assignment operator, there are many ways to make it part of the parser. One method is to add a **level1()** to the parser, as shown here:

```
/* process an assignment */
void level1(result)
float *result;
```

```
{
  float hold;
  int slot,ttok_type;
  char temp_token[80];

  if(tok_type==VARIABLE) {
    /* save old token */
    strcpy(temp_token, token);
    ttok_type = tok_type;

    slot = toupper(*token)-'A';
    get_token();
    if(*token != '=') {
      putback(); /* return current token */
      /* restore old token ~ not assignment */
      strcpy(token, temp_token);
      tok_type = ttok_type;
    }
    else {
      get_token(); /* get next part of exp */
      level2(result);
      vars[slot] = *result;
      return;
    }
  }

  level2(result);
}
```

As you can see, the function must look ahead to determine whether an assignment is actually being made. This is because a variable name always precedes an assignment, but not every variable name implies an assignment expression. That is, the parser will accept "A=100" as an assignment, but is also smart enough to know that "A/10" is an expression.

Here is the entire enhanced parser:

```
/* recursive descent parser for floating point expressions
   which may include variables */
#include "math.h"
#include "ctype.h"

#define DELIMITER  1
#define VARIABLE   2
#define NUMBER     3

extern char *prog;  /* holds expression to be analyzed */
char token[80];
char tok_type;

float vars[26]= {     /* 26 user variables, A-Z */
  0.0, 0.0, 0.0, 0.0, 0.0, 0.0, 0.0, 0.0, 0.0, 0.0,
  0.0, 0.0, 0.0, 0.0, 0.0, 0.0, 0.0, 0.0, 0.0, 0.0,
  0.0, 0.0, 0.0, 0.0, 0.0, 0.0
};
```

```
void get_exp(),level2(), level3(), level4(), level5();
void level6(), primitive(), get_token(), arith(), unary();
void serror(), putback(), level1();

float find_var();

/* entry point into parser */
void get_exp(result)
float *result;
{
  get_token();
  if(!*token) {
    serror(2);
    return;
  }
  level1(result);

}

/* process an assignment statement */
void level1(result)
float *result;
{
  float hold;
  int slot, ttok_type;
  char temp_token[80];

  if(tok_type==VARIABLE) {
    /* save old token */
    strcpy(temp_token, token);
    ttok_type=tok_type;

    slot = toupper(*token)-'A';
    get_token();
    if(*token != '=') {
      putback();  /* return current token */
      /* restore old token - not assignment */
      strcpy(token, temp_token);
      tok_type = ttok_type;
    }
    else {
      get_token();  /* get next part of exp */
      level2(result);
      vars[slot] = *result;
      return;
    }
  }

  level2(result);

}

/*  add or subtract two terms */
void level2(result)
float *result;
{
  register char  op;
  float hold;
```

```
    level3(result);
    while((op = *token) == '+' || op == '-') {
      get_token();
      level3(&hold);
      arith(op, result, &hold);
    }
}

/* multiply or divide two factors */
void level3(result)
float *result;
{
  register char  op;
  float hold;

  level4(result);
  while((op = *token) == '*' || op == '/' || op == '%') {
    get_token();
    level4(&hold);
    arith(op, result, &hold);
  }
}

/* process integer exponent */
void level4(result)
float *result;
{
  float hold;
  level5(result);
  if(*token== '^') {
    get_token();
    level4(&hold);
    arith('^', result, &hold);
  }
}

/* unary + or - */
void level5(result)
float *result;
{
  register char  op;

  op = 0;
  if((tok_type==DELIMITER) && *token=='+' || *token=='-') {
    op = *token;
    get_token();
  }
  level6(result);
  if(op)
    unary(op, result);
}

/* process parenthesized expression */
void level6(result)
float *result;
{
  if((*token == '(') && (tok_type == DELIMITER)) {
    get_token();
```

```
      level1(result);
      if(*token != ')')
        serror(1);
      get_token();
  }
  else
    primitive(result);
}

/* find value of number or variable */
void primitive(result)
float *result;
{

  switch(tok_type) {
  case VARIABLE:
    *result = find_var(token);
    get_token();
    return;
  case NUMBER:
    *result = atof(token);
    get_token();
    return;
  default:
    serror(0);
  }
}

/* perform the specified arithmetic */
void arith(o, r, h)
char o;
float *r, *h;
{
  register int t, ex;

  switch(o) {
    case '-':
      *r = *r-*h;
      break;
    case '+':
      *r = *r+*h;
      break;
    case '*':
      *r = *r * *h;
      break;
    case '/':
      *r = (*r)/(*h);
      break;
    case '%':
      t = (*r)/(*h);
      *r = *r-(t*(*h));
      break;
    case '^':
      ex = *r;
      if(*h==0) {
        *r = 1;
        break;
```

```
      }
      for(t=*h-1; t>0; --t) *r = (*r) * ex;
      break;
   }
}


void unary(o, r)
char o;
float *r;
{
  if(o=='-') *r = -(*r);
}

/* return a token to its resting place */
void putback()
{

  char *t;

  t = token;
  for(; *t; t++) prog--;
}


/* find the value of a variable */
float find_var(s)
char *s;
{
  if(!isalpha(*s)){
    serror(1);
    return 0;
  }
  return vars[toupper(*token)-'A'];
}

/* display an error message */
void serror(error)
int error;
{
  static char *e[]= {
      "syntax error",
      "unbalanced parentheses",
      "no expression present"
        };
  printf("%s\n", e[error]);
}

/* get a token */
void get_token()
{

  register char *temp;

  tok_type = 0;
  temp = token;

  while(isspace(*prog)) ++prog;    /* skip over white space */
```

```
    if(is_in(*prog, "+-*/%^=()")){
      tok_type = DELIMITER;
      *temp++ = *prog++;
      /* advance to next position */
    }
    else if(isalpha(*prog)) {
      while(!isdelim(*prog)) *temp++ = *prog++;
      tok_type = VARIABLE;
    }
    else if(isdigit(*prog)) {
      while(!isdelim(*prog)) *temp++ = *prog++;
      tok_type = NUMBER;
    }

    *temp = '\0';

}

/* return true if c is a delimiter */
isdelim(c)
char c;
{
   if(is_in(c, " +-/*%^=()") || c==9 || c=='\r' || c==0)
     return 1;
   return 0;
}

is_in(ch, s)
char ch, *s;
{
   while(*s) if(*s++==ch) return 1;
   return 0;
}
```

You may still use the same simple **main( )** function that you did for the simple parser. With the enhanced parser, you can now enter expressions like

$$A = 10/4$$
$$A - B$$
$$C - A*(F-21)$$

Syntax Checking in a Recursive Descent Parser

In expression parsing, a *syntax error* is a situation in which the input expression does not conform to the strict rules required by the parser. Usually this is caused by human error—most commonly by typing mistakes. For example, the following expressions will not be parsed correctly by the parsers in this chapter:

$$10**8$$
$$(10-5)*9)$$
$$/8$$

The first expression has two operators in a row; the second has unbalanced parentheses; and the last has a division sign starting an expression. None of these conditions are allowed by the parsers. Because syntax errors can cause the parser to give erroneous results, it is necessary to guard against them.

As you have studied the code to the parsers, you have probably noticed the **serror( )** function, which is called in certain situations. Unlike many other parsers, the recursive descent method makes syntax checking easy because, for the most part, syntax errors occur in either **primitive( )**, **find—var( )**, or **level6( )**, where parentheses are checked. The syntax checking as it now stands has only one problem: the entire parser is not aborted on syntax error. This can cause multiple error messages to be generated.

The best way to implement **serror( )** is to have it execute a **longjmp( )** routine. Turbo C comes with a pair of companion functions called **setjmp( )** and **longjmp( )**. The effect of these two functions is to allow a program branch to a *different* function. Therefore, in **serror( )** you would execute a **longjmp( )** to some safe point in your program outside the parser.

If you leave the code the way it is, all that will happen is that multiple syntax error messages may be issued. This could be an annoyance in some situations, but a blessing in others because multiple errors will be caught. Generally, however, you will want to enhance the syntax checking before using it in commercial programs.

Converting Turbo
Pascal to Turbo C

CHAPTER 11

Why would anyone want to convert programs written in Turbo Pascal into Turbo C? The reasons might be because many great Turbo Pascal programs already are written and many long-time Turbo Pascal users who are moving up to Turbo C want to bring their existing code along. Whatever the reasons, the task of translating Turbo Pascal programs into Turbo C is fairly easy once you know a few tricks. As presented later in this chapter, it also is possible to use a simple computer program to assist you in your efforts.

The Turbo C user manual contains an excellent chapter that focuses on helping Turbo Pascal users move to Turbo C. It examines many of the specific differences between the languages. If you haven't read this section of the manual, you might want to do so before continuing. In the discussion that follows, the focus is on the actual translation process—the "how to" of translation.

Structured, but Different

Turbo Pascal and Turbo C have many similarities, especially in their control structures and use of standalone subroutines with local variables. These similarities make it possible to perform a large number of one-to-one translations. Often you can simply substitute the equivalent Turbo C keyword or function name for the keyword or function in Turbo Pascal. Because of this substitution potential, it is possible to use the computer to assist with the translation process.

Even though Turbo Pascal and Turbo C are similar, you should keep in mind two major differences between them. First, Turbo Pascal is much more restrictive and, in some ways, more limited than Turbo C. For example, Turbo Pascal makes it difficult to write system-level programs because its strong type-checking does not allow the various type conversions usually needed. Second, and more important, Turbo Pascal is formally *block-structured*, whereas C is not. The term "block structured" refers to the ability of a language to create logically connected units of code that can be referenced as one block. It also means that procedures can have other procedures (known only to the outer procedure) nested inside. Although C is commonly referred to as block-structured because it allows the easy creation of blocks of code, it does not allow functions to be defined inside other functions. For example, the following Turbo Pascal code is valid:

```
procedure A;
  var x:integer;

  procedure B;
  begin
    writeln('inside proc b');
  end;

begin
  writeln('starting A');
  B;
end;
```

As you can see, **procedure B** is defined inside of **procedure A**. This means that **procedure B** is known only to **procedure A** and may only be used by **procedure A**. Outside of **procedure A**, another **procedure B** could be defined without conflict. The same code translated into C would have to have two functions. They would be the following:

```
A()
{
  printf("starting A\n");
  B();
}

B()
{
  printf("inside function B\n");
}
```

Also, because **B()** is no longer shielded by **A()**, you must make sure that there are no other functions called **B()** anywhere else in the program.

Another difference between Turbo Pascal and C is that all Turbo Pascal variables, functions, and procedures must be declared before they are used. This means that in Turbo Pascal, forward references are not allowed without the **forward** statement. In C, all variables must be declared before they are used, but functions may be referenced before they are declared. For example, the **sum** procedure must be declared as **forward** in this Turbo Pascal program:

```
program sample;

procedure sum(a,b: integer); forward;

procedure add;
var
  i, j: integer;
begin
  writeln('enter two numbers');
  readln(i); readln(j);
  sum(i,j);
end;

procedure sum(a, b: integer);
begin
  writeln(a+b);
end;

begin
  add;
end.
```

In Turbo C, this program will look like this:

```
main()
{
  add();
}
```

```
add()
{
  int i, j;

  printf("enter two numbers\n");
  scanf("%d%d", &i, &j);
  sum(i, j);
}

sum(a, b)
int a, b;
{
  printf("%d", a+b);
}
```

However, it is important to remember that in C you have to declare a function prior to calling it when the function returns a type other than integer. Also, you may use function prototypes in C to cause the compiler to check the types of the arguments to a function against the types of the parameters. This strong type checking is optional in Turbo C, but it is required in Turbo Pascal.

An Identifier Comparison
Between Turbo Pascal
and Turbo C

Consider how some common Turbo Pascal statements compare to Turbo C statements. Table 11-1 shows a comparison between Turbo Pascal keywords and Turbo C keywords and operators. Many of the Turbo Pascal keywords have no Turbo C equivalent. This is because Turbo Pascal uses keywords where Turbo C uses operators to accomplish the same thing. Sometimes, Turbo Pascal is simply wordier than Turbo C. (The Turbo C user manual contains a complete cross-reference of all Turbo Pascal/Turbo C identifiers.)

In addition to the keywords, Turbo Pascal has several built-in *standard identifiers* that can be used directly in a program. These identifiers may be functions (**writeln**, for example), or global variables (such as **MaxInt**), which are used to hold information about the state of the system. Turbo Pascal uses

Table 11-1.   Turbo Pascal Keywords Compared to C Keywords

Turbo Pascal	C
and	&&
array	
begin	{
case	switch
const	const
div	/ (using integers)
do	
downto	
else	else
end	}
file	
forward	extern (on occasion)
for	for
function	
goto	goto
if	if
in	
label	
mod	%
nil	(sometimes \0)
not	!
of	
or	‖
packed	
procedure	
program	
record	struct
repeat	do
set	
then	
type	typedef
to	
until	while (as in do/while)
var	
while	while
with	

Table 11-2. Some Turbo Pascal Standard Identifiers and Turbo C Equivalents

Turbo Pascal	C
boolean	char or integer
byte	char
char	char
EOF	EOF (in stdio library)
false	0
flush	flush() (in stdio library)
integer	int
read	scanf() and others
real	float
true	any non-zero value
write	printf()

Table 11-3. Turbo Pascal and C Operators

Turbo Pascal	C	Meaning
+	+	addition
−	−	subtraction
*	*	multiplication
/	/	division
div	/	integer division
mod	%	modulus
:=	=	assignment
=	==	equals as a condition
<	<	less than
>	>	greater than
>=	>=	greater than or equal
<=	<=	less than or equal
<>	!=	not equal

standard identifiers to specify data types as in **real, integer, boolean,** and **char**. Table 11-2 shows several of the more common Turbo Pascal standard identifiers with their C equivalents. In addition to those shown, a number of Turbo Pascal's built-in library functions have equivalents in Turbo C.

In addition to the keywords, built-in functions, and variables, Turbo Pascal differs from Turbo C in its operators. Table 11-3 shows the Turbo Pascal operators and the Turbo C equivalents.

Converting Turbo Pascal Loops into C Loops

Because program control loops are fundamental to most programs, consider how loops in Turbo Pascal compare to loops in Turbo C. Turbo Pascal has three built-in loops: **for, while,** and **repeat-until**. Turbo C has corresponding loops for each of these.

The Turbo Pascal **for** has the general form

for <initial value> to <target value> do statement;

The Turbo Pascal **for** is much more limited than the Turbo C **for** because it does not allow increments other than 1 (or −1 if the **downto** is used). Unlike the flexible design in C, the loop condition in Turbo Pascal is rigidly tied to the counting mechanism. However, these differences are minor when translating from Turbo Pascal into C because the Turbo Pascal **for** is simply a subset of **for** in Turbo C. For example,

```
for x:=10 to 100 do writeln(x);
```

can be translated into C as

```
for(x=10;x<=100;++x) printf("%d\n",x);
```

The Turbo Pascal **while** and the Turbo C **while** are virtually the same.

However, the Turbo Pascal **repeat-until** and the Turbo C **do-while** require the use of different keywords. Also, the loop test condition must be "reversed" because the Turbo Pascal **until** implies that a loop runs *until* something *becomes* true, whereas the Turbo C **do-while** loops *while* the loop condition *is* true. A sample translation of both these types of loops is shown here:

```
Turbo Pascal                Turbo C

while x<5 do                while(x<5)
begin                       {
   writeln(x);                 printf("%d\n",x);
   read(x);                     x=getnum();
end;                        }

repeat                      do {
   read(x);                    x=getnum();
   writeln(x);                 printf("%d\n",x);
until x>5;                  } while(x<=5);
```

Remember to watch out for the **repeat-until** to **do-while** translation. You must reverse the sense of the test condition.

The **case** *and* **if** *Statements*

For the most part you can directly translate the Pascal **case** statement into the C **switch** statement. For example, these two fragments are functionally equivalent:

```
Turbo Pascal                Turbo C

case choice of              switch(choice) {
  'E': enter;                  case 'E': enter();
                                 break;
  'D': display;               case 'D': display();
                                 break;
  'Q': quit;                  case 'Q': quit();
end;                        }
```

The only time you will have problems is when the **case** statement uses a range. The C **switch** statement cannot accept a range. For example, the following **case** statement cannot be directly translated into a C **switch** statement:

```
case time of
  0..6: sleep;
  7..8: getready;
  9..17: work;
  18..20: rest;
  21..24: sleep;
end;
```

To translate this sort of statement you must use a series of **if** statements.

To translate Turbo Pascal **if** statements into Turbo C **if** statements is straightforward and no exceptions will occur.

Records Versus Structures

Aside from variant records, you should have no trouble translating a Turbo Pascal **record** into a Turbo C structure. To translate a variant record into a structure requires you first to create a union that will contain the variant part of the record and then to make this union an element of the structure. For example, this variant record

```
type
  PayType = (salaried, hourly, LaidOff);

  employee = record
    name: string[40];
    age: integer;
    case PayMethod: PayType of
      salaried: (MonthyWage: real);
      hourly: (HourlyRate: real);
      LaidOff: (NoWage: boolean);
  end;
```

would be translated into Turbo C like this:

```
union PayMethod {
  float MonthyWage, HourlyWage;
  char NoWage;
};

enum PayType {Hourly, Monthy, InActive};

struct employee {
  char name[40];
  int age;
  enum PayType method;
  union PayMethod Pay;
}
```

Any program using this structure must manually set the **method** field in accordance with what is actually in the **pay** union.

Variant records are not considered good programming practice because of the high likelihood for error, and it is best to avoid using them.

A Sample Translation

To give you the flavor of the translation process, convert the following simple Turbo Pascal program into Turbo C:

```
program test (input,output);
var qwerty: real;

procedure func2 (x: integer);
begin
      writeln(x*2);
end;

function func1 (w: real): real;
begin
      func1:=w/3.1415;
      qwerty:=23.34
end;

begin
      qwerty:=0;
      writeln(qwerty);
      writeln('hello there');
      func2(25);
      writeln(func1(10));
      writeln(qwerty:2:4);
end.
```

The Turbo Pascal program has one function and one procedure declared. Since functions and procedures are the same in C, do not be concerned with the difference, except to return the value properly. Therefore, the **func2** procedure becomes the following:

```
func2(x)
int x;
{
  printf("%d", x*2);
}
```

The **func1** function becomes

```
float func1(w)
float w;
{
   qwerty=23.34;
   return w/3.1415;
}
```

Notice that because **func1( )** is returning a **float**, you must explicitly declare it by placing the type declaration **float** in front of the name **func1**.

Next, the **program** code (which starts with the first **begin** that is not inside another function or procedure) must be converted into the **main( )** function. It becomes

```
main()
{
   qwerty=0;
   printf("%f",qwerty);
   printf("hello there\n");
   func2(25);
   printf("%f\n",func1(10));
   printf("%2.4f\n",qwerty):
}
```

The last thing you must do is declare the global variable **qwerty** as a **float**. After you do this and put the pieces together, you have the program translated into Turbo C as shown here:

```
float qwerty;

main()
{
   qwerty=0;
   printf("%f",qwerty);
   printf("hello there\n");
   func2(25);
   printf("%f\n",func1(10));
   printf("%2.4f\n",qwerty):
}

func2(x)
int x;
{
   printf("%d", x*2);
}

float func1(w)
float w;
{
   qwerty=23.34;
   return w/3.1415;
}
```

Using the Computer to Help Convert Turbo Pascal to C

You can construct a computer program that accepts source code in one language and outputs it in another. The best way to do this is to actually implement a complete language parser for the source language. Instead of generating code, however, the program outputs the destination language in source form. Occasionally you can find advertisements for such products in computer magazines, and their prices reflect the complexity of the task. To help you in your conversion efforts, you can use a simple program to perform only some of the simpler translations. This program can be thought of as "computer assist" and can make conversion jobs easier.

The basic idea behind a computer assist translator is that it will accept a program in the source language as input and automatically perform the one-to-one conversions into the destination language, leaving the more difficult conversion up to you. For example, in Turbo Pascal, to assign **count** the value of 10, you would write the following:

```
count:=10;
```

In Turbo C, the statement is the same, except without a colon. The computer assist program can change the ":=" assignment statement in Turbo Pascal to the "=" for use with Turbo C. But the ways Turbo Pascal and C access disk files are different, and there is no easy way to automatically perform such a conversion. The translations that cannot be done easily are left to you.

The first thing the translator needs is a function that returns a token at a time from the input file. The **get__token( )** function developed in Chapter 10 can be modified for this use and is shown here:

```
get_token()
{
  register char *temp;

  tok_type = 0; tok = 0;
  temp = token;

  if(*prog=='\n') {
    *temp++ = '\r';
    *temp++ = '\n';
```

```
  *temp = '\0';
  prog++;
  tok_type = DELIM;
  return;
}

if(*prog=='\0') {
  *temp = '\0';
  tok_type = DELIM;
  return;
}
while(isspace(*prog)) ++prog;   /* skip over white space */

/* relational equals */
if(*prog=='=') {
  prog++;
  strcpy(token, "==");
  tok_type = OP;
  return;
}

/* assignment */
if(*prog==':') {
  prog++;
  if(*prog=='=')
  {
    *temp++ = '=';
    prog++;
  }
  else *temp++ = ':';

  *temp = '\0';
  tok_type = OP;
  return;
}

/* strings */
if(is_in(*prog, "'")) {
  *temp++ = '"';  prog++;
  while(!is_in(*prog, "'")) *temp++ = *prog++;
  *temp = '"'; temp++; *temp = '\0'; prog++;
  tok_type = STRING;
  return;
}

/* other operators  */
if(is_in(*prog, "+-*;.,/^%()")){
  *temp = *prog;
  prog++; /* advance to next position */
  if(*temp=='.') *temp = ' ';
  temp++;
  *temp = '\0';
  tok_type = OP;
  return;
}

/* variables */
if(isalpha(*prog)) {
  while(isalpha(*prog)) *temp++ = *prog++;
  *temp = '\0';
```

```
   tok_type = IDENTIFIER;
   return;
}

/* numbers */
if(isdigit(*prog)) {
  while(!isdelim(*prog)) *temp++ = *prog++;
  tok_type = NUMBER;
  *temp = '\0';
  return;
}
prog++;  /* unknown character */
}
```

The Turbo Pascal assignment ":=" is converted into Turbo C "=", and the "=" is converted into its C equivalent "==" inside **get__token( )**. This conversion simplifies the coding of other parts of the program, as you will see.

The second important routine is the one that translates Turbo Pascal keywords and some functions into their C counterparts. The **translate( )** shown here uses the two-dimensional array **trans** to look up Turbo Pascal identifiers, and then return their Turbo C counterparts:

```
char * trans[][2] = {
  "and", "&&",
  "begin", "{",
  "case", "switch",
  "div", "/",
  "do", "do",
  "else", "else",
  "end", "}",
  "forward", "extern",
  "for", "for",
  "function", "\n",
  "goto", "goto",
  "if", "if",
  "then", " ",
  "mod", "%",
  "nil", "'\0'",
  "not", "!",
  "procedure", "\n",
  "record", "struct",
  "repeat", "do",
  "until", " while",
  "while", "while",
  "writeln", "printf",
  "read", "scanf",
  "readln", "scanf",
  "write", "printf",
  "real", "float",
  "integer", "int",
  "char", "char",
  "", ""
};
```

```
/* translate Turbo Pascal indentifiers into Turbo C */
translate(s)
char *s;
{
  register int i;

  for(i=0; *trans[i][0]; i++)
    if(!strcmp(s, trans[i][0])) {
      strcpy(s, trans[i][1]);
      return;
    }
}
```

You can easily add new identifiers to the list to expand what the program translates. An improved version of this function requires a sorted list of identifiers in **trans** and then uses a binary search to find the proper entry. If you try to implement this improvement yourself, notice that some words (such as **program**) have no equivalent in C. In this case, a newline is substituted. The reason a null string is not used is that it is reserved to indicate the end of the file.

The entire translation program is shown here:

```
/* computer assisted Turbo Pascal to C converter */

#include "stdio.h"
#include "ctype.h"

#define OP        1
#define IDENTIFIER 2
#define VAR       3
#define NUMBER    4
#define DELIM     5
#define STRING    6

char token[80];
int tok_type;
int tok;

char s[10000];  /* holds source file */
char *prog;

char * trans[][2] = {
  "and", "&&",
  "begin", "{",
  "case", "switch",
  "div", "/",
  "do", "do",
  "else", "else",
  "end", "}",
  "forward", "extern",
  "for", "for",
  "function", "\n",
```

```
     "goto", "goto",
     "if", "if",
     "then", " ",
     "mod", "%",
     "nil", "'\0'",
     "not", "!",
     "procedure", "\n",
     "record", "struct",
     "repeat", "do",
     "until", " while",
     "while", "while",
     "writeln", "printf",
     "read", "scanf",
     "readln", "scanf",
     "write", "printf",
     "real", "float",
     "integer", "int",
     "char", "char",
     "",""
};

main(argc, argv)
int argc;
char *argv[];
{
   FILE *fp1, *fp2;
   char *p;
   int indent=0, i;

   prog = s;

   if(argc!=3) {
     printf("usage: input output");
     exit(1);
   }

   if((fp1=fopen(argv[1], "r"))==0) {
     printf("cannot open input file\n");
     exit(1);
   }

   if((fp2=fopen(argv[2], "w"))==0) {
     printf("cannot open output file\n");
     exit(1);
   }

   while((*prog=getc(fp1))!=EOF)
     prog++; /* read in source */

   *prog = '\0';
   prog = s;

   for(;;) {
     get_token();
     if(!*token) break;  /* end of input file */
     p = token;
     /* if token is an indentifier then translate it */
     if(tok_type==IDENTIFIER) translate(token);
```

```
      while(*p) putc(*p++, fp2); /* write it */
      /* put a space between tokens */
      if(*token!='\r') putc(' ', fp2);

      /* indent code to proper level */
      if(*token=='\r') {
        for(i=0; i<indent; i++) {
          putc(' ', fp2);
          putc(' ', fp2);
        }
      }

      if(*token=='}') indent--;
      if(*token=='{') indent++;
    }
    fclose(fp1); fclose(fp2);
  }
get_token()
{

    register char *temp;

    tok_type = 0; tok = 0;
    temp = token;

    if(*prog=='\n') {
      *temp++ = '\r';
      *temp++ = '\n';
      *temp = '\0';
      prog++;
      tok_type = DELIM;
      return;
    }

    if(*prog=='\0') {
      *temp = '\0';
      tok_type = DELIM;
      return;
    }
    while(isspace(*prog)) ++prog;  /* skip over white space */

    /* relational equals */
    if(*prog=='=') {
      prog++;
      strcpy(token, "==");
      tok_type = OP;
      return;
    }

    /* assignment */
    if(*prog==':') {
      prog++;
      if(*prog=='=')
      {
        *temp++ = '=';
        prog++;
      }
      else *temp++ = ':';
```

```
    *temp = '\0';
    tok_type = OP;
    return;
}

/* strings */
if(is_in(*prog, "'")) {
  *temp++ = '"';  prog++;
  while(!is_in(*prog, "'")) *temp++ = *prog++;
  *temp = '"'; temp++; *temp = '\0'; prog++;
  tok_type = STRING;
  return;

  }

  /* other operators  */
  if(is_in(*prog, "+-*;.,/^%()")){
    *temp = *prog;
    prog++; /* advance to next position */
    if(*temp=='.') *temp = ' ';
    temp++;
    *temp = '\0';
    tok_type = OP;
    return;
  }

  /* variables */
  if(isalpha(*prog)) {
    while(isalpha(*prog)) *temp++ = *prog++;
    *temp = '\0';
    tok_type = IDENTIFIER;
    return;
  }

  /* numbers */
  if(isdigit(*prog)) {
    while(!isdelim(*prog)) *temp++ = *prog++;
    tok_type = NUMBER;
    *temp = '\0';
    return;
  }
  prog++;  /* unknown character */
}

isdelim(c)
char c;
{
  if(is_in(c, " ;,+-/*^%()") || c==9 || c=='\r' || c==0)
    return 1;
  return 0;
}

is_in(ch, s)
char ch, *s;
{
  while(*s) if(*s++==ch) return 1;
  return 0;
}
```

```
/* translate Turbo Pascal indentifiers into Turbo C */
translate(s)
char *s;
{
  register int i;

  for(i=0; *trans[i][0]; i++)
    if(!strcmp(s, trans[i][0])) {
      strcpy(s, trans[i][1]);
      return;
    }
}
```

In essence, the conversion assist program from Turbo Pascal to Turbo C reads in the entire source code of the Turbo Pascal program, takes a token at a time from it, performs any translations it can, and writes out a Turbo C version. Except for a few operator changes, the standard **strcmp( )** function is used to detect translatable tokens and **strcpy( )** functions convert them to the proper Turbo C tokens. The program, as written, is case-sensitive and expects the Turbo Pascal identifiers to be in lowercase. You may want to alter this, depending upon how the Turbo Pascal code is written. The translation program automatically indents the translated code by two spaces for each new level.

To see how such a simple program could make life easier, consider the following Turbo Pascal program:

```
program test (input,output);

procedure f1(x: integer);
begin
    writeln(x*2);
end;

function f2 (w: real): real;
begin
    if w=100 then writeln('w is 100 inside f2');
    f2:= w/3.1415;
end;

begin
    writeln('hello there');
    f1(25);
    writeln(f2(10));
end.
```

After running this Turbo Pascal program through the translator program, the pseudo-C output is

```
test ( input , output ) ;
f1 ( x : int ) ;
{
  printf ( x * 2 ) ;
  } ;

f2 ( w : float ) : float ;
{
  if w == 100 printf ( " w is 100 inside f2 " ) ;
  f2 = w / 3.1415;
  } ;

{
  printf ( " hello there " ) ;
  f1 ( 25 ) ;
  printf ( f2 ( 10 ) ) ;
  }
```

As you can see, it is not C code, but considerable typing has been saved. All you need do is edit it a line at a time and correct the differences.

Final Thoughts on Translating

Although translating programs can be the most tedious of all programming tasks, it is also one of the most common. One of the best overall approaches is to first learn to use the program you are translating and to understand the way it works. Once you know how it operates, recoding it is easier because you know whether your new version is working correctly. Also, when you know the program you are translating, the job becomes more interesting because it is not just a simple symbol substitution process.

Efficiency, Porting, and Debugging

CHAPTER 12

The ability to write programs that use system resources efficiently, are error-free, and are easily transportable to a new computer is the mark of a professional programmer. It is also this ability that transforms computer science into the "art of computer science," because so few formal techniques are available to ensure success. This chapter presents some of the methods by which you may achieve efficiency, program debugging, and portability.

Efficiency

When it pertains to a computer program, the term *efficiency* refers to the program's speed of execution, its use of system resources, or both. System resources include RAM, disk space, printer paper, and basically anything that can be allocated and used up. Whether or not a program is efficient is sometimes a subjective judgment—it depends on the situation. Consider a

312 Advanced Turbo C

sorting program that uses 128K of RAM, requires 2 megabytes of disk space, and has an average run time of 7 hours. If this program is sorting only 100 addresses in a mailing-list database, then the program is not very efficient. However, if the program is sorting the New York telephone directory, then it is probably quite efficient.

Another consideration when you are concerned with efficiency is that optimizing one aspect of a program will often degrade another. For example, making a program execute faster often means making it bigger if you use in-line code to eliminate the overhead of a function call. Also, if you make a program smaller by replacing in-line code with function calls, you slow down the program execution. Making more efficient use of disk space by compacting the data often makes disk access slower.

This problem even affects the code generator of Turbo C. This is why Turbo C allows you to decide whether it will optimize for speed or for memory. These and other types of efficiency trade-offs can be frustrating—especially to the nonprogramming end-user, who cannot see why one thing should affect the other.

In light of these problems, you may wonder how efficiency can be discussed at all. There are also some programming practices that are always efficient—or at least more efficient than others. There are also a few techniques that make programs both faster and smaller.

The Increment and Decrement Operators

Discussions on the efficient use of C almost always start by considering the increment and decrement operators. Remember that the increment operator ++ increases its argument by one, and the decrement operator −− decreases its argument by one. The increment operator essentially replaces this type of assignment statement:

```
x = x + 1;
```

The decrement operator replaces assignment statements of this type:

```
x = x - 1;
```

Besides the obvious advantage of reducing the number of keystrokes, the increment and decrement operators have another glorious advantage: they execute faster and need less RAM than their statement counterparts. This is because of the way object code is generated by the compiler.

As is the case for most common microcomputers, it is often possible to increment or decrement a word of memory using explicit load and store instructions. For Turbo C to take advantage of this you use the ++ or −− operators. If you do not, unneeded load and store instructions will be used. For example, this program

```
main()
{
  int t=0;

  t++;

  t = t+1;
}
```

produces the following assembly language code when compiled with the −S (generate assembly listing) option. (The comment lines that begin with asterisks were added by the author.)

```
        name    test
_text   segment byte public 'code'
dgroup  group   _bss,_data
        assume  cs:_text,ds:dgroup,ss:dgroup
_text   ends
_data   segment word public 'data'
_d'     label   byte
_data   ends
_bss    segment word public 'bss'
_b'     label   byte
_bss    ends
_text   segment byte public 'code'
_main   proc    near
        push    si
; Line 3
; Line 4
; Line 5
        xor     si,si
; Line 6
; Line 7
; ***** This is the t++ statement
        inc     si
; Line 8
;***** This is the t=t+1 statement.  Notice that
;***** three instructions are used: one to load t into a
;***** register, one to increment it, and one to store it.
        mov     ax,si
        inc     ax
        mov     si,ax
; Line 9
'1:
```

```
          pop       si
          ret
_main     endp
_text     ends
_data     segment  word public 'data'
_s'       label     byte
_data     ends
_text     segment  byte public 'code'
          public    _main
_text     ends
          end
```

As you can see, both the load and store instructions are absent from the increment statement, which means smaller code that executes faster.

Using Register Variables

There are two reasons you should use **register** variables for loop control wherever possible. First, because the variable is held in an internal register of the CPU, its access time is short—much shorter than if it were held in memory. Second, the speed with which the critical loops of a program execute sets the pace for the overall speed of the program.

To see how the code differs between a **register** variable and a regular memory variable, the following program was compiled to an assembly language listing:

```
int j;

main()
{
  register int i;

  for(i=0; i<100 ;i++) ;

  for(j=0; j<100; j++) ;

}
```

The resulting assembly code file is shown here. The comments (lines beginning with the asterisks) were added by the author.

```
          name      test
_text     segment  byte public 'code'
dgroup    group    _bss,_data
          assume   cs:_text,ds:dgroup,ss:dgroup
_text     ends
_data     segment  word public 'data'
_d'       label     byte
```

```
_data    ends
_bss     segment word public 'bss'
_b'      label   byte
_bss     ends
_text    segment byte public 'code'
_main    proc    near
         push    si
; Line 4
; Line 5
; Line 6
;******* This is the initialization of the register
;******* controlled loop.  Notice that SI is cleared
;******* using a subtract instruction.
         xor     si,si
         jmp     short '5
'4:
'3:
;******* a register increment
         inc     si
'5:

;******* Only a register comparison is necessary
;******* to access SI's value.
         cmp     si,100
         jl      '4
'2:
; Line 7
;******* Here is the initialization of the memory
;******* controlled loop.  Notice that a memory access
;******* is required to clear the variable.
         mov     word ptr dgroup:_j,0
         jmp     short '9
'8:
'7:
;******* Here, a memory access increment is needed.
         inc     word ptr dgroup:_j
'9:
;******* Another memory access required to check the
;******* control variable's value.
         cmp     word ptr dgroup:_j,100
         jl      '8
'6:
; Line 8
'1:
         pop     si
         ret
_main    endp
_text    ends
_bss     segment word public 'bss'
         public  _j
_j       label   word
         db      2 dup (?)
_bss     ends
_data    segment word public 'data'
_s'      label   byte
_data    ends
_text    segment byte public 'code'
         public  _main
_text    ends
         end
```

To understand the time differences, assume an 8088 processor executes this program. The register-controlled loop uses the **inc si** instruction to increment the control variable. This requires only 2 system clock ticks. On the other hand, the memory-controlled loop must use **inc word ptr dgroup:＿j**, which requires 29 clock ticks — almost a 15-to-1 increase.

Turbo C automatically makes the first two integer variables in a function into **register** types, if no other **register** variables are present. This process is called a compiler *optimization* and is used to increase the overall speed of execution.

Because you can have only two register variables, it is important to choose the correct loops for use by the variables. In the following fragment, you would use **register** variables for the two inner loops, but not for the outer loop:

```
for(i=0; i<100; i++) {
  .
  .
  .
  for(j=0; j<1000; j++) {
    .
    .
    .
  }
  for(k=0; k<10; k++) ...;
}
```

You choose the inner loops because they will both be executed 100 times. This means that **j** will be accessed 100,000 times and **k** will be accessed 1000 times, while **i** is accessed only 100 times.

Pointers Versus Array Indexing

Another technique you can use that always produces both smaller and faster code is substituting pointer arithmetic for array indexing. Take a look at the following two code fragments, which both do the same thing:

```
array indexing          pointer arithmetic

                        p=array;
for(;;) {               for(;;) {
```

```
a=array[t++];            a=*(p++);
  •                        •
  •                        •
  •                        •
}                        }
```

With the pointer method, after **p** has been loaded with the address of **array**, perhaps in an index register (such as SI on the 8086 processor), only an increment must be performed each time the loop repeats. However, the array-index version forces the program to compute the array index based on the value of **t**—a more complex task. The disparity between array indexing and pointer arithmetic grows as multiple indexes are used. Each index requires its own sequence of instructions, whereas the pointer arithmetic equivalent can use simple addition.

As a precaution, you may want to use array indexes when the index is derived through a complex formula and when the use of pointer arithmetic would obscure the meaning of the program. It is usually better to degrade performance slightly than to sacrifice clarity.

Use of Functions

Always remember that the use of standalone functions with local variables forms the basis of structured programming. Functions are the building blocks of C programs, and they are one of C's strongest assets. Do not let anything that is discussed in this section be construed otherwise. Now that you have been warned, you should know a few aspects of C functions and their effects on the size and speed of your code.

First and foremost, Turbo C is a *stack-oriented language:* all local variables and parameters to functions use the stack for temporary storage. When a function is called, the return address of the calling routine is placed on the stack as well. This allows the subroutine to return to the location from which it was called. When a function returns, this address—as well as all local variables and parameters—must be removed from the stack. The process of pushing this information onto the stack is generally referred to as the *calling sequence* and the process of popping information off the stack is called the *returning sequence.* These sequences take time—sometimes quite a bit of time.

To understand how a function call can slow down your program, look at the two code fragments shown on the following page.

```
version 1                        version 2
for(x=1;x<100;++x) {             for(x=1;x<100;++x) {
  t=compute(x);                    t=abs(sin(q)/100/3.1416);
}                                }

float compute(q)
int q;
{
  return abs(sin(q)/100/3.1416);
}
```

Although each loop performs the same function, Version 2 is much faster because the overhead of the calling and returning sequences has been eliminated by using in-line code.

Consider another example.

```
main()
{
    int x;

    x=max(10,20);
}

max(a,b)
int a,b;
{
  return a>b ? a : b;
}
```

When this program is compiled using the −S option, it produces the assembly code listing shown here. The calling and return sequences are indicated by comments (lines beginning with asterisks) added by the author. As you can see, they amount to a sizable amount of the code in the program.

```
            name     test
  _text     segment  byte public 'code'
dgroup      group    _bss,_data
            assume   cs:_text,ds:dgroup,ss:dgroup
  _text     ends
  _data     segment  word public 'data'
  _d`       label    byte
  _data     ends
  _bss      segment  word public 'bss'
  _b`       label    byte
  _bss      ends
  _text     segment  byte public 'code'
  _main     proc     near
            push     bp
            mov      bp,sp
```

```
        dec     sp
        dec     sp
; Line 3
; Line 4
; Line 5
; **********************************************************
; ***** the calling sequence:
        mov     ax,20
        push    ax
        mov     ax,10
        push    ax
; **********************************************************
        call    near ptr _max
; **********************************************************
; ***** end of the returning sequence
        pop     cx
        pop     cx
; **********************************************************
        mov     word ptr [bp-2],ax
; Line 6
`1:
        mov     sp,bp
        pop     bp
        ret
_main   endp
_max    proc    near
; **********************************************************
; ***** more of the calling sequence
        push    bp
        mov     bp,sp
; **********************************************************
; Line 10
; Line 11
        mov     ax,word ptr [bp+6]
        cmp     word ptr [bp+4],ax
        jle     `4
        mov     ax,word ptr [bp+4]
        jmp     short `3
`4:
        mov     ax,word ptr [bp+6]
`3:
`2:
; Line 12
; **********************************************************
; ***** the returning sequence
        pop     bp
        ret
; **********************************************************
_max    endp
_text   ends
_data   segment word public 'data'
_s`     label   byte
_data   ends
_text   segment byte public 'code'
        public  _max
        public  _main
_text   ends
        end
```

Now, you may think you should write programs that have just a few large functions so they run quickly. In the majority of cases, however, the slight time differential will not be meaningful, and the loss of structure will be acute. But there is another problem. Replacing functions that are used by several routines with in-line code will make your program very large because the same code is duplicated several times. Keep in mind that subroutines were invented primarily as a way to make efficient use of memory. As a rule of thumb, making a program faster means making it bigger, while making it smaller means making it slower.

In the final analysis, it only makes sense to use in-line code instead of a function call when speed is of absolute priority. Otherwise, the liberal use of functions is definitely recommended.

Porting Programs

It is common for a program written on one machine to be transported to another computer with a different processor, operating system, or both. This process is called *porting* and can be either very easy or extremely hard, depending on the way the program was originally written. A program is *portable* if it can be easily ported. A program is not easily portable if it contains numerous *machine dependencies* —code fragments that will work only with one specific operating system or processor. Turbo C has been designed to allow the creation of portable code, but it still requires care and attention to detail to actually achieve that goal. This section examines a few specific problem areas and offers some solutions.

Using #*define*

Perhaps the simplest way to make programs portable is to make *every* system- or processor-dependent "magic number" into a #**define** macro-substitution directive. These "magic numbers" include buffer sizes for disk accesses, special screen and keyboard commands, memory allocation information, and anything else that has even the slightest possibility of changing when the program is ported. These defines will not only make the "magic numbers" obvious to the person doing the porting, but they also simplify editing; their values will have to be changed only once instead of throughout the program.

For example, here are two functions that use **fread()** and **fwrite()** to read and write information from a disk file:

```
f1()
{
  fwrite(buf,128,1,fp);
}

f2()
{
  fread(buf,128,1,fp);
}
```

The problem is that the buffer size, 128, is hard-coded into both the **fread()** and the **fwrite()** statements. This might be acceptable for one operating system, but less than optimal for another. A better way to code this function is shown here:

```
#define buf_size 128

f1()
{
  fwrite(buf,buf_size,1,fp);
}

f2()
{
  read(buf,buf_size,1,fp);
}
```

In this case, only the define would have to change and all references to **buf_size** would be automatically corrected. This version not only makes it easier to change, but it also avoids many editing errors. Remember that there will probably be many references to **buf_size** in a real program, so the gain in portability is often substantial.

Operating System Dependencies

Virtually all commercial programs have code in them that is specific to the operating system. For example, a spreadsheet program might make use of the IBM PC's video memory to allow fast switching between screens, or a graphics package may use special graphics commands that are only applicable to that operating system. Some operating-system dependencies are necessary for fast, commercially viable programs. However, there is no reason to hard-code any more dependencies than necessary.

As suggested earlier, disk file functions can sometimes contain implicit machine dependencies. The **fread()** and **fwrite()** functions found in the standard library, for example, can work with various buffer sizes, but an operating system may require an even multiple of some number to operate most efficiently. Therefore, a buffer size of 128 might be fine for CP/M 2.2 but may not be acceptable for MS-DOS. In this case, the buffer size should be defined, as discussed previously.

When you must use system calls to access the operating system, it is best to do them all through one master function so that you only have to change it to accommodate a new operating system and can leave the rest of the code intact. For example, if system calls were needed to clear the screen and clear to end-of-line, and to locate the cursor at an x,y coordinate, then you would create a master function like **op_sys_call()**, shown here:

```
void op_sys_call(op,x,y)
char op;
int x,y;
{
  switch(op) {
    case 1: clear_screen();
    break;
    case 2: clear_eol();
    break;
    case 3: goto_xy(x,y);
    break;
  }
}
```

Only the code that forms the actual functions would have to change, leaving a common interface intact.

Differences in Data Sizes

As you may know, the size of a word in a 16-bit processor is 16 bits and in a 32-bit processor it is 32 bits. Because the size of a word tends to be the size of an integer, never make assumptions about the size of a data type when writing portable code. Use **sizeof** whenever your program needs to know the length in bytes of something. For example, this function writes an integer to a disk file and works on any computer:

```
void write_int(i)
int i;
{
  fwrite(&i, sizeof(int), 1, stream);
}
```

However, sometimes it is not possible to create portable code even with **sizeof**. For example, this function, which swaps the bytes in an integer, works on an 8088-based computer but fails on a 68000. This function cannot be made portable because it is based upon the fact that integers in the 8088 are 2 bytes long, while integers in the 68000 are 4 bytes long.

```
void swap_bytes(x)
int *x;
{
  union sb {
    int t;
    unsigned char c[2];
  } swap;

  unsigned char temp;

  swap.t = *x;
  temp = swap.c[1];
  swap.c[1] = swap.c[0];
  swap.c[0] = temp;
  *x = swap.t;
}
```

Debugging

To paraphrase Thomas Edison, programming is 10% inspiration and 90% debugging. Good programmers are usually good debuggers. Certain types of bugs can occur easily while using C.

Order of Process Errors

When the increment and decrement operators are used in programs written in C, the order in which the operation takes place is affected by whether these operators precede or follow the variable. Consider the two statements at the top of the next page.

Version 1	*Version 2*
y=10;	y=10;
x=y++;	x=++y;

These two statements are not the same. The first one assigns the value of 10 to **x** and then increments **y**. The second increments **y** to 11 and then assigns the value 11 to **x**. Therefore, in Version 1, **x** contains 10; in Version 2, **x** contains 11. The rule is that increment and decrement operations occur before other operations if they precede the operand; otherwise, they occur afterward.

An order-of-process error usually occurs when changes are made to an existing statement. For example, you may enter the statement

```
x = *p++;
```

which assigns the value pointed to by **p** to **x** and then increments the pointer **p**. However, say that later you decide that **x** really needs the value pointed to by **p** squared. To do this you rewrite the statement as follows:

```
x = *p++ * (*p);
```

However, this version does not work, because **p** has already been incremented. The proper solution is to write

```
x = *p * (*p++);
```

Errors like this can be hard to find. There may be clues, such as loops that do not run correctly or routines that are off by one. If you have any doubt that a statement is correct, recode it in a form you are certain will work.

Pointer Problems

A common error in C programs is the misuse of pointers. Pointer problems fall into two general categories: misunderstanding of indirection and the pointer operators; and the accidental use of invalid pointers. To solve the first type of problem, you must understand the C language; to solve the second, you must always verify the validity of a pointer before you use it.

The following illustrates a typical pointer error that C programmers make:

```
#include "stdlib.h"

main()   /* this program is WRONG */
{
  char *p;

  *p = (char *) malloc(100); /* this line is wrong */

  gets(p);
  printf(p);

}
```

This program will most likely crash, probably taking with it the operating system. It will crash because the address returned by **malloc()** was not assigned to **p**, but to the memory location pointed to by **p**, which is completely unknown in this case. To correct this program, you must substitute

```
p = (char *) malloc(100); /* this is correct */
```

for the incorrect line.

The program has a second and more insidious error: there is no run-time check on the address returned by **malloc()**. Remember, if memory is exhausted, then **malloc()** will return null, which is never a valid pointer in C. The malfunction caused by this type of bug is difficult to find because it occurs rarely, only when an allocation request fails. Prevention is the best way to deal with this. Here is a corrected version of the program, which now includes a check for pointer validity:

```
#include "stdlib.h"

main()   /* this program is now correct */
{
  char *p;

  p = (char *) malloc(100); /* this is correct */

  if(p==NULL) {
    printf("out of memory\n");
    exit(1);
  }

  gets(p);
  printf(p);
}
```

"Wild" pointers are extremely difficult to track down. If you are making assignments to a pointer variable that does not contain a valid pointer address, your program may appear to function correctly sometimes but crash at other times. Statistically, the smaller your program, the more likely it will run correctly even with a stray pointer, because very little memory is in use. As your program grows, failures become more common, but as you try to debug you will be thinking about recent additions or changes to your program, not about pointer errors. Hence, you will probably look in the wrong spot for the bug.

One indication of a pointer problem is that errors tend to be erratic. Your program will work right one time and wrong another. Sometimes other variables will contain garbage for no explainable reason. If these problems occur, check your pointers. As a matter of procedure, you should check all pointers when bugs begin to occur.

Although pointers can be troublesome, they are also one of the most powerful and useful aspects of the C language, and they are worth whatever trouble they may cause. Make the effort early on to learn to use them correctly.

One final point to remember about pointers is that you must initialize them before they are used. Consider the following code fragment:

```
int *x;
*x = 100;
```

This will be a disaster because you do not know where **x** is pointing. Assigning a value to that unknown location is probably destroying something of value—such as other code or data for your program.

Redefining Functions

You can—but should not—call your functions by the same names as those in the C standard library. Most compilers will use your function over the one in the library. One of the worse occurrences of the redefinition problem is when a standard library function is redefined, but the standard function is *not* used directly in the program. Rather it is used indirectly by another standard function. Consider the following:

```
char text[1000];

main()
{
   int x;

   scanf("%d",&x);
      .
      .
      .
}

getc(p)   /* return char from array */
{
   return text[p];
}
   .
   .
   .
```

This program will not work with most compilers because **scanf()**, a standard C function, will probably call **getc()**, a standard C function redefined in the program. This problem can be difficult to find, because you have no clue you have created a side effect. It will simply seem that **scanf()** is not working correctly.

The only way to avoid such problems is never to give a function you have written the same name as one in the standard library. If you are not sure, append your initials to the start of the name, as in **hs—getc()** instead of **getc()**.

"One Off" Errors

By now you know that all C array indexes start at 0. A common error involves using a **for** loop to access the elements of an array. Consider the following program, which is supposed to initialize an array of 100 integers:

```
main()   /* this program will not work */
{

   int x, num[100];

   for(x=1; x<=100; ++x) num[x]=x;
}
```

The **for** loop in this program is wrong for two reasons. First, it does not initialize **num[0]**, the first element of array **num**. Second, it goes one past the end of the array; **num[99]** is the last element in the array and the loop runs to 100. The correct way to write this program is

```
main()  /* this is right */
{
   int x, num[100];

   for(x=0; x<100; ++x) num[x]=x;
}
```

Remember, an array of 100 has elements 0 through 99.

Boundary Errors

The Turbo C run-time environment and many standard library functions have very little or no run-time boundary checking. For example, it is possible to index an array beyond its dimensions. Consider the following program that is supposed to read a string from the keyboard and display it on the screen:

```
main()
{
   int var1;
   char s[10];
   int var2;

   var1 = 10;  var2 = 10;
   get_string(s);
   printf("%s %d %d", s, var1, var2);
}

get_string(string)
char *string;
{
   register int t;

   printf("enter twenty characters\n");
   for(t=0; t<20; ++t) {
     *s++ = getchar();
   }
}
```

Here there are no direct coding errors. However, an indirect error arises when **get_string()** is called with s. The s is declared to be 10 characters long, but **get_string()** will read 20 characters, causing s to be overwritten.

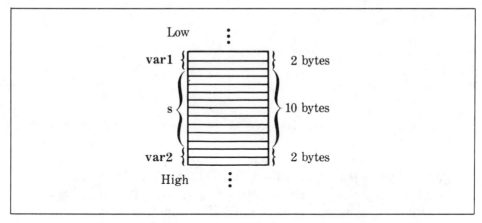

Figure 12-1. The variables **var1**, **var2**, and s in memory

The actual problem is that while s may display all 20 characters correctly, either **var1** or **var2** will not contain the correct value. Turbo C must allocate a region of memory for local variables from the stack. The variables **var1**, **var2**, and s will be located in memory as shown in Figure 12-1.

When s is overwritten, the additional information is placed into the area that is reserved for **var2**, destroying any previous contents. Therefore, instead of printing the number 10 for both integer variables, the program will display something else for the one destroyed by the overrun of s. This will cause you to look for the problem in the wrong place. Also, the return address of the function call in this specific instance may also be overwritten and cause a crash.

Function Declaration Omissions

Any time a function returns a value type other than integer, the function must be declared to do this inside any function that uses it. Consider the following program that multiplies two floating-point numbers together:

```
main() /* this is wrong */
{
  float x, y;

  scanf("%f%f", &x, &y);
  printf("%f", mul(x, y));
```

```
}

float mul(a, b)
float a, b;
{
  return a*b;
}
```

Although **main()** expects an integer value from **mul()**, **mul()** returns a floating-point number. You will get meaningless answers, because **main()** will only copy two bytes out of the eight needed for a **float**. Although the compiler will catch this error if these functions are both in the same file, it cannot catch the error if these functions are in separately compiled modules.

To correct this program, declare **mul()** in **main()**, as shown here:

```
main() /* this is correct */
{
  float x, y, mul();

  scanf("%f%f", &x, &y);
  printf("%f", mul(x, y));
}
float mul(a, b)
float a, b;
{
  return a*b;
}
```

Adding **mul()** to the **float** declaration list tells **main()** it should expect a floating point value to be returned from **mul()**.

Calling Argument Errors

You must be sure to match whatever type of argument a function expects with the type you give it. Remember, for instance, that **scanf()** expects to receive the *addresses* of its arguments, not their values. For example, this code is wrong:

```
int x;
char string[10];

scanf("%d%s", x, string);
```

This code is correct:

```
scanf("%d%s",&x,string);
```

Remember, strings already pass their addresses to functions, so you should not use the & operator on them.

If the formal parameters of a function are of type **float**, you must pass floating-point variables to the function. For example, the following program will not function correctly:

```
main() /* this program is wrong */
{
  int x, y;

  scanf("%d%d", &x, &y);
  printf("%d", div(x, y));
}

float div(a, b)
float a, b;
{
  return a/b;
}
```

You cannot use a floating-point function, such as **div()**, to return an integer value, and you cannot expect **div()** to operate correctly—it expects floating-point numbers, not integers. Remember that a cast can always be used to change one type to another if necessary. Turbo C may provide type checking for this type of situation if you use function prototypes.

Stack-Heap Collisions

A *stack-heap collision* occurs when the stack runs into the heap. When this occurs the program either completely dies or continues executing at a bizarre point. This second symptom is because data is accidentally being used as a return address. The worst thing about stack-heap collisions is that they generally occur without any warning and crash the program so completely that debugging code cannot execute. Another problem is that a stack-heap collision often appears to be a wild pointer and thus misleads you. The only piece of advice that can be offered is that most stack-heap collisions are caused by runaway, recursive functions. If your program uses recursion and you experience unexplainable failures, check the terminating conditions in your recursive functions.

General Debugging Theory

Everyone has a different approach to programming and debugging. However, some techniques have proved to be better than others. In the case of debugging, incremental testing is considered to be the least costly and most time-effective method, even though it can appear to slow the development process at first. To understand what incremental testing is, you must first understand what it is not.

In the early days of computers, programmers were taught to prepare their programs in advance, submit them for execution, and then interpret results. This process is called *batch programming*. It was necessary when computers were scarce, but it is seldom used today because there are many computers that support an interactive programming environment. Batch programming required programmers to expend an enormous amount of time and mental energy to develop a program—indeed, a painful experience. Because all testing had to be done in batch mode as well, it was very difficult to try all possible conditions in which a program could fail. This lack of thorough testing led to the pervasive "computer error" problems so common in many early computer installations.

Today batch programming is virtually extinct because it cannot support an interactive *incremental testing* environment, or the process of always having a working program. That is, very early in the development process an *operational unit* (a piece of working code) is established. As new code is added to this unit, the code is tested and debugged. In this way, the programmer can easily find errors, because the errors most likely will occur in the newly added code, or in the way that it interacts with the operational unit.

Debugging time can be computed according to the following formula:

$$DebugTime = (NumOfLines + X)^2$$

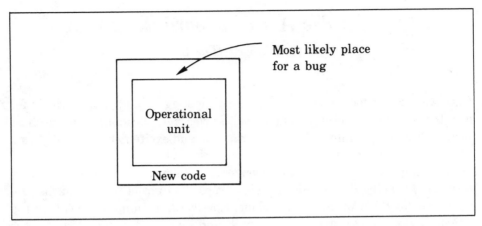

Figure 12-2.   Most likely location of a bug during incremental testing

where **NumOfLines** is the total number of lines of code in which a bug could occur and **X** is some programmer-dependent constant. As you can see, debugging time is a squared quantity. With incremental testing, it is possible to restrict the number of lines of code to only those that are newly added, or those not part of the operational unit. This situation is shown in Figure 12-2.

Incremental testing theory is generally based on probability and areas. As you know, *area* is a squared dimension. Therefore, as your program grows, there is an *n*-squared area in which you must search for bugs. While debugging, you as a programmer want the smallest possible area to deal with. Through incremental testing you can subtract the area already tested from the total area, thereby reducing the region that may contain a bug.

In large projects, several modules may have only mild interaction. In these cases, you may establish several operational units to allow concurrent development.

Incremental testing is important for two reasons. First, incremental testing greatly reduces debugging time because errors are easier to find. Second, incremental testing speeds up the development process because design errors can be caught early in the project before all the code is written. Incremental testing is simply the process of always having working code. As soon as it is possible to run a piece of your program, you should do so and completely test that section. As you add to the program, continue to test the new sections and test the way they connect to the known operational code. In this way you will be concentrating any possible bugs to a small area of code.

The Art of Program
Maintenance

Once a program has been written, tested, debugged, and judged ready for use, the program's development phase is over and the maintenance phase begins. Most programmers enjoy the glamour and excitement of developing a new program but try to avoid being the person who maintains the program because the maintenance phase never ends. When a program (even a very large one) is being developed, there is always the light at the end of the tunnel. Someday the program will be done. However, the maintenance phase is a daily grind of quirks, anomalies, errors, and bugs that never ends. For the maintenance programmer, the thrill of accomplishment is rarely felt. However, as bleak as it may seem, program maintenance can be one of the most challenging and rewarding tasks if approached correctly.

The maintenance programmer is in charge of correcting bugs and source-code protection.

Fixing Bugs

All nontrivial programs have bugs—one of the unprovable but irrefutable truths of computer science. Because all the easy bugs are found during the development stage, the bugs the maintenance programmer must find and fix are often obscure and only surface under devilishly complex (and difficult to re-create) circumstances.

There are basically three types of bugs: those that you will fix (Category I), those that you would like to fix (Category II), and those that you just will not worry about (Category III.)

Category I bugs crash the system, scribble on the disk, or destroy data. For example, the bug that causes a database program to occasionally destroy the database disk file simply must be fixed because it renders the program unusable.

Category II bugs are fixed only when no Category I bugs need to be fixed. An example is the bug that rarely causes a word processor to incorrectly reformat a paragraph. Nothing is lost, the program doesn't die, and the user will make a manual adjustment. For the most part, Category II bugs are annoyances to the user, but they can be worked around. These bugs should be fixed, and will be fixed, but they do not receive a high priority.

Category III bugs generally are nuisances, such as a word processor that always spits out an extra sheet of paper at the end of a print session. Another example might be when the program documentation says the program will work one way and it actually works a different way. These types of bugs are rarely fixed, not because they shouldn't be, but because there are always too many Category I and Category II bugs.

If you can organize the reported bugs into these three categories, you can budget your time accordingly.

Source-Code Protection

The maintenance programmer is often in charge of the program source code. Although most companies will place a copy of the source of the current version of the program in a bank box, it is usually out of date if ever needed. Generally, the code in the bank is viewed as the code of last resort. In actuality, the maintenance programmer is in charge of protecting and not losing the company's source code.

The most common period of program development during which source code is lost occurs during the bug-fixing process. For example, assume programmer A "fixes" a bug. Unknown to A, in the process an editing error is made that deletes five lines of code elsewhere in the file. Programmer A compiles the program and checks to see if the bug is fixed. The bug appears fixed, so programmer A copies the "fixed" source code from the work directory back into the storage directory. Now five lines of code are missing and the program definitely has a new bug. But before this is discovered, programmer B (whose job it is to backup the hard disk) copies the incorrect copy of the program onto an offsite storage disk. Now the old source code is nonexistent.

The only way to prevent this scenario is never to destroy old versions of the program. The real error (aside from sloppy editing) was that programmer B overwrote the offsite storage media.

Here is the way you must handle an evolving program's source code to prevent its loss. First, create three directories. The first directory contains the currently released version of the program. This directory is only updated when a new release is made. The second directory contains the latest stable, but unreleased, version of the program. The third directory contains the evolving code.

Second, perform offsite storage backups on a regular basis (perhaps weekly) and always use a new diskette (or tape). Keep on file all previous backups. In this way, the offsite storage never will be more than five days out of date if it is needed for a recovery.

Turbo C
Memory Models

A P P E N D I X   A

One of Turbo C's most confusing aspects is that you can compile a C program using six different memory models defined by the 8086 family of processors. On other types of processors, Turbo C may not have this ability. Each model organizes the computer's memory differently and governs the size of the code or the data, or both. Because the model you use has a profound effect on the way a program may access the system resources — especially memory — this appendix begins with an overview of the various memory models. It then develops a program that allows you to inspect and to change any part of the RAM in your system.

This appendix specifically addresses Turbo C on the 8086 family of processors. The discussion of the Turbo C memory models assumes that you know somewhat how the 8086 CPU operates. However, you can still understand the difference between the various memory models in a practical sense, even if you don't understand the underlying principles.

The 8086 Family
of Processors

Before you can understand the way the various memory models work, you need to understand how processors in the 8086 address memory. (For the rest of this appendix, the CPU referred to will be the 8086, but the information applies to all processors in this family, including 8088, 80186, 80286, and the 80386.)

The 8086 CPU contains 14 registers into which information is placed for processing or program control. The registers fall into the following four categories:

- General-purpose registers
- Base pointer and index registers
- Segment registers
- Special-purpose registers

All the registers in the 8086 CPU are 16 bits (2 bytes) wide.

The *general-purpose registers* are the "workhorse" registers of the CPU. Values are placed in these registers for processing, including arithmetic operations (such as adding or multiplying), comparisons (including equality, less than, and greater than), and branch (jump) instructions. Each of the general-purpose registers may be accessed in either of two ways: as a 16-bit register or as two 8-bit registers.

The *base pointer* and *index registers* are used to provide support for such things as relative addressing, the stack pointer, and block move instructions.

The *segment registers* are used to support the segmented memory scheme in the 8086. The CS register holds the current code segment, the DS holds the current data segment, the ES holds the extra segment, and the SS holds the stack segment. These segments are discussed in more detail later in this appendix.

Finally, the *special-purpose registers* are the flag register, which holds the state of the CPU, and the instruction pointer, which points to the next instruction for the CPU to execute.

Figure A-1 shows the layout of the 8086 registers.

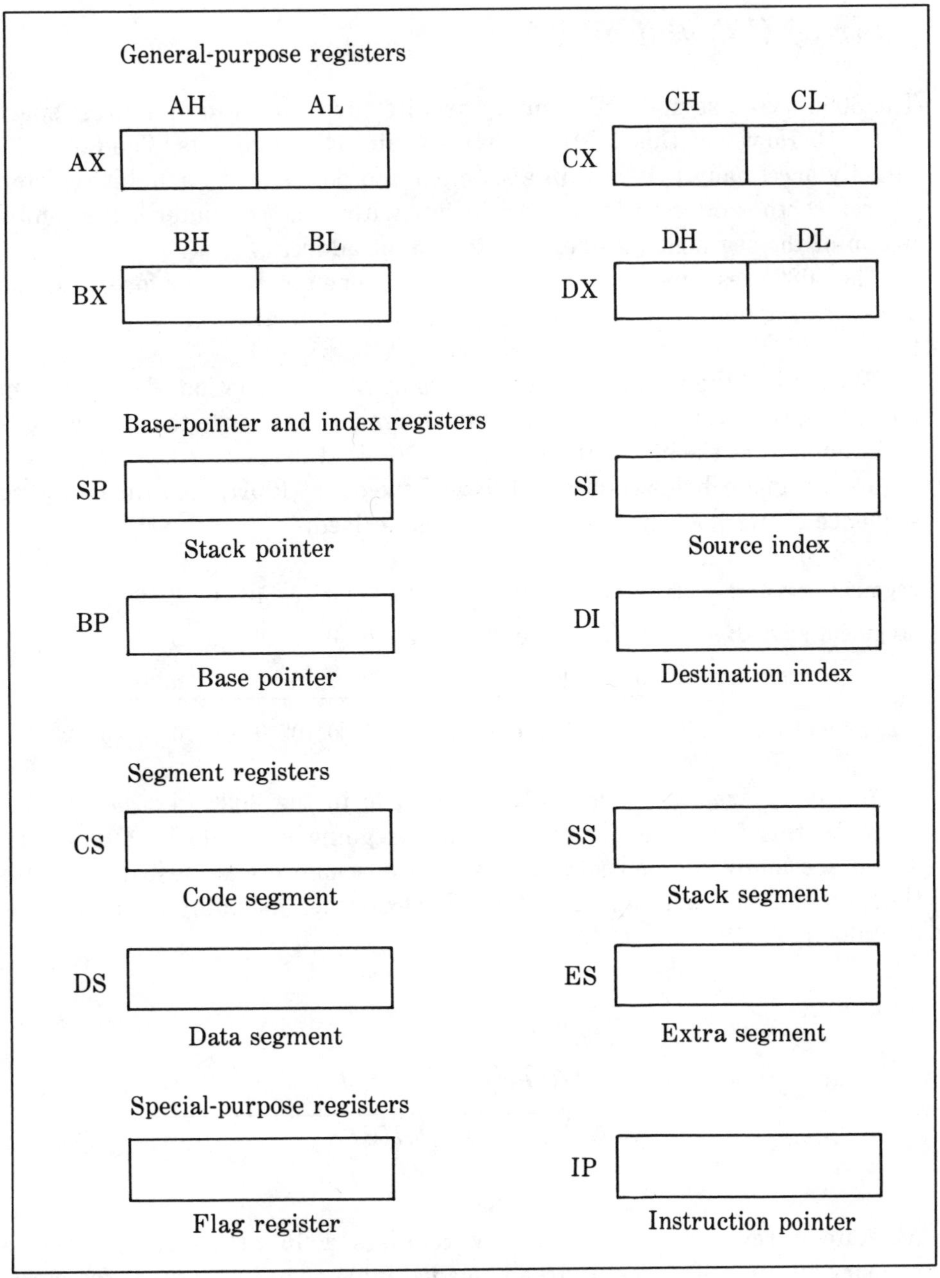

Figure A-1. The 8086 CPU registers

Address Calculation

The 8086 uses a segmented memory architecture with a total address space of 1 MB. However, this 1 MB is divided into 64K segments. The 8086 can directly access any byte within a segment and does so with a 16-bit register. Therefore, the address of any specific byte within the computer is the combination of the segment number and the 16-bit address.

The 8086 uses four segments: one for code, one for data, one for stack, and one extra segment. All segments must start on addresses that are even multiples of 16.

To calculate the actual byte referred to by the combination of the segment and offset, you first shift the value in the segment register to the left by 4 bits and then add in the offset. This makes a 20-bit address. For example, if the segment register holds the value 10H and the offset 100H, then the following sequence shows how the actual address is derived:

```
segment register:   0 0 0 0  0 0 0 0  0 0 0 1  0 0 0 0
segment shifted:    0 0 0 0  0 0 0 1  0 0 0 0  0 0 0 0
        offset:     0 0 0 0  0 0 0 1  0 0 0 0  0 0 0 0
                   _____
segment+offset      0 0 0 0  0 0 1 0  0 0 0 0  0 0 0 0  (200H)
```

Addresses are most commonly referred to in the 8086 in *segment:offset* form. In this form the outcome of the foregoing example is 0010:0100H. There are many segment:offsets that can describe the same byte because the segments may overlap each other. For example, 0000:0010 is the same as 0001:0000.

16-Bit Versus
32-Bit Pointers

As stated previously, the 8086 only requires a 16-bit address to access memory within the segment already loaded into one of its segment registers. To access memory outside that segment, however, both the segment register and the offset must be loaded with the proper values. This effectively means that a 32-bit address is required. The difference between the two is that it takes twice as long to load two 16-bit registers as it does to load one. Hence your programs run much slower.

Memory Models

Turbo C for the 8086 family of processors can compile your program six different ways, and each way organizes the memory differently in the computer. The six models are called tiny, small, medium, compact, large, and huge.

Tiny Model

The tiny model compiles a C program so that all the segment registers are set to the same value and all addressing is done using 16 bits. This means that the code, data, and stack must all be within the same 64K segment. This method of compilation produces the smallest, fastest code. Programs compiled using this version may be converted into ".COM" files using the DOS command EXE2BIN.

Small Model

The small model is Turbo C's default mode of compilation and is useful for a wide variety of tasks. Although all addressing is done using only the 16-bit offset, the code segment is separate from the data, stack, and extra segments (which are in their own segments). This means that the total size of a program compiled this way is 128K split between code and data. The addressing time is the same as that for the tiny model, but the program can be twice as big. Most programs you write fall into this model category.

Medium Model

The medium model is for large programs where the code exceeds the one segment restriction of the small model. Here, the code may use multiple segments and requires 32-bit pointers. The stack, data, and extra segments are in their own segment, however, and use 16-bit addresses. This is good for large programs that use little data.

Compact Model

The complement of the medium model is the compact model. In this version, program code is restricted to one segment, but data may occupy several segments. This means that all accesses to data require 32-bit addressing, but accesses to the code use 16-bit addressing. This is good for programs that require large amounts of data, but little code.

Large Model

The large model allows both code and data to use multiple segments. However, the largest single item of data (such as an array) is limited to 64K. This model is used when you have both large code and data requirements. It also runs much slower than any of the previous versions.

Huge Model

The huge model is the same as the large model with the exception that individual data items may exceed 64K. This makes run-time speed degrade further.

Selecting a Model

You should generally use the small model, unless there is a reason to do otherwise. Select the medium model if you have a significant amount of program code, but not much data. Use the compact model if you have a significant amount of data and not much program code. If you have a large amount of both code and data, then use the large model. If you need single data items larger than 64K, use the huge model. Remember, both the large and huge models run substantially slower than the other models.

Overriding a Memory Model

It is unfortunate that even a single reference to data in another segment requires that you use the compact model rather than the small model. This slows the execution of the entire program, even though only an isolated part of the program actually needs a 32-bit pointer.

This sort of situation generally appears in a variety of ways. For example, it is necessary to use 32-bit addressing to access the video RAM. The solution to this and other related problems is the *segment override* type modifiers added by Turbo C. They are

near   far   huge
_cs   _ds   _es   _ss

These modifiers may only be applied to pointers or to functions. When they are applied to pointers, they affect the way data is accessed. When applied to functions, these modifiers affect the way the function is called and returned from.

These modifiers follow the base type and precede the variable name. For example, the following code declares a **far** pointer called **f_pointer:**

```
char far *f_pointer;
```

Let's look at these now.

far

The most often used model override is the **far** pointer. This override is common when you need to access some region of memory that is (or may be) outside the data segment. However, if the program is compiled for one of the large data models, *all access* to data becomes slow—not just accesses to the region of memory outside the current data segment. The solution to this problem is to explicitly declare **far** pointers to memory outside the current data segment. In this way, only those references to objects actually outside the current data segment incur the additional overhead.

The use of **far** functions is less common and is generally restricted to specialized programming situations where a function may lie outside the current code segment (in ROM, for example). In these cases, the use of **far** ensures that the proper calling and returning sequences are used.

One important aspect of **far** pointers implemented in Turbo C is that pointer arithmetic only affects the offset. This means that when a **far** pointer with the value 0000:FFFF is incremented, its new value will be 0000:0000 and not 0001:0000. Therefore, even though the pointer can access objects not in its own data segment, it may not access objects larger than 64K.

As implemented in Turbo C, two **far** pointers should not be used in a relational expression because only their offsets will be checked. You can have two different pointers that actually contain the same physical address, but that have different segments and offsets. If you need to compare 32-bit pointers, you must use **huge** pointers.

near

A **near** pointer is a 16-bit offset that uses the value of the appropriate segment to determine the actual memory location. The **near** modifier forces Turbo C to treat the pointer as a 16-bit offset to the segment contained in DS. You will use a **near** pointer when you have compiled a program using either the medium, large, or huge memory model.

If you use **near** on a function, you cause that function to be treated as if it were compiled using a small model. When you compile a function using either the tiny, small, or compact models, all calls to the function place a 16-bit return address on the stack. If you use a large model, a 32-bit address is pushed on the stack. Therefore, in programs that are compiled for the large model, a highly recursive function should be declared as **near** to conserve stack space and speed up execution time.

huge

The **huge** pointer is like the **far** pointer with two additions. First, its segment is normalized so that comparisons between **huge** pointers are meaningful. Second, a **huge** pointer may be incremented any number of times. The **huge** pointer does not suffer from a wrap-around problem as do **far** pointers.

The __cs, __ds, __es, and __ss modifiers tell Turbo C which segment register to use when evaluating a pointer. For example, the following code instructs Turbo C to use the extra segment when using **ptv**:

```
int _es *ptr;
```

You will need to use these segment register overrides few, if any, times.

A Review of
Turbo C

APPENDIX B

This appendix serves as an aid to the inexperienced Turbo C programmer by clarifying aspects of the language. As such, it is a reference guide and not a tutorial.

The Origins of C

The C language was invented and first implemented by Dennis Ritchie on a DEC PDP-11 using the UNIX operating system. The C language is the result of a development process that started with an older language called BCPL, which is still in use primarily in Europe. BCPL, developed by Martin Richards, influenced a language called B, which was invented by Ken Thompson and which led to the development of C.

For many years, the *de facto* standard for C was the one supplied with the UNIX Version 7 operating system and described in *The C Programming Language* written by Brian Kernighan and Dennis Ritchie (Englewood Cliffs: Prentice-Hall, Inc., 1978). As the popularity of microcomputers increased, a great number of C implementations were created. Most of these implementations were highly compatible with each other on the source-code level. However, because no standard existed, discrepancies did exist.

To correct this situation, a committee was established in the summer of 1983 to begin work on the creation of an ANSI standard that would finally define the C language. As of this writing, the proposed standard is almost complete and its adoption by ANSI is expected in 1987. (Turbo C implements the proposed ANSI C standard.)

C as a Structured Language

C is commonly considered to be a structured language, with some similarities to ALGOL and Pascal. Although the term block-structured language does not strictly apply to C in an academic sense, C is informally part of that language group. The distinguishing feature of a block-structured language is *compartmentalization of code and data.* This means the language can section off and hide from the rest of the program all information and instructions necessary to perform a specific task. Generally, compartmentalization is achieved by subroutines with local variables, which are temporary. In this way, it is possible to write subroutines so that the events occurring within them cause no side effects in other parts of the program. Excessive use of global variables (variables known throughout the entire program) may allow bugs to creep into a program by allowing unwanted side effects. In C, all subroutines are discrete functions.

Functions are the building blocks of C in which all program activity occurs. They allow specific tasks in a program to be defined and coded separately. After debugging a function that uses only local variables, you can rely on the function to work properly in various situations without creating side effects in other parts of the program. All variables declared in that particular function will be known only to that function.

In C, using blocks of code also creates program structure. A *block of code* is a logically connected group of program statements that can be treated as a unit. It is created by placing lines of code between opening and closing curly braces, as shown here:

```
if(x<10) {
  printf("Invalid input - retry");
  done = 0;
}
```

In this example, the two statements after the **if** between curly braces are both executed if **x** is less than 10. These two statements together with the braces represent a block of code. They are linked together: one of the statements cannot execute without the other also executing. In C, every statement can be either a single statement or a block of statements. The use of code blocks creates readable programs with logic that is easy to follow.

C is a programmer's language. Unlike most high-level computer languages, C imposes few restrictions on what you can do with it. By using C a programmer can avoid using assembly code in all but the most demanding situations. In fact, one motive for the invention of C was to provide an alternative to assembly language programming.

Assembly language uses a symbolic representation of the actual binary code that the computer directly executes. Each assembly language operation maps into a single operation for the computer to perform. Although assembly language gives programmers the potential for accomplishing tasks with maximum flexibility and efficiency, it is notoriously difficult to work with when developing and debugging a program. Furthermore, since assembly language is unstructured by nature, the final program tends to be "spaghetti code," a tangle of jumps, calls, and indexes. This makes assembly language programs difficult to read, enhance, and maintain.

Initially, C was used for systems programming. A *systems program* is part of a large class of programs that form a portion of the operating system of the computer or its support utilities. For example, the following are commonly called systems programs:

- Operating systems
- Interpreters
- Editors
- Assemblers
- Compilers
- Database managers

As C grew in popularity, many programmers began to use C to program all tasks because of its portability and efficiency. Since there are C compilers for virtually all computers, it is easy to take code written for one machine and then compile and run it on another machine with few or no changes. This portability saves both time and money. C compilers also tend to produce tight, fast object code—faster and smaller than most BASIC compilers, for example. With the advent of the speedy and efficient Turbo C, it is difficult to justify using any other language.

Perhaps the real reason that C is used in all types of programming tasks is because programmers like it. C has the speed of assembler and the extensibility of FORTH, while having few of the restrictions of Pascal. A C programmer can create and maintain a unique library of functions that have been tailored to his or her own personality. Because C allows—and indeed encourages—separate compilation, large projects are easily managed.

A Review of Turbo C

As defined by the proposed ANSI standard, the 32 keywords shown in Table B-1, combined with the formal C syntax, form the C programming language.

In addition to these keywords, Turbo C has added the following to the IBM PC version to allow greater control over the way memory and other system resources are used:

_cs	_ds	_es	_ss
cdecl	far	huge	interrupt
near	pascal		

All C keywords are in lowercase letters. In C, uppercase or lowercase makes a difference; that is, **else** is a keyword, ELSE is not.

Variables—Types and Declaration

C has five built-in data types, as shown in Table B-2. With the exception of **void,** all of these data types may be modified through the use of the C type modifiers:

signed
unsigned
short
long

Variable names are strings of letters from 1 to 32 characters in length. For clarity, the underscore may also be used as part of the variable name (for example, **first＿time**). Remember that in C, uppercase and lowercase are different—**test** and **TEST** will be two different variables.

All variables must be declared prior to use. The general form of the declaration is

type **variable＿name;**

Table B-1.   List of Keywords

auto	**double**	**int**	**struct**
break	**else**	**long**	**switch**
case	**enum**	**register**	**typedef**
char	**extern**	**return**	**union**
const	**float**	**short**	**unsigned**
continue	**for**	**signed**	**void**
default	**goto**	**sizeof**	**volatile**
do	**if**	**static**	**while**

Table B-2.   Data Types and C Keyword Equivalents

Data Type	**C Keyword Equivalent**
character	**char**
integer	**int**
floating point	**float**
double floating point	**double**
value-less	**void**

For example, to declare **x** to be a float, **y** to be an integer, and **ch** to be a character, you would type

```
float x;
int y;
char ch;
```

In addition to the built-in types, you can create combinations of built-in types by using **struct** and **union**. You can also create new names for variable types by using **typedef**.

A *structure* is a collection of variables grouped and referenced under one name. The general form of a structure declaration is

> **struct struct＿name** {
>   *element 1;*
>   *element 2;*
>   .
>
>   .
>
>   .
>
> } **struct＿variable;**

As an example, the following structure has two elements: **name**, a character array, and **balance**, a floating-point number.

```
struct client {
  char name[80];
  float balance;
};
```

To reference individual structure elements, the dot operator is used if the structure is global or declared in the function referencing it. The arrow operator is used in all other cases.

When two or more variables share the same memory, a **union** is defined. The general form for a **union** is

> **union union＿name** {
>   *element 1;*
>   *element 2;*
>   .
>
>   .
>
>   .
>
> } **union＿variable;**

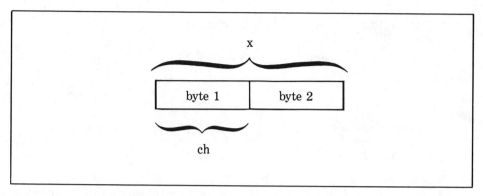

Figure B-1. The **union t** in memory

The elements of a **union** overlay each other. For example, the following declares a **union t** that looks like Figure B-1 in memory:

```
union tom {
  char ch;
  int x;
} t;
```

The individual variables that comprise the **union** are referenced using the dot operator. The arrow operator is used with pointers.

Another type of variable that can be created, called an *enumeration*, is a list of objects or values (depending upon how you interpret it). An *enumeration type* is a specification of the list of objects that belong to the enumeration. When a variable is declared to be of an enumeration type, then its only values may be those defined by the enumeration.

To create an enumeration, you must use the keyword **enum**. For example, the following short program defines an enumeration of cities called **cities**, and the variable **c** of type **cities**. Finally, the program assigns **c** the value "Houston."

```
enum cities {Houston, Austin, Amarillo };
enum cities c;

main()
{
  c=Houston;
}
```

The general form of an enumeration type is

$$\textbf{enum}\ \textit{name}\ \{\ \textit{list of values}\ \};$$

The Storage-Class Type Modifiers

The type modifiers **extern, auto, register, const, volatile,** and **static** are used to alter the way C creates storage for the variables that follow.

If the **extern** modifier is placed before a variable name, the compiler knows that the variable has been declared elsewhere. The **extern** modifier is most commonly used when two or more files share the same global variables.

An **auto** variable is created upon entry into a block and is destroyed upon exit. For example, all variables defined inside a function are **auto** by default. Although seldom used, **auto** variables can be valuable in specialized or dedicated systems where RAM is in short supply.

The **register** modifier can only be used on local integer or character variables. This modifier causes the compiler to attempt to keep that value in a register of the CPU instead of being placed in memory, which makes all references to that variable extremely fast. Throughout this book, **register** variables were used for loop control. For example, the following function uses a **register** loop control:

```
f1()
{

   register int t;

   for(t=0;t<10000;++t) {
       •
       •
       •
   }
}
```

Variables of type **const** may not be changed during your program's execution. The compiler is free to place variables of this type into ROM. For example, the following line

```
const int a;
```

creates an integer called **a** that cannot be modified by your program, but can be used in other types of expressions. A **const** variable receives its value either from an explicit initialization or by some hardware-dependent means. The inclusion of **const** type variables aids in the development of applications for ROM.

The modifier **volatile** tells the compiler that a variable's value may be changed in ways not explicitly specified by the program. For example, a global variable's address may be passed to the clock routine of the operating system and used to hold the real time of the system. In this situation, the contents of the variable are altered without any explicit assignment statements in the program. In order to achieve higher performance, Turbo C automatically optimizes certain expressions by assuming that the contents of a variable are unchanged inside that expression. The **volatile** modifier prevents this assumption in those rare instances where this is not true.

You can add the **static** modifier to any of the previously mentioned variables. The **static** modifier instructs the C compiler to keep a local variable in existence during the lifetime of the program, instead of creating and destroying it. Remember that the values of local variables are discarded when a function finishes and returns. Using **static** maintains their values between function calls.

Addressing Type Modifiers

Turbo C has added the following modifers that may be applied to pointers so that you can explicitly control — and override — the default addressing mode used to compile your program:

> **_cs _ds _es _ss**
> **far   near huge**

Use of these modifiers is discussed in Appendix A.

Arrays

You can declare arrays on any of the previously mentioned data types. For example, to declare an integer array **x** of 100 elements, you write

```
int x[100];
```

This creates an array that is 100 elements long with the first element being 0 and the last being 99. For example, the following loop loads the numbers 0 through 99 into array **x**:

```
for(t=0;t<100; t++) x[t]=t;
```

Multidimensional arrays are declared by placing the additional dimensions inside additional brackets. For example, to declare a 10 × 20 integer array, you write

```
int x[10][20];
```

Operators

Turbo C has a rich set of operators that can be divided into the following classes: *arithmetic*, *relational and logical*, *bitwise*, *pointer*, *assignment*, and *miscellaneous*.

Arithmetic Operators

C has the seven arithmetic operators shown in Table B-3.
   The precedence of these operators is

$$\begin{array}{ll} \text{highest} & ++ \quad -- \quad - \text{ (unary minus)} \\ & * \; / \; \% \\ \text{lowest} & + \quad - \end{array}$$

Operators on the same precedence level are evaluated left to right.

Relational and Logical Operators

Relational and logical operators are used to produce TRUE/FALSE results and are often used together. In C, any nonzero number evaluates TRUE; however, a C relational or logical expression produces the number 1 for

Table B-3. Arithmetic Operators

Operator	Action
−	Subtraction, unary minus
+	Addition
*	Multiplication
/	Division
%	Modulo division
−−	Decrement
++	Increment

Table B-4. Relational and Logical Operators

Relational Operators	
Operator	Meaning
>	Greater than
>=	Greater than or equal
<	Less than
<=	Less than or equal
==	Equal
!=	Not equal

Logical Operators	
Operator	Meaning
&&	AND
||	OR
!	NOT

TRUE and 0 for FALSE. The rational and logical operators are shown in Table B-4.

The precedence of these operators is

highest	!
	> >= < <=
	== !=
	&&
lowest	||

For example, the following expression evaluates TRUE:

```
(100<200) && 10
```

Bitwise Operators

Unlike most other programming languages, C provides bitwise operators that manipulate the actual bits inside a variable. The bitwise operators can only be used on integers or characters. They are shown in Table B-5.

The truth tables for the AND, OR, and XOR are as follows:

```
& | 0 | 1
--+---+---
0 | 0 | 0
1 | 0 | 1
```

```
| | 0 | 1
--+---+---
0 | 0 | 1
1 | 1 | 1
```

```
^ | 0 | 1
--+---+---
0 | 0 | 1
1 | 1 | 0
```

These rules are applied to each bit in a byte when the bitwise AND, OR, and XOR operations are performed. For example,

```
  0 1 0 0    1 1 0 1
& 0 0 1 1    1 0 1 1
---------    -------
  0 0 0 0    1 0 0 1


  0 1 0 0    1 1 0 1
| 0 0 1 1    1 0 1 1
---------    -------
  0 1 1 1    1 1 1 1


  0 1 0 0    1 1 0 1
^ 0 0 1 1    1 0 1 1
---------    -------
  0 1 1 1    0 1 1 0
```

Table B-5.   Bitwise Operators

Operator	Meaning
&	AND
¦	OR
^	XOR
~	One's complement
>>	Right shift
<<	Left shift

In a program, you use the **&**, ¦ and ^ like any other operator, as shown here:

```
main()
{
  char x,y,z;

  x = 1; y = 2; z = 4;

  x = x & y;  /* x now equals zero */

  y = x ¦ z;  /* y now equals 4 */

}
```

The one's complement operator (~) inverts all the bits in a byte. For example, if the character variable **ch** has the bit pattern

$$0\ 0\ 1\ 1\quad 1\ 0\ 0\ 1$$

then

```
ch=~ch;
```

places the bit patter

$$1\ 1\ 0\ 0\quad 0\ 1\ 1\ 0$$

into **ch**.

The right shift and left shift operators move all bits in a byte or a word right or left by some specified number of bits. As bits are shifted, 0s are brought in. The number on the right side of the shift operator specifies the number of positions to shift. The general forms of the shift operators are

variable >> number of bit positions
variable << number of bit positions

For example, given the bit pattern

0 0 1 1   1 1 0 1

a shift right yields

0 0 0 1   1 1 1 0

while a single shift left produces

0 1 1 1   1 0 1 0

A shift right is effectively a division by 2 and a shift left is a multiplication by 2. The following code fragment will first multiply and then divide the value in **x**:

```
int x;
x=10;
x=x<<1;
x=x>>1;
```

Because of the way negative numbers are represented inside the machine, you must be careful when you try to use a shift for multiplication or division. Moving a 1 into the most significant bit position causes the computer to think that the number is a negative number.

Remember: the bitwise operators are used to modify the value of a variable—they differ from the logical and relational operators, which produce a TRUE or FALSE result.

The precedence of the bitwise operators is as follows:

highest	~
	>> <<
	&
	^
lowest	|

Pointer Operators

Pointer operators are important in C: not only do they allow strings and arrays to be passed to functions, but they also allow C functions to modify their calling arguments. The two pointer operators are **&** and *****. (Unfortunately, these operators use the same symbols as the multiply and bitwise AND, which are completely unrelated to them.)

The **&** operator returns the address of the variable it precedes. For example, if the integer **x** is located at memory address 1000, then

```
y = &x;
```

places the value 1000 into **y**. The **&** can be read as "the address of." For example, the previous statement could be read as "Place the address of **x** into **y**."

The ***** operator takes the value of the variable it precedes and uses that value as the address of the information in memory. For example,

```
y = &x;
*y = 100;
```

places the value 100 into **x**. The ***** can be read as "at address." In this example, it could be read as, "Place the value 100 at address **y**." The ***** operator can also be used on the right-hand side of an assignment. For example,

```
y = &x;
*y = 100;
z = *y/10;
```

places the value of 10 into **z**.

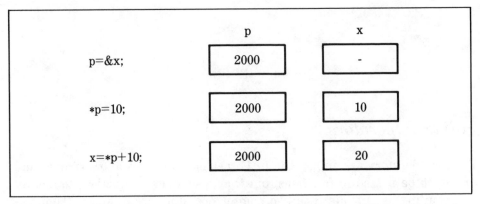

Figure B-2. Pointer operations for character pointer **p** and integer **x**, with **x** at memory location 2000

These operators are called pointer operators because they are designed to work on *pointer variables*. A pointer variable holds the address of another variable; in essence, it "points" to that variable as shown in Figure B-2.

Pointers of Type *void*

A pointer of type **void** is a generic pointer and can be used to point to any type of object. This implies that a pointer of any type can be assigned to pointers of type **void** (and vice versa) if you use the appropriate type casts. To declare a **void** pointer you use a declaration similar to the following:

```
void *p;
```

The **void** pointer is particularly useful when various types of pointers are manipulated by a single routine.

Assignment Operators

In C, the assignment operator is the single equal sign. However, C allows a convenient "shorthand" for assignments of the general type

$$variable1 = variable1\ operator\ expression;$$

For example,

$$x = x+10;$$
$$y = y/z;$$

Assignments of this type can be shortened to the general form

variable1 operator = expression;

In the case of the two examples, they can be shortened to

$$x += 10;$$
$$y /= z;$$

The shorthand notation is used often in C programs written by experienced C programmers, so you should become used to it.

The ? Operator

The ? operator is a ternary operator that is used to replace **if** statements of the general type

if *expression1* **then** x=*expression2*
else x=*expression3*

The general form of the ? operator is

variable = expression1 ? expression2 : expression3;

If *expression1* is TRUE, then the value of *expression2* is assigned to *variable*; otherwise, *variable* is assigned the value of *expression3*. For example,

```
x = (y<10) ? 20 : 40;
```

assigns to **x** either the value of 20 if **y** is less than 10 or the value of 40 if **y** is not.

The ? operator exists because a C compiler can produce very efficient code for this statement—much faster than the equivalent **if/else** statement.

Miscellaneous Operators

The . (dot) operator and the → (arrow) operator are used to reference individual elements of structures and unions. The dot operator is used when the structure or union is global or when the referencing code is in the same function as the structure or union declaration. The arrow operator is used when only a pointer to a structure or a union is available. For example, consider the following global structure:

```
struct date_time {
   char date[16];
   int time;
} tm;
```

To assign the value "3/12/88" to element **date** of structure **tm**, you would write

```
strcpy(tm.date, "3/12/88");
```

The , (comma) operator is used mostly in the **for** statement. It causes a sequence of operations to be performed. When it is used on the right side of an assignment statement, the value of the entire expression is the value of the last expression of the comma-separated list. For example, consider the following:

```
y=10;

x = (y=y-5,25/y);
```

After execution, **x** has the value 5 because the original value of **y** (10) is reduced by 5, and then that value is divided into 25, yielding a result of 5.

Although **sizeof** is also considered a keyword, it is a compile-time operator used to determine the size of a data type in bytes, including user-defined structures and unions. For example,

```
int x;

printf("%d", sizeof(x));
```

prints the number 2.

Parentheses are considered operators that increase the precedence of the operations inside of them. Square brackets perform array indexing.

A *cast* is a special operator that forces the conversion of one data type into another. The general form is

$$(type)\ variable$$

For example, for the integer **count** to be used in a call to **sqrt()**, which is the square root routine in C's standard library and requires a floating-point parameter, a cast forces **count** to be treated as type **float**:

```
float y;
int count;

count = 10;

y = sqrt((float)count);
```

Figure B-3 lists the precedence of all C operators. Note that all operators — except the unary operators and ? — associate from left to right. The unary operators (*, &, −, and ?) associate from right to left.

Functions

A Turbo C program is a collection of one or more user-defined functions. One of the functions must be **main( )** because execution begins at this function. Historically, **main( )** is usually the first function in a program; however, it could go anywhere.

The general form of a C function is

> **type function_name**(*parameter list*)
> *parameter declaration*
> {
>   *body of function*
> }

```
Highest  ()  □  →  .
         ! ~ ++ -- - (type) * & sizeof
         * / %
         + -
         << >>
         < <= > >=
         == !=
         &
         ^
         |
         &&
         ||
         ?:
         =  +=  -=  *=  /=  %=  >>=  <<=  &=  ^=  |=
Lowest   ,
```

Figure B-3.   Precedence of C operators

If the function has no parameters, no parameter declaration is needed. The type declaration is optional. If no explicit type declaration is present, the function defaults to integer. All functions terminate and return to the calling procedure automatically when the last brace is encountered. You may force return prior to that using the **return** statement.

Except those declared as **void**, all functions return a value. The type of the return value must match the type declaration of the function. If no explicit type declaration has been made, then the return value is defaulted to integer. If a **return** statement is part of the function, then the value of the function is the value in the **return** statement. If no **return** is present, then the function returns 0. For example,

```
f1()
{
  int x;

  x = 100;
  return(x/10);
}
```

returns the value 10, whereas

```
f2()
{
  int x;

  x = 100;
  x = x/10;
}
```

returns the value 0 because no explicit **return** statement is encountered.

If a function is going to return a value other than an integer, then its type must reflect this fact. Also, it will be necessary to declare the function prior to any reference to it by another piece of code. This can best be accomplished by making a function declaration in the global definition area of the program. The following example shows how the function **fn()** is declared to return a floating-point value:

```
float fn();

main()
{
  .
  .
  .
  printf("%f", fn());
  .
  .
  .
}

float fn()
{
  return 12.23;
}
```

Because all functions, except those declared as **void**, have values, they may be used in any arithmetic statement. For example, beginning C programmers tend to write code like this:

```
x = sqrt(y);

z = sin(x);
```

whereas a more experienced programmer would write:

```
z = sin(sqrt(y));
```

Remember that in order for the program to determine the value of a function, it must be executed. This means that the following code reads keystrokes from the keyboard until a "u" is typed:

```
while((ch=getche())!='u') ;
```

This code works because **getche( )** must be executed to determine its value, which is the character typed at the keyboard.

The Scope and Lifetime of Variables

C has two general classes of variables: global and local. A global variable is available for use by all functions in the program, while a local variable is known and used only by the function in which it was declared. In some C literature, global variables are referred to as *external variables* and local variables are called *dynamic* or *automatic variables*. This appendix uses the terms *global* and *local* because they are the generally accepted terms.

A global variable must be declared outside of all functions, including the **main( )** function. Global variables are usually placed at the top of the file before **main( )**, because this makes the program easier to read and because a variable must be declared before it is used. A local variable is declared inside a function after the function's opening brace. For example, the following program declares one global variable, **x**, and two local variables, **x** and **y**.

```
int x;

main()
{
  int y;

  y = get_value();
  x = 100;
  printf("%d %d", x, x*y);
}

f1()
{
  int x;

  scanf("%d", &x);
  return x;
}
```

This program multiplies the number entered from the keyboard by 100. Note that the local variable **x** in **f1()** has no relationship to the global variable **x**, because local variables that have the same name as global variables always take precedence over the global ones.

Global variables exist during the entire program. Local variables are created when the function is entered and are destroyed when the function is exited. This means that local variables do not keep their values between function calls. You can use the **static** modifier, however, to preserve values between calls.

The formal parameters to a function are also local variables, and except for receiving the value of the calling arguments, they behave and can be used like any other local variable.

The *main()* Function

As previously mentioned, all C programs must have a **main()** function. When execution begins, **main()** is the first function called. You must not have more than one function called **main()**. When **main()** terminates, the program is over and control passes back to the operating system.

The only parameters that **main()** is allowed to have are **argc** and **argv**. The variable **arg C** holds the number of command-line arguments. The variable **argv** holds a character pointer to those arguments. *Command-line arguments* are the information that you type in after the program name when you execute a program. For example, when you compile a Turbo C program, you type

TCC MYPROG.C

where **MYPROG.C** is the name of the program you wish to compile.

The value of **argc** is always at least 1, because C considers the program name to be the first argument. The variable **argv** must be declared as an array of character pointers. This is shown in the following short program, which prints your name on the screen:

```
main(argc, argv)
int argc;
char *argv[];
{
    if(argc<2)
      printf("enter your name on the command line.\n");
    else
      printf("hello %s\n",argv[1]);
}
```

Notice that **argv** is declared as a character pointer array of unknown size. The Turbo C compiler automatically determines the size of the array that is necessary to handle all of the command-line arguments.

Command-line arguments give your programs a professional look and feel, as well as allowing the programs to be placed into a batch file for automatic usage.

Statement Summary

This section is a brief synopsis of the keywords in Turbo C. The memory model keywords (**far**, **near**, **huge**, **_es**, **_ds**, **_ss**, and **_cs**) are discussed in Appendix A.

auto

The **auto** keyword creates temporary variables that are created upon entry into a block and are destroyed upon exit. For example,

```
main()
{
  for(;;) {
    if(getche()=='a') {
      auto int t;
      for(t=0; t<'a'; t++)
        printf("%d ", t);
    }
  }
}
```

In this example, the variable **t** is created only if you type an "a." Outside of the **if** block, **t** is completely unknown and any reference to it generates a compile-time syntax error.

break

The **break** keyword is used to exit from a **do**, **for**, or **while** loop, bypassing the normal loop condition. It is also used to exit from a **switch** statement.

The following is an example of **break** in a loop:

```
while(x<100) {
  x = get_new_x();
  if(keystroke()) break;    /* key hit on
                               keyboard */
  process(x);

}
```

In this example, if a key is pressed, the loop terminates no matter what the value of **x** is.

A **break** always terminates the innermost **for**, **do**, **while**, or **switch** statement, regardless of the way these might be nested. In a **switch** statement, **break** effectively keeps program execution from "falling through" to the next **case**. (Refer to the discussion on **switch** for details.)

case

Refer to the discussion on **switch**.

cdecl

The **cdecl** keyword is specific to Turbo C and is not part of the ANSI standard. It forces Turbo C to compile a function so that its parameter passing conforms with the standard C calling convention. You only use **cdecl** when compiling an entire file while using the Pascal option and when you want a specific function to be compatible with C.

const

The **const** modifier tells the compiler that the variable that follows may not be modified.

char

The **char** data type declares character variables. For example, to declare **ch** to be character type, you write

```
char ch;
```

continue

The **continue** keyword is used to bypass portions of code in a loop and force the conditional test to be performed. For example, the following **while** loop simply reads characters from the keyboard until an "s" is typed:

```
while(ch=getche()) {
  if(ch!='s') continue;  /* read another char */
  process(ch);
}
```

The call to **process( )** will not occur until **ch** contains the character "s".

default

The **default** keyword is used in the **switch** statement to signal a default block of code to be executed if no matches are found in the **switch**. (See the discussion of **switch**.)

do

The **do** loop is one of three loop constructs available in C. The general form of the **do** loop is

> **do** {
>   *statement block*
> } **while**(*condition*);

If only one statement is repeated, the braces are not necessary, but they do add clarity to the statement.

The **do** loop is the only loop in C that always has at least one iteration, because the condition is tested at the bottom of the loop.

A common use of the **do** loop is reading disk files.The following code reads a file until an EOF is encountered:

```
do {
  ch=getc(fp);
  store(ch);
} while(!feof(fp));
```

double

The **double** data type specifier declares double-precision floating-point variables. To declare **d** to be of type **double**, you write

```
double d;
```

else

See the discussion of **if**.

enum

The **enum** type specifier creates enumeration types. An enumeration is simply a list of objects, and an enumeration type specifies what that list of objects is. Further, an enumeration type variable may only be assigned values that are part of the enumeration list. For example, the following code declares an enumeration called **color**, declares a variable of that type called **c**, and performs an assignment and a condition test:

```
enum color {red, green, yellow};
enum color c;

main()
{
  c=red;
  if(c==red) printf("is red\n");
}
```

extern

The **extern** data type modifier tells the compiler that a variable is declared elsewhere in the program. This modifier is often used in conjunction with separately compiled files that share the same global data and are linked together. In essence, **extern** notifies the compiler of a variable without re-declaring it.

As an example, if **first** were declared in another file as an integer, then in subsequent files the following declaration would be used:

```
extern int first;
```

float

The **float** data type specifier declares floating-point variables. To declare **f** to be of type **float**, you write

```
float f;
```

for

The **for** loop allows automatic initialization and incrementing of a counter variable. The general form is

> **for**(*initialization*; *condition*; *increment*) {
>   *statement block*
> }

If the *statement block* is only one statement, the braces are not necessary.

    Although the **for** allows a number of variables, generally the *initialization* is used to set a counter variable to its starting value. The *condition* is generally a relational statement that checks the counter variable against a termination value, and *increment* increments (or decrements) the counter value.

    The following code prints the message "hello" ten times:

```
for(t=0; t<10; t++) printf("hello\n");
```

The next example waits for a keystroke after printing "hello":

```
for(t=0; t<10; t++) {
  printf("hello\n");
  getche();
}
```

goto

The **goto** keyword causes program execution to "jump" to the label specified in the **goto** statement. The general form of **goto** is

> **goto** *label*;
> .
> .
> .
> *label*:

    All labels must end in a colon and must not conflict with keywords or function names. Furthermore, a **goto** can only branch within the current function, and not from one function to another.

The following example prints the message "right," but not the message "wrong":

```
goto lab1;
  printf("wrong");
lab1:
  printf("right");
```

if

The general form of the **if** statement is

$$\begin{aligned}
&\textbf{if}(\textit{condition})\ \{\\
&\quad \textit{statement block 1}\\
&\}\\
&\textbf{else}\ \{\\
&\quad \textit{statement block 2}\\
&\}
\end{aligned}$$

If single statements are used, then the braces are not needed. The **else** is optional.

The condition may be any expression. If that expression evaluates to any value other than 0, then *statement block 1* executes; otherwise, if it exists, *statement block 2* executes.

The following code fragment can be used for keyboard input and to look for a "q," which signifies "quit."

```
ch=getche();
if(ch=='q') {
  printf("program terminated");
  exit(0);
}
else  proceed();
```

int

The **int** type specifier declares integer variables. For example, to declare **count** as an integer, you write

```
int count;
```

interrupt

The **interrupt** type specifier is specific to Turbo C and is not part of the ANSI standard. It declares functions that are used as interrupt service routines.

long

The **long** data type modifier declares double-length integer variables. For example, to declare **count** as a long integer, you write

```
long int count;
```

pascal

The **pascal** keyword is specific to Turbo C and is not defined by the ANSI standard. It forces Turbo C to compile a function so that its parameter passing convention is compatible with Pascal, rather than Turbo C.

register

The **register** declaration modifier forces either an integer or a character to be stored in a register of the CPU, instead of being placed in memory. It can only be used on local variables. To declare **i** as a register integer, you write

```
register int i;
```

return

The **return** keyword forces a return from a function and can be used to transfer a value back to the calling routine.

For example, the following function returns the product of its two integer arguments:

```
mul(a, b)
int a, b;
{
  return(a*b);
}
```

Remember that as soon as a **return** is encountered, the function returns and skips any other code in the function.

sizeof

The **sizeof** keyword is a compile-time operator that returns the length of the variable it precedes. For example, the following prints a 2:

```
printf("%d", sizeof(int));
```

The principal use of **sizeof** is aiding the generation of portable code when that code depends upon the size of the C built-in data types.

signed

The **signed** type modifier ensures a **signed** data type.

short

The **short** data type modifier declares 1-byte integers. For example, to declare **sh** as a short integer you write

```
short int sh;
```

static

The **static** data type modifier instructs the compiler to create permanent storage for the local variable that it precedes. This enables the specified variable to maintain its value between function calls. For example, to declare **last_time** as a **static** integer, you write

```
static int last_time;
```

struct

The **struct** keyword creates complex or conglomerate variables (called *structures*) that are made up of one or more elements of the seven basic data types. The general form of a structure is

```
struct structname {
 type element1;
 type element2;
       .
       .
       .
 type elementn;
} structure_variable_name;
```

The individual elements are referenced by using the dot or arrow operator.

switch

The **switch** statement is C's multiway branch statement. It is used to route execution one of several different ways. The general form of the statement is

```
switch(variable) {
 case (constant1): statement set 2;
   break;
 case (constant2): statement set 1;
   break
    .
    .
    .
 case (constant n): statement set n;
   break;
 default: default statements;
}
```

The length of each *statement set* may be from one to several statements. The **default** portion is optional.

The **switch** works by checking the **variable** against all the constants. As soon as a match is found, that set of statements is executed. If the **break** statement is omitted, then execution continues until the end of the **switch**. Think of **case** as a label. Execution will continue until a **break** statement is found, or the **switch** ends.

The following example can be used to process a menu selection:

```
ch = getche();

switch (ch) {
  case 'e': enter();
      break;
  case 'l': list();
      break;
  case 's': sort();
      break;
  case 'q': exit(0);
  default: printf("unknown command\n");
      printf("try again\n");

}
```

typedef

The **typedef** keyword creates a new name for an existing data type. The data type may be either one of the built-in types, or a structure or union name. The general form of **typedef** is

> **typedef** *type—specifier new—name*;

For example, to use the word **balance** in place of **float**, you write

```
typedef float balance;
```

union

The **union** keyword assigns two or more variables to the same memory location. The form of the definition and the way an element is referenced are the same as for **struct**. The general form is

```
union union_name {
  type element1;
  type element2;
       .
       .
       .
  type elementN;
} union variable_name;
```

unsigned

The **unsigned** data type modifier tells the compiler to eliminate the sign bit of an integer and to use all bits for arithmetic. This has the effect of doubling the size of the largest integer, but restricts it to only positive numbers. For example, to declare **big** to be an unsigned integer, you write

```
unsigned int big;
```

void

The **void** type specifier is primarily used to explicitly declare functions that return no (meaningful) value. It is also used to create **void** pointers (pointers to **void**), which are generic pointers capable of pointing to any type of object.

volatile

The **volatile** modifier tells the compiler that a variable may have its contents altered in ways not explicitly defined by the program. These may include variables that are changed by hardware such as real-time clocks, interrupts, or other inputs.

while

The **while** loop has the general form

```
        while(condition) {
           statement block
        }
```

If a single statement is the object of the **while**, then the braces may be omitted.

The **while** tests its *condition* at the top of the loop. Therefore, if the *condition* is FALSE to begin with, the loop will not execute at all. The *condition* may be any expression.

The following example of a **while** reads 100 characters from a disk file and stores them into a character array:

```
t = 0;
while(t<100) {
  s[t]=getc(fp);
  t++;
}
```

The Turbo C Preprocessor

Turbo C includes several preprocessor commands that give instructions to the compiler.

#define

The #**define** command is part of the C preprocessor. It can perform macro-substitutions of one piece of text for another throughout the file in which it is used. The general form of the directive is

#**define** *name string*

Notice that no semicolon appears in this statement.

For example, if you wish to use the word TRUE for the value 1 and the word FALSE for the value 0, you would declare the following two macro #**defines**:

#**define** TRUE 1
#**define** FALSE 0

This causes the compiler to substitute a 1 or a 0 each time the name TRUE or FALSE is encountered.

#error

The *#error* preprocessor directive forces the compiler to stop compilation when it is encountered. It is used primarily for debugging. Its general form is as follows:

#error *message*

When **#error** is encountered, Turbo C displays the message and the line number.

#include

The **#include** preprocessor directive instructs the compiler to read and compile another source file. The source file to be read in must be enclosed between double quotation marks or angle brackets. For example, the following code instructs the C compiler to read and compile the header for the disk file library routines.

```
#include "stdio.h"
```

#if, #ifdef, #ifndef, #else, #elif, #endif

These preprocessor directives selectively compile various portions of a program. These are of the greatest use to commerical software houses that provide and maintain many customized versions of one program. The general idea is that if the expression after an **#if**, **#ifdef**, or **#ifndef** is true, then the code that is between one of the preceding and an **#endif** will be compiled; otherwise it will be skipped over. The **#endif** directive marks the end of a **#if** block. The **#else** can be used with any of the above in a manner similar to the **else** in the C **if** statement.

The general form of #**if** is

> #**if** *constant expression*

If the *constant expression* is TRUE, then the block of code will be compiled.
The general form of #**ifdef** is

> #**ifdef** *name*

If the **name** has been defined in a #**define** statement, the block of code following the statement will be compiled.
The general form of #**ifndef** is

> #**ifndef** *name*

If **name** is currently undefined by a #**define** statement, then the block of code is compiled.

For example, here is the way some of the preprocessor directives work together:

```
#define ted 10

main()
{
#ifdef ted
  printf("Hi Ted\n");
#endif
  printf("bye bye\n");
#if 10<9
  printf("Hi George\n");
#endif
}
```

This code prints "Hi Ted" and "bye bye" on the screen, but not "Hi George."
The #**elif** directive creates an if-else-if statement. Its general form is

> #**elif** *constant-expression*

The #**elif** may be used with the #**if**, but not the #**ifdef** or #**ifndef** directives.

The Turbo C
Standard Library

Unlike most other languages, C does not have built-in functions to perform disk I/O, console I/O, and a number of other useful procedures. The way these things are accomplished in C is by using a set of predefined library functions supplied with the compiler. This library is usually called the "C Standard Library." Library functions can be used by your program at your discretion. Turbo C automatically links the functions during the link process.

Turbo C contains a large number of library functions and these are fully described in the Turbo C user manual. Also, *C: The Complete Reference* by Herbert Schildt (Berkeley: Osborne/McGraw-Hill, 1987) discusses the library functions in considerable detail.

T R A D E M A R K S

DEC™ PDP-11	Digital Equipment Corporation
DOS®	International Business Machines Corporation
Dow Jones®	Dow Jones & Co., Inc.
IBM® PC	International Business Machines Corporation
Microsoft® C	Microsoft Corporation
Microsoft® Macro Assembler	Microsoft Corporation
MS-DOS®	Microsoft Corporation
Turbo C®	Borland International, Inc.
Turbo Pascal®	Borland International, Inc.
UNIX®	AT&T

INDEX

V

Variables
    adding to a parser, 281
    errors in declaring, 328
    register, 314
    scope and lifetime of, 368
    statistical, 166
    types and declaration of, 350-356
Variance, 173
Video I/O functions, 105-107
void, 381
    pointers of type, 362
volatile, 354, 381

W

while, 381
    loops, Turbo C and Turbo Pascal,
      296
writepoint( ), 139

X

XOR, 218, 220, 358

The manuscript for this book was prepared and
submitted to Osborne/McGraw-Hill in electronic form.
The acquisitions editor for this project was Jeffrey Pepper,
the technical reviewer was Deuce Dubois, and
Lyn Cordell was the project editor.

Text type is Century Expanded. Display is set in Eras Demi.

Cover art is by Bay Graphics Design Associates. Cover
supplier is Phoenix Color Corporation. This book was
printed and bound by R. R. Donnelley & Sons
Company, Crawfordsville, Indiana.

Other related Osborne/McGraw-Hill titles include:

Advanced Turbo Prolog™
Version 1.1
by Herbert Schildt

Herb Schildt now applies his expertise to Borland's remarkable Turbo Prolog™ language development system, specifically designed for fifth-generation language programming and the creation of artificial intelligence on your IBM® PC. *Advanced Turbo Prolog*™ has been extensively revised to include Turbo Prolog version 1.1. The new Turbo Prolog Toolbox™, which offers more than 80 tools and 8,000 lines of source code, is also described in detail. Schildt focuses on helping you progress from intermediate to advanced techniques by considering typical AI problems and their solutions. Numerous sample programs and graphics are used throughout the text to sharpen your skills and enhance your understanding of the central issues involved in AI. Expert systems, problem solving, natural language processing, vision and pattern recognition, robotics, and logic are some of the applications that Schildt explains as he leads you to Turbo Prolog mastery.

$21.95 p
0-07-881285-2, 350 pp., 7³/₈ x 9¹/₄
The Borland-Osborne/McGraw-Hill
Programming Series

Turbo Pascal® Programmer's Library
by Kris Jamsa and Steven Nameroff

You can take full advantage of Borland's famous Turbo Pascal® with this outstanding collection of programming routines. Now revised to cover Borland's new Turbo Pascal Numerical Methods Toolbox™, the *Turbo Pascal® Programmer's Library* includes a whole new collection of routines for mathematical calculations. You'll also find new date and time routines. Kris Jamsa, author of *DOS: The Complete Reference* and *The C Library*, and Steven Nameroff give experienced Turbo Pascal users a varied library that includes utility routines for Pascal macros as well as routines for string and array manipulation, records, pointers, and pipes. You'll find I/O routines and a discussion of sorting that covers bubble, shell, and quick-sort algorithms. And there's even more ... routines for the Turbo Toolbox® and the Turbo Graphix Toolbox® packages. It's all here to help you become the most effective Turbo Pascal programmer you can be.

$21.95 p
0-07-881286-0, 625 pp., 7³/₈ x 9¹/₄
The Borland-Osborne/McGraw-Hill
Programming Series

Using Turbo C®
by Herbert Schildt

Here's the official book on Borland's tremendous new C compiler. *Using Turbo C*® is for all C programmers, from beginners to seasoned pros. Master programmer Herb Schildt devotes the first part of the book to helping you get started in Turbo C. If you've been programming in Turbo Pascal® or another language, this orientation will lead you right into Turbo C fundamentals. Schildt's emphasis on good programming structure will start you out designing programs for greater efficiency. With these basics, you'll move on to more advanced concepts such as pointers and dynamic allocation, compiler directives, unions, bitfields, and enumerations, and you'll learn about Turbo C graphics. When you've finished *Using Turbo C*®, you'll be writing full-fledged programs that get professional results.

$19.95 p
0-07-881279-8, 350 pp., 7³/₈ x 9¹/₄
The Borland-Osborne/McGraw-Hill
Programming Series

Using REFLEX®: THE
DATABASE MANAGER
by Stephen Cobb

Using REFLEX® THE DATABASE MANAGER, the first book in *The Borland-Osborne/McGraw-Hill Business Series*, is a comprehensive guide to Borland's analytical database program for the IBM® PC.REFLEX® offers something for everyone: powerful graphical representation of data for analysis and strong reporting capabilities. If you're a beginner, this book gives in-depth descriptions of all REFLEX features along with clear, step-by-step examples of their use. If you're an advanced user, you'll find practical and inventive REFLEX applications, as well as power tips and sophisticated techinques. Cobb, an experienced computer instructor and consultant, shows you how to take full advantage of REFLEX by using SuperKey®, the software that lets you build powerful macros to streamline computing tasks. Cobb reviews REFLEX Workshop™, a new series of adaptable business templates and provides applications that you can use right away. You'll also learn about data transfer between REFLEX and Lotus® 1-2-3®, dBASE®, and other database programs. With Cobb's expert techniques, greater REFLEX-ability will be at your command for any task you choose.

$21.95 p
0-07-881287-9, 400 pp. 7³/₈ x 9¹/₄
The Borland-Osborne/McGraw-Hill
Business Series

Using SPRINT™: The Professional Word Processor
by Kris Jamsa and Gary Boy

Borland's fabulous new word processing system puts you in first place with increased capabilities for users at every level in your office. Now Jamsa and Boy show you how to SPRINT™ with this fast-paced user guide. You'll learn the basics in not time since SPRINT emulates the command sets of WordPerfect® and WordStar®: it also supports file conversion for XyWrite™II and III, MultiMate®, and MultiMate Advantage™, as well as WordStar®, WordStar® 2000, and WordPerfect®. You'll find out how to customize menus with the Soft User Interface and how to use SPRINT's full text editor, desktop publishing capabilities, automatic text recovery, and built-in spelling checker/thesaurus. Jamsa and Boy pay special attention to programming with SPRINT's macros so you can speed-up word processing routines with a simple keystroke. *Using SPRINT™* puts you ahead in the race with the skills you need to take full advantage of Borland's new professional word processor.

$21.95p
0-07-881291-7, 350 pp., 7⅜ x 9¼

The Borland-Osborne/McGraw-Hill Business Series

Advanced Turbo Pascal®
by Herbert Schildt

Advanced Turbo Pascal® is the book you need to learn superior programming skills for the leading Pascal language development system. Revised and expanded, *Advanced Turbo Pascal®* now covers Borland's newly released Turbo Database Toolbox®, which speeds up database searching and sorting, and the Turbo Graphix Toolbox®, which lets you easily create high-resolution graphics. And, *Advanced Turbo Pascal®* includes techniques for converting Turbo Pascal for use with Borland's hot new compiler, Turbo C®. Schildt provides many programming tips to take you on your way to high performance with Turbo Pascal. You'll refine your skills with techniques for sorting and searching; stacks, queues, linked lists and binary trees; dynamic allocations; expression parsing; simulation; interfacing to assembly language routines; and efficiency, porting, and debugging. For instruction and reference, *Advanced Turbo Pascal®* is the best single resource for serious programmers.

$21.95p
0-07-881283-6, 350 pp., 7⅜ x 9¼

The Borland-Osborne/McGraw-Hill Programming Series

C: The Complete Reference
by Herbert Schildt

Once again Osborne's master C programmer and author Herb Schildt, shares his insight and expertise with all C programmers in his latest book, *C: The Complete Reference*. Designed for both beginning and advanced C programmers, this is an encyclopedia for C terms, functions, codes, applications, and more. *C: The Complete Reference* is divided into five parts, each covering an important aspect of C. Part one covers review material and discusses key words in C. Part two presents an extensive summary of C libraries by category. Part three concentrates on various algorithms and C applications and includes information on random number generators as well as artificial intelligence and graphics. Part four addresses interfacing efficiency, porting, and debugging. Finally, part five is for serious programmers who are interested in C++, C's latest direction. The book also includes complete information on the proposed ANSI standard.

$24.95p
0-07-881263-1, 740 pp., 7⅜ x 9¼

C Made Easy
by Herbert Schildt

With Osborne/McGraw-Hill's popular "Made Easy" format, you can learn C programming in no time. Start with the fundamentals and work through the text at your own speed. Schildt begins with general concepts, then introduces functions, libraries, and disk input/output, and finally advanced concepts affecting the C programming environment and UNIX™ operating system. Each chapter covers commands that you can learn to use immediately in the hands-on exercises that follow. If you already know BASIC, you'll find that Schildt's C equivalents will shorten your learning time. *C Made Easy* is a step-by-step tutorial for all beginning C programmers.

$18.95p
0-07-881178-3, 350 pp., 7⅜ x 9¼

Advanced C
by Herbert Schildt

Herbert Schildt, author of *C Made Easy*, now shows experienced C programmers how to develop advanced skills. You'll find thorough coverage of important C programming topics including operating system interfacing, compressed data formats, dynamic allocation, linked lists, binary trees, and porting. Schildt also discusses sorting and searching, stacks, queues, encryption, simulations, debugging techniques, and converting Pascal and BASIC programs for use with C. A complete handbook, *Advanced C* is both a teaching guide and a lasting resource.

$19.95p
0-07-881208-9, 350 pp., 7⅜ x 9¼

The C Library
by Kris Jamsa

Design and implement more effective programs with the wealth of programming tools that are offered in *The C Library*. Experienced C programmers will find over 125 carefully structured routines ranging from macros to actual UNIX™ utilities. There are tools for string manipulation, pointers, input/output, array manipulation, recursion, sorting algorithms, and file manipulation. In addition, Jamsa provides several C routines that have previously been available only through expensive software packages. Build your skills by taking routines introduced in early chapters and using them to develop advanced programs covered later in the text.

$18.95p
0-07-881110-4, 220 pp., 7³/₈ x 9¹/₄

Artificial Intelligence Using C
by Herb Schildt

With Herb Schildt's newest book, you can add a powerful dimension to your C programs—artificial intelligence. Schildt, a programming expert and author of seven Osborne books, shows C programmers how to use AI techniques that have traditionally been implemented with Prolog and LISP. You'll utilize AI for vision, pattern recognition, robotics, machine learning, logic, problem solving, and natural language processing. Each chapter develops practical examples that can be used in the construction of artificial intelligence applications. If you are building expert systems in C, this book contains a complete expert system that can easily be adapted to your needs. Schildt provides valuable insights that allow even greater command of the systems you create.

$21.95p
0-07-881255-0, 360 pp., 7³/₈ x 9¹/₄

Available at fine bookstores and computer stores everywhere.

For a complimentary catalog of all our current publications contact: Osborne/McGraw-Hill, 2600 Tenth Street, Berkeley, CA 94710

Phone inquiries may be made using our toll-free number. Call 800-227-0900 or 800-772-2531 (in California). TWX 910-366-7277.

Prices subject to change without notice.

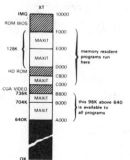
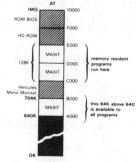